Butterflies and Bullshit

By

Natalie Newman

Cover design by Taher

2nd edition- December 2011

Copyright © 2011 by Natalie Newman

All rights reserved

Triple N Publishing Company ~Duluth, MN

www.wordpress.com/natalienewmansworld

Printed in the United States of America

This book is dedicated to

*To God- my Creator and true source of everything. Thank you for letting me be Me.

*To all the beautiful Angels from above who are beside me through every moment I face with loving guidance.

* To my beautiful children Dakota, Nathalia, and Diego who have given me a reason to live and smile through every day. You are the best and I love you all so much.

*To Erik- My beautiful soul mate who broke down all my walls, challenged me to face all my pain filled fears, loved me perfectly so I could heal myself and have the strength to write this book. I love you so very much.

*To LouAnn for the space and place to finish this book. I am so grateful to you, Love you!

*To my amazing friends who have been earth angels to me through my entire life. You are the greatest friends on earth. Thank you!

*To my incredibly strong family that pushes me to be better. I am so lucky to be a part of your lives.

*To everyone who reads this book, because you are all family to me. One Blood, One Love, One People!

* And to all the people who were put in my path to make things miserable, to challenge me and help me become so strong. Thank You!

Forward

By Tara- USA

The day I met Natalie was the day, without even realizing, that my whole life would change. Maybe it did not change at that exact moment, weeks, or even months. But down the road was when I needed Natalie the most. Without even realizing it, that was the day I met my angel.

Natalie has helped me in more ways than I will ever know. Not with just advice, but in prayer, support, love, guidance, and pushing me to be the strong woman I am today. She believed in me and she gave me the faith I needed.

I was at a point in my life where I wanted "out". I was turning towards death. Thinking no one cared and no one was there for me. I was screaming at the top of my lungs for help. Just to have someone hear me, to understand me, and to just listen. Everyone had turned on me for the choices and the mistakes I had made. I was in so much pain, so much hurt. There was so much anger and sadness inside me. I wanted out of life!

It was at that moment Natalie reached out to me. She told me she knew something was wrong and I was all she thought about. We talked for hours. Her words of wisdom helped me. She gave me the encouragement to be the mother my children needed me to be. She believed in me! I made choices on what I knew was best for my children. I was ridiculed by people who were supposed to be there for me and help support the choices I make. The way we voice our opinions on people, judge people and how our actions affect people is hurtful. Natalie has taught me how to be strong, how to love myself, how to follow my heart and my gut.

As we become older, we realize who our true friends are. We have people come in and out of our lives. To me, Natalie is more than my friend. She is my angel. I believe God had us cross paths not just as friends, coworkers, or a place to hang out, but as a gift!

Natalie was my angel sent from God. She came to help me get through this rough time in my life. She helped me remember to always keep faith no matter how bad life may get. Natalie is my gift from God and I will be forever grateful to have someone so beautiful in my life.

Angels are everywhere, to guide us, to watch over us, and to protect us. Who is your angel?

I love you Natalie xo

Tara

By Joom- Thailand

My dear Natalie,

    First of all, congratulations! You did awesome work on this book Natalie. You are a very strong woman and a very kind person who think about sharing this and making this book. To make us be more considerate about the significant of life and educate ourselves better. It must be hard to be the ROCK Natalie Newman nowadays. You discuss about many good point in life in the book.

    Fear is the dangerous feeling which happens to everybody that's for sure. Then it leads to judgment. I like when you said that pointing the finger at another for whatever reason we don't want to look at ourselves or for other to look at our bad behavior. Look! In the same time you point one finger to another, you point the rest of your fingers to yourselves too. I agree with you about fear creates anger and rage inside us. They are a disaster for your life if you let those feelings keep growing inside you. Most of people from Thailand believe that anger will turn you to be a crazy/insane person! So only the crazy/insane people will not able to control their anger. We should take it easy with our life.

    I think you have it right to talk about religion and God in your book Natalie. As you said there are so many conflicts about the different religions. And there are many people who were killed just because they do not believe in the same with one another. I think there are many people who are dying and suffering enough from this religion thing. My belief and from the truth of life from the Buddhist way, we all have the same God, but he just has a different name to called him from the different parts of our world. I think we believe and have faith to the same God who loves us, wants to teach and guide the way to live our life well and happy. I'm sure every religion in this planet have the same teaching and same goal. It doesn't matter what religion you are, but it does matter if you are good and do good things which are the significant and the purpose of God.

Another important issue to consider if you want to live life more smoothly is attachments. We should just make our life stay in the middle way, not too high or not to low on the earth, not too tight and not too loose. Make our life more balanced. Most of all, try to lose your attachments more and more. Attachment will lead to FEAR, anger, and judgment at some point. I like when you said, "Remember that there was a time when you COULD live without that thing or that person. Nothing is irreplaceable; a habit is not a need." That is so true!!! When we are born we just came without anything or any materials and by the end we all die without taking anything with us either. Nothing belongs to us forever. In my opinion we should drop our attachment to all things more and just enjoy everything, even the little things. It's my pleasure to do everything for you when you need me, Natalie, I love you. You are always kind to me and comfort me when I need it. Your book will be master piece work that is very significant for all people who are still lost and need to find the way to be happy. Hope you have the fun life with your new and different CHAPTER of your life.

Love,
Joom

By Maria- Romania

Natalie,

    I have read your chapters at least 3 times each and all I can say is, besides being very emotional, I can see that you put all your being in writing this book. It's very inspiring, just like you. I don't know all the details of the things that you've been through, but I can realize that it has been hard. You still managed to find yourself and keep yourself strong and positive. You are one strong woman and I'm sure that through this book you will be a source of inspiration for people. Always keep your head up and try your best at everything even though it's hard. This is a lesson I have learned from you Natalie, even though we've spent so little time together.

    You just have this positive energy that you convey to all the people around you. And now through this book you can do it on a larger scale. I just hope that this book will sell so that you can open as many Natalie's Garage as you can. What you said to me about raising money for helping women - it's wonderful and I would like to help with whatever means necessary. Believe me Romania is a country who really needs something like that. I would like to say much more but even the language is limited to convey all these feelings. Good luck with your book and keep me informed about your progress.

Love, Peace and Hugs!
Maria

Table of Contents

Part 1- My Crazy Life

Introduction- Bullshit..................................14

Chapter 1- Born into Pain..........................24

Chapter 2- Sex, Drugs and Rock-n-Roll.................32

Chapter 3- Run Natalie, RUN....................43

Chapter 4- Behind Closed Doors..............54

Chapter 5- The Divine Intervention of Natalie......65

Chapter 6- The Search for Natalie..................74

Chapter 7- My Sweet Serbian Suicide...................86

Chapter 8- I'm Surrounded by Angels I call Friends..96

Chapter 9- Along Came a Swede Who Injected His Seed of Addiction Inside Her................................107

Chapter 10- It Takes a Strong Man to Handle a Broken Woman...120

Conclusion to Part 1- Butterflies..................145

Part 2- What I Learned Along the Way

Introduction– Part 2..153

Chapter 1- Change Your Thoughts to Beautify Your Life......155

Chapter 2- Numb and Dumb is How They Want You.............165

Chapter 3- You Wrote the Book of Your Life..........................175

Chapter 4- I can Learn, Let Go and Grow…………………...187

Chapter 5- Without the Darkness You will Never Search for the Light..204

Chapter 6- The Soul Never Ends..217

Chapter 7- Children- My Promise from God I will Always Have a Friend..…..228

Chapter 8- Love Comes When We Stop Searching for It..242

Chapter 9- God Gave Us People to Love and Things to Use, not People to Use and Things to Love………………………..253

Chapter 10- The World Opens for Us All………....................265

Chapter 11- Imagine..274

Chapter 12- Connecting to the World Waiting for You...286

My last words to you-...291

Introduction
Bullshit

Life: nothing but an adventure into the unknown. One minute my life was like a dream. The next minute it fell into a pit of hell. Was it all just an illusion I created to make everything feel good? I don't know anything about anything right now. As I look at this moment I have no answers, no words, just complete confusion. I have lived in this illusion that my faith in God will get me through. That God is my only true source of everything. Am I willing to risk it all on the illusion that God will take care of me and that God's plans for me are greater than my dreams? At this point I have EVERYTHING to lose. So a choice must be made now.

I am not perfect in any way, HELL NO! Every time I think my ass is doing well and everything is wonderful, BAM. I get hit with the reality stick right between the eyes. I managed to mess everything up along the way. Thank God I learn fast from my mistakes. I hate pain. I don't want to feel it over and over again for the same thing. Yet, it seems to be what I keep doing. I am constantly banging my head against the wall. Making the same mistakes but at higher levels each time. How the hell did I get here when I tried so goddamn hard to do my best? Now I am sitting here questioning everything. I am lost, spinning in dizziness and confusion. I have no idea even which direction to swim. Everything keeps trying to pull me down. I feel like I am drowning fast.

It is August 28, 2011. I look at this moment now and wonder how the hell did I get HERE? How have I screwed up so bad to get myself HERE? How did I survive through all the horrible disasters in my life and still only be HERE. I never believed I would live to see 25 years old. I almost didn't because of abuse, drug addiction, depression, and suicidal tendencies. I am now 41 years old. It seems I still don't know anything. I am sitting here now telling myself I need to write it all out. Hoping it will lead to figuring out how the hell I am going to survive and get out of this mess.

My physical self is exhausted. I don't take care of myself because I am too busy taking care of everyone else. I don't eat well, dehydrated, and in terrible physical pain from the emotional pain I carry around. I seriously need to think about myself and take care of this temple I live in. I am not getting any younger. God gave me the gift of this beautiful body and I abuse it by never taking care of it.

My mental health is at a point of either they lock my ass up for being insane or everything is really beautiful. I can't get help from mental health professionals because every time I see a therapist either I outsmart them or they tell me I have overcome so much on my own. They ask why I even need them. My levels of thinking are far above most professionals. Yet, I just can't seem to figure out if I really am crazy with all this madness I see in my head. Or, is my life really filled with so much magic and beauty.

My emotional health is a roller coaster ride from Heaven to Hell. Sometimes that ride can happen 2-3 times a day. Sometimes that ride is within a minute. Life hands me my ass so fast. I just try my best to ride it and stay centered. Most times it is not my own problems. Others just fill me with sadness because of their moment or situation. I absorb other's pain and emotions so very easily. I try so hard to be my best and fail. My result seems to only create more confusion within myself. Self-esteem becomes an issue and I begin to wonder why the hell I even try when I can never get it right.

My spiritual health is growing and very healthy. But, is that all an illusion too? What is real and what have I created in my head? I work my butt off to stay centered to get through the moments I am put through. The questions are: Will smiling, loving and trusting in God get me through life?

Can I truly survive on my faith in God and the Universe alone? Or, am I completely delusional? Does God really exist? Does God love a person like me who doesn't seem to listen and keeps making huge mistakes every day? Should I listen to my friends that tell me to stop living in a dream and give up my faith that God is taking care of me? Should I swoop down to the level most humans are spiritually? Most people are non-believers living in a world of negative reality. I love my relationship with God and the Angels. Truly, I don't know any other way at the moment.

I look at my children. They are so beautiful, happy, healthy, strong, intelligent, nice, popular, and loved. They love me so very much. How did they get like that? Their fathers show them so much negative. Yes, they love their children. But, they are not quite aware of what they have dragged their children through. However, I am not here to point fingers at anyone. I am not one to talk. I am so wrapped up in my own shit trying to survive, I forget about what I have put them through. They have stood beside me while I fight this battle through hell trying to save my life.

As for my relationship, well that is kind of how I got HERE. Love: confuses us, destroys us, kills us, hurts us, blinds us, and yet we cannot live without it. We lose track of who WE are and we hang on so tightly. What we really need is to let go. Now I am stuck in the middle of the road being pulled in two directions. I feel like I am going to be split in half. I do not know whether to let him go or hang on.

My beautiful man lives in Sweden and I am in the USA. We have been together 15 months and have no physical relationship. He has come here twice for a total of 7 weeks. We survive on video calls and trust. I love this man more than any human on earth, except my children. He is perfect in every way for me. I have given up everything I had trying to help and guide him. Trying my best to love him unconditionally through every dark and painful moment he has to go through. In the process, I enabled his behavior and allowed him to disrespect me for 15 months.

I know in my heart he did not want to be like this. But at this point he has destroyed almost all of my trust. He disrespects my time. I wait for him patiently and sometimes for days. I beg and plead with him over and over to just be nice for a moment so I can save my life. That is when he screws up the worse and hurts me so deeply. I am hurt and angry because I wasted my precious time when I could have been doing something so much better.

Now, it has snowballed into something huge. It forced both of us to look deep inside ourselves about everything. I chose to work very hard and change everything he managed to see wrong with me. Yet, he just lived in denial with his ego, aggression and stubbornness pointing the finger at me every time a problem arose. Yes, he did work very hard on himself in so many ways. But, it seemed he worked on every other part of his life instead of our relationship. That is why I felt like I was the problem and I worked so damn hard on changing myself. I just could not make him happy.

Like everyone, I have been patiently waiting for the "right one" to show up. When we start a new relationship we have to learn, change, and suffer to understand each other. Then question ourselves if this really is the "right one". I feel in my heart he is the right one and that I love him. But what the hell do I have to go through before I can't take anymore? If I walk away, then I will wonder if I gave up too soon or if it could have worked. When a relationship strips you of your freedom, integrity and is sucking the life out of you, is it love? When do you stop giving them chances?

Another big problem I have is I love so intensely I destroy everything. I tried so hard to love him that I forgot about myself, my life, my friends, my home, my financial situation and my kids. I was swimming in pain because of his actions, my reactions and the difficult lessons I was learning through it all. Now I look around and say "Holy Shit Natalie, what have you done?" I put everything I had into love and now I am on a hairline of losing everything I have. Was the suffering worth it? Can I still get my ass out of this mess? Does he think I have the rest of my life to wait for him to change? I am tired of fighting the same fight over and over with little results.

Finally, the other day my Swede had an epiphany about how he was treating me. He blurted out everything I have been thinking, feeling, and saying to myself through this entire mess. I dreamed of this day for over a year hoping he would wake up and see it. I expected it to be a moment of happiness because then we could finally move forward. Instead, it was a slap in the face. He was holding up a mirror of all the shit I put up with. Questioning what I am doing and what I have done to everything in my life. He questioned what kind of woman I was to stand there and take all his abuse trying to love him. Once again, allowing myself to be a victim like I have my entire life. I felt stupid, embarrassed, ashamed, and all alone. I just wanted to run so far and never stop. I just can't get ANYTHING right.

I don't know whether I should stand beside him or walk away. I don't know if I can stay with him while he is dealing with his horrible moment of realization. I will definitely carry his pain and keep spiraling down. I don't know if I even have the strength anymore, especially now. Yet, the world is heaven on earth when we are together and getting along. That man is my very best friend. I have never trusted anyone to know everything about me. I did tell him everything about me and he still loves me so very, very much. I don't want to or know how to live without him. He has grown into such a beautiful man, but his darkness is so deep.

Furthermore, I am not sure I can save him. I am not sure if I have any more energy to do it. I may have to walk away into the unknown and walk alone. All I know is the pain has almost destroyed me. I have to decide which way to turn before it is too late. I may have to let go of my greatest love to find myself and save my damn life. How do you handle that? What the hell do you do?

We have many soul mates in life. Most are here to teach us lessons to elevate us to a greater love. But, also a greater love and respect for ourselves. If we don't learn, we stay trapped until we do. Where do you draw the line of being content, not needing, wanting and deserving better? If you keep setting higher standards for yourself and walk away, did you just miss out on the "right one" because you didn't have patience or understanding? Love is the most risky and confusing shit on earth.

Now I have to pay for my actions loving someone, pick up the mess, swallow my pride, and go forward. My heart is blown into a million pieces. Did I work so hard to help him become such a wonderful man for some other woman to benefit from my suffering? Or do I just face the fact that maybe it is some other woman he needs? I just want what is best for him. That's what love is about, even if it doesn't include you. I became the woman I am today because of his actions. But, also because I wanted to suit his needs. Maybe that wasn't what he needed. Back to the old saying- "If you love something, set it free. If it comes back to you, it's yours. If it doesn't, it never was." I guess I may need to just suck it up and let go. What the hell do I have to lose? I have already lost almost everything. Is it time to close this door and heal myself before I do lose it all?

So now let's move into my financial situation at this moment. I was basically forced to quit my job 3 years ago because they said I couldn't have the manager position I was already working. The General Manager said it was because I had children. Discrimination- yes, but how the hell do you prove when it is your word against theirs? Then I lost my driver's license because someone from Serbia was driving a car in someone else's name. There was no insurance and I got the ticket. I cannot get my license back because I have to get insurance on myself for a year. The amount is about $1200. I don't have a vehicle anymore because they all died.

So yes, I can get a job but I live 8 miles in the woods from the nearest town. I could walk approximately 6 hours a day and 16 miles to get there. Hell yeah, I would have a great ass and legs that's for sure. But, let's be realistic. Six months of the year it is winter here. The only way I can make money is if I find a way to do it from home. Almost every business at home takes money to start in some way.

My home is months behind on payments. My electric is supposed to get shut off at any moment. I spent the money for the house payment to buy necessities for living, food, phone, and internet. I need the phone in case of emergencies because my son is deathly allergic to bees and it is summer. I need the internet to write, keep my relationship going, have contact with my friends so I can mentally and emotionally survive. My house is falling apart and needs a lot of work. Winter is around the corner and it gets so damn cold here. I need to insulate it. If my water pipes freeze I have to walk away because it is almost impossible to crawl under the house and fix those pipes.

The house is still in both my ex and my name. He is finally at the point that he wants me to buy him out. However, I can't even need to make more money to pay the payments. I have nowhere to go with my children if money doesn't happen. If my electric gets shut off my ex would be right there to take these kids with social services. If the phone gets shut off I can't get my son a ride to the emergency room, he could die.

So, now as I told you, I am left with nothing. Winter is just a blink of an eye away and I burn wood to heat my house. I have enough wood for about 2 weeks. I need enough for 7 months. We have enough food to survive about a week. Also, school starts in 1 week. I don't have a dime to buy anything for my children. I feel like such a loser parent. My heart is so broken because I cannot provide the things my children need. I do provide for my children all their needs, but nothing extra.

If money doesn't come I will be knee deep in shit with no home or children. I paid the phone company only half the bill six days ago. I didn't have the rest. Much to my surprise, they shut off my phone. It is the beginning of my end? Or is it the end of life being like this? Will I swim to shore or drown fighting against everything trying to pull me down? Do I just give up and surrender? Or do I keep fighting with everything I have? This is my story and the lessons I have learned. I pray the answers will unfold as I write it. I am going to take you on my journey to find these answers and myself. Sometimes you find yourself in the middle of nowhere, and sometimes, in the middle of nowhere you find yourself.

~And maybe a happy ending doesn't include a guy, maybe it's you **on your own,** picking up the pieces and starting over, freeing yourself up for something better in the future. Maybe the happy ending is just moving on.

~When I was 5 years old, my mother always told me that happiness was the key to life. When I went to school, they asked me what I wanted to be when I grew up. I wrote down 'happy'. They told me I didn't understand the assignment, and I told them they didn't understand life. ~ John Lennon

~Remember that the first impression that you get from someone isn't necessarily a true reflection of their personality. There are still many layers beneath the surface that must be uncovered before the true depth of a person is known. Don't assume that you know everything about a person just from your first encounter. You may end up disregarding someone completely unless you stop worrying about the attention being focused on you, and start thinking more about the other person.

~Reputations are just history in rumor form, you can change it

~ Love is the light that dissolves all walls between souls, families and nations. ~ Paramahansa Yogananda

~ We don't receive wisdom; we must discover it for ourselves after a journey that no one can take for us or spare us. ~ Marcel Prous

Part 1
My Crazy Life

"I am Me. In all of the world, there is no one else exactly like me. Everything that comes out of me is authentically mine, because I alone chose it. I own everything about me: my body, my feelings, my mouth, my voice, all my actions, whether they be to others or myself. I own my fantasies, my dreams, my hopes, my fears. I own my triumphs and successes, all my failures and mistakes. Because I own all of me, I can become intimately acquainted with me. By so doing, I can love me and be friendly with all my parts. I know there are aspects about myself that puzzle me, and other aspects that I do not know -- but as long as I am friendly and loving to myself, I can courageously and hopefully look for solutions to the puzzles and ways to find out more about me. However I look and sound, whatever I say and do and whatever I think and feel at a given moment in time is authentically me. If later some parts of how I looked, sounded, thought, and felt turn out to be unfitting, I can discard that which is unfitting, keep the rest, and invent something new for that which I discarded. I can see, hear, feel, think, say, and do. I have the tools to survive, to be close to others, to be productive, and to make sense and order out of the world of people and things outside of me. I own me, and therefore, I can engineer me. I am me, and I am Okay." ~Virginia Satir

Chapter 1
Born into Pain

The morning of October 4, 1969 was a beautiful day of 86F or 30C. At that moment my soul entered this body as baby Natalie Newman took her first breath. When a baby takes its first breath is when the spirit enters the body with a "Lifetime Plan". The lies and the hell were already spinning in place the moment I entered this body. God had made me and my parents had adopted me this life.

When I was two years old my mother and father divorced. I never had seen my father again from that moment on. My mother remarried my step-dad and he was the man who raised me. With him came my step-brother and sister. Not much later my mother had a baby boy and I just became more like a third wheel.

Furthermore, my life was never normal. Holidays were spent watching everyone get drunk and my grandfather grabbing every female family member's breasts. I knew in my heart at 4 years old this was not correct. Yet, everyone excused his behavior. I still cannot rid myself of those sick visions. I was always observing everyone around me and questioning everything they did.

At 7 years old my mother gave birth to my sister and 13 months later another sister. Seems everyone was a bit too busy at this time in life to pay attention to what was really going on. My parents would drop my brother and I off overnight with our grandparents very frequently. Instantly, the sexual molestation began. By the grace of God he was not able to achieve an erection, probably due to his age. It was continuous oral sex and threats if I told anyone. I knew it was wrong but yet it gave a good feeling. It was enormously confusing emotions for a young child.

The sexual molestation continued throughout the years. My grandmother just ignored it while being in the same room. I used to cry and beg to my parents to please not leave me there with my grandparents. Then, out the door they went exposing me to this unbearable sickness. I had seen him rape my best childhood friend while I was in the same room. The neighbor girl said she seen him walking around the garage naked.

There was child pornography and sex toys everywhere, even under the trees in the yard. It was so damn humiliating for me to live like this. NOBODY did anything about it. My disbelief in how everyone handled it made me start believing this was a normal thing. So I began to tell myself it was okay. Yet, I felt confused, ashamed, guilty, dirty, and alone with no support.

For all those years I was being repetitively put into this man's sick and twisted hands at least once a week. He was an alcoholic and sex abuser. My grandmother just looked away trying to be a high society woman covering her ass and ignoring the truth. Everyone just turned their heads to what was happening to me.

Also, at 8 years old the school suggested that my mother put me up two grades in school. They said I was too smart for my class. I would finish my work and then I was bored. So I would start talking or causing trouble out of boredom. The school did not know what else to do with me. Thankfully, my mother refused and kept me with my friends.

At eleven years old I had hidden the truth from everyone. I was one of the popular girls in my grade. I lived in a very small community of 3600 people. Everyone knows EVERYONE. Which can be a good thing but also a very bad thing. People love to lie and spread rumors.

On a very cold and snowy Christmas Eve, at about eleven at night, my parents got a phone call and left the house. I was sleeping on the couch when they returned. They woke me and asked me some questions. Because it was such a life changing and explosive moment the only memory I have was saying to them, "Well he did it to the neighbor girl too". I remember my step-father losing his mind saying he was going to kill him.

The next day police officers were asking me a million questions about everything my grandfather had done and anything I knew about what he had done. They posted his arrest in the local newspaper. They wrote what he had done and what he was charged with.

As if my world wasn't already damaged enough with the incest, by the time we had returned to school from the Christmas/ New Year's vacation, the gossip had spread like wildfire. There was not many who did not know what had happened or that something had happened to me. The parents told their children they could not be around me because I was a bad, dirty girl and had very bad things happen to me. Everyone pointed their fingers at me laughing and whispering. If assholes could fly, this town would be an airport.

I went from Miss Popular to the bad-girl slut in an instant. I knew in my heart I did nothing wrong but society kept telling me different. My entire family, aunts, uncles, grandparents and cousins split in every direction. At this time my great-grandmother was still alive and she was my favorite person on earth. The last sane thing she said was, "I am going to kill him." Then she went completely insane, which broke my heart into a million pieces and she died soon after that.

My parents started drinking and fighting. My father would come home and rip the door off the wall trying to get my mother. Hell had arisen in every single inch of my life. I was left with nothing but a dark hole in my soul. I kept thinking maybe if I had not said anything, everyone would not blame me. My grandfather was right when he said it would destroy everybody's life if I told.

I had never even kissed a boy and I had managed to earn the worst reputation in town. I really do not even think the children I grew up with even understood why they called me those names. They just followed the rumors and what their parents said. As you know children can be the cruelest humans on earth at times. It is what their parents teach them.

I would go to church every Sunday and people would start talking about me. I would look around the entire congregation and think, "How can you talk to God, still call me names and blame ME? How can you say you believe in God, judge me, and not know God loves EVERYONE?" Jesus said, "Do not judge another unless you want to be judged."

At this moment I had now hit a dangerous suicidal level at 11 years old and I began to dream of being dead. I just shoved it deep inside where nobody could see it. My grandmother at one point told me it would make me a better person and the next door neighbor called me the "devil's spawn". But for some reason, I took pride in the neighbor saying that and still do to this day. They said that girl is a problem, nothing but a goddamn problem. People were so cruel and most of them religious with closets full of their own skeletons.

My world was exploding in a million pieces and I began to learn the art of escapism. I began to see a beautiful man in my dreams and daydreams. I would imagine he was my husband. I dreamed of this European man who saved me and loved me more than anything on earth. I saw him in times of ancient Greece. I was laid on a stone table while he massaged me and said beautiful things to me. I could feel the way he held me and how he passionately kissed me. I could see how beautiful he was physically and how we made love together like magic. I imagined how he made me laugh, I could hear how he talked to me and his words were beautifully romantic. He treated me like I was a Queen.

This man would be in my thoughts every day of my life and

still is to this day. My soul stops every time I have thoughts about him. I wished so badly that dream would come true and he could rescue me from this hell. As the reality lights went off in my mind, I tore myself apart saying I would never deserve a man like that. So I would always try to forget about him remembering the things others said about me. I felt nobody would want a disgusting person like me.

The court system sentenced my grandfather to nine years of probation and nine years of Alcoholics Anonymous once a week. He never spent a day in jail for what he had done to me or the torture he had done to others. He was allowed to continue with his sickness. He was completely free. I was imprisoned in hell trying to survive every day of my life.

I was told years later by the County Attorney that he was always parked at the playground at the elementary school watching the children. Only God knows if he did anything to another child, but I pray the ignorance of that judge did not cause another child to suffer because of this man. I was the 4th generation of incest in my family that I know of. It was a normal part of all their lives I guess, but I made a very important vow to myself not to continue this insanity. This continuous pattern generation after generation was stopping with me. I was not going to continue the madness, secrets and lies. I also decided I never wanted to have children so nobody could ever hurt them.

At 12 years old, I really don't remember very much about our home life during that year. I am not sure what happened to our parents but that is when I became a mother. I assumed the responsibility of taking care of my brother and little sisters. Our parents were never home. Our family was very poor, we did not have much food and we never ate much. It is here when my body developed the ability to not have the feeling of hunger. To this day I still fight the battle of making myself eat. I just forget about it. Sometimes I do not eat for days because I do not feel hunger or think about eating.

My mother also made the decision to continue to take us

to our grandparents' house. She felt bad for her mother and told me that it was not her fault it happened. So continuously week after week I had to see this man and relive every second of this nightmare over and over and over. There was no way to get away from it. There was no way to escape this hell. It was everywhere I went. I will never understand my mother's choices to continue to be a part of this asshole's life. But we just kept going to visit them.

We also spent birthdays and holidays with him. He never touched me again but I never left myself in a situation where he could. I stayed close to my parents. It was not very nice to grow up having to constantly look over your shoulder. It was complete mental torture that never ended. I had to relive it over and over. Everyone looked away at what he had done. Yet, I was being made fun of by children in school, pointed at by society, living in hell trying to survive and drowning in the fear of it happening again. My childhood was stripped from me.

However, I was lucky enough to grow up on a road that was one mile long out in the country. The children I grew up with were wild, crazy and fun. We were always adventuring through the woods and playing by the rivers. It was the perfect escape for my mind to have them in my life. I do not think they will ever understand how much I appreciate them to this day. I found my freedom being alone in nature. It is where my heart was free from everything and everyone. I would go far out somewhere, sit alone and just talk to myself.

Nature was my therapist. I did not have a healthy childhood. Age 8 years old until age 11, I was having sex with my grandfather. Then the community turned on me and sadly at twelve I became a 2nd mother. The environment of nature was where I could go get lost, escape the world, and dream of a beautiful, loving, peaceful future. Without those crazy and fun neighbor kids I am sure I would have killed myself. There was nothing to live for.

Yet, as a very young child I magically was given this

amazing gift to heal my mind, let go and move on. Life was definitely not fair but somehow I survived though it, sometimes barely breathing, but I always kept my head above water.

Now as you can expect coming into the teen years I turned to drugs and alcohol to escape my lonely hell. Addiction of all kinds can be added to the potpourri of problems I already had. I found a way to make myself feel better even if it was just for a moment. Now this is where the real party begins.

~The world will not be destroyed by evil, but by those who watch them without doing anything. ~ Albert Einstein

~I look just like the girls next door... if you happen to live next door to an amusement park." ~Dolly Parton

~I'd rather be hated for who I am, than loved for who I am not." ~Kurt Cobain

~The most important kind of freedom is to be what you really are. You trade in your reality for a role. You trade in your sense for an act. You give up your ability to feel, and in exchange, put on a mask. There can't be any large-scale revolution until there's a personal revolution, on an individual level. It's got to happen inside first. ~Jim Morrison

~Who are you to judge the life I live? I know I'm not perfect and I don't live to be, but before you start pointing fingers make sure your hands are clean! ~Bob Marley

~Some people think that to be strong is to never feel pain, in reality, the strongest people are the ones who feel it, understand it and accept it. ~ Unknown~

~Be careful because sometimes when someone comes back for a second chance, is because they aren't done hurting you yet.

~Your heart can break, your soul can ache, your confidence can shake, your smile can be fake, but your life is never a mistake.

Chapter 2
Sex, Drugs and Rock-n-Roll

When you see a child whose behavior is out of control, do not point the finger at them and be astonished at the way they are behaving. Stop and think about what hell they are surviving to make them behave this way. Children do not just go out of control. Something has forced them out of control. Someone created the monster. Ask yourself what pain is so deep inside this person to cause them to act out like this. Try to see the hell deep inside of them. All they want is attention, someone to help them, and most of all to be loved. You could save someone and help them to live a better life if you just try to hold out your hand to them.
~ Natalie Newman

Being a teen in the 80's was all about big hair, sex, drugs and rock-n-roll. We had smokers' bathrooms in the school. They were a haven for selling and doing drugs. When you hear the song 'Smoking in the Boys Room' it is the perfect explanation for what was happening. It was a cloud of marijuana and pockets full of speed. It was in my teens when I learned music was my medicine. We walked around with our big boom boxes all drugged up, head banging to hot, heavy metal hairbands. I spent my entire teen years running as fast as I could consuming as much drugs and alcohol as possible. Nothing or nobody could hold me down or stop me. I just wanted to party and forget the tortured side of me. I wanted to die.

Finally, at 15 years old I lost my virginity for real. Now it was time to welcome a whole new level of self-abuse. Adding sex to the game gave me a new power I had never quite experienced before. Suddenly, I began to realize I could control men and use them to empower myself. Sex had caused me so much pain and now I found it could give me power. It was a sick and twisted way to think. But, I had not been taught the rules of sex properly.

I don't know what it is about men but all I have to do is walk by or look them straight in the eyes and they are mine. I learned that my seductive, naughty, eyes along with my great personality were a formula that men do not have a resistance to and it was thrilling. Today I NEVER look a man in the eyes unless I want it. I know my eyes are dangerous. Men became my little toys from that point on. The eyes worked for everything, including a lot of free drugs and alcohol. The art of manipulation had been born in to my life.

There was never a moment of sobriety. Just shove as many different kinds of drugs into my body and as much of it as I could do at once. Then add a half gallon of whiskey to that. I did not care if I died. I was aiming for that. I had spent the first 15 years of my life in pain so I decided I wanted to party until I ended it. Partying was a release and a band aid for the hell. I never for one second believed I was going to see 25 years old and honestly I DID NOT want to.

School for me was just a landing strip at the airport to flying high. I had to get there in order to take off and get as high as possible with my friends. Needless to say, the last day of ninth grade the police raided a house looking for some friends and me. We were just taking off on a fabulous LSD trip. We were loaded into the police car and off to school we went. Not for one second could I keep a straight face. They kicked me out of school and told me to never come back. I had skipped 2/3 of the school year to go get messed up.

Also, I was always running away from home to escape the nightmare. My mother would walk the rivers and through woods looking for me. She was tormented by my endless need to run and never knew if I was alive or dead. My mother would call the police after I was missing for 3-4 days. The police would bring me home every time. I would walk in the front door and while they talked to my mother I would go straight out the back door immediately. I would run as fast as I could for miles through the woods to get back to the city, my friends, more alcohol and more drugs. I only wanted freedom, intoxication, fun and friends.

At twenty two years of age I was in a bar and the entire law enforcement was there. One of the police officers said out loud, with a moment of dead silence in the entire building, "Natalie, you are the only girl every cop has taken home." Red-faced I laughed because I knew what he meant, but I am sure it added to the rumors about me. I also made a contract with myself that when my grandfather dies I am going to throw one hell of a wild party and dance for days with people I love.

August of my fifteenth year of age was my first trip to inpatient drug treatment. I was a horrible mess. I had been awake for 5 days, anorexic (never ate), and stripped from the security of the chaos I had created. When I entered the treatment center they told me I was pregnant.

Because of all the legal paperwork my mother had to tell me the truth about the lies she had told me for my entire life to that point. I found out my step-father had never adopted me but they had given me his last name. I felt like someone had put a gun to my head and pulled the trigger. Everything about my life was a lie at that very second. I had to make a decision about the baby immediately. I had to have an abortion that week or it was too late. I knew in my heart at 15 years old that I did not want a child. I already felt I had my children because I had been raising my brother and sisters. I know I did a horrible job with them. They were also living in my hell and so very young.

I also knew that I had not stopped pouring drugs and alcohol into my system for over a year. Therefore, I was not healthy at all. That was no way to start a life for a baby even if I had adopted it out. I knew because of my behavior something would be wrong with it. I chose the abortion and my drug treatment began. I was spun out in every direction and it was the first time in my high speed life of destruction I had come to a complete halt. I knew I had no plans of sobering up. So I took advantage of the program to work on myself, learn a few things and get the hell out of there.

Well to my surprise, my mother decided to put me in a foster home in a big city 20 miles away. I left that 28 day treatment center to a new home with a woman I had never met. I was starting at new school and with no friends. My family did not even want me anymore. Well, that was the way I had seen it. The last thing I said to my mother before I started this new life was "You are not my damn family, my friends are my only true family." Believe it or not, it really has not changed all these years of my life. I love my family yes, but not very close to any of them. I was completely alone and wondering what I had done to deserve this.

I started a new school that was triple the size of the last one I was in. I turned 16 and I was looking for some fun. Oh hell yeah, I found it immediately. This high school was nothing but rich kids. The parents had really good drugs or they could afford to buy them. So, I let it all begin again. I partied like a rock star for two years at that school. I had great friends to help me through it. I occasionally got to go home on home visits but I always screwed that up.

I had parents, foster-mother, social workers, counselors, psychologists and psychotherapists all trying to dig in my head continuously trying to help me. I felt like a mental science experiment. I felt none of them really knew anything about what had happened to me. First session with them was always telling them my life history. Then I would look at whoever was trying to save me next and ask "Has this ever happened to you? Have you ever been sexually abused, raped or any of the hell I have been through?" 99% of the time they replied NO. I always shook my head and laughed. Calmly I would reply to them, "Then how the hell can you tell me how I feel when you read it in a damn book? How will you ever understand me if you haven't felt it and lived through it yourself?" I learned to reverse it back to them by this point in my life. I seriously believed that only the damaged should counsel the damaged. Painless people should not counsel the pained. Just like sober people shouldn't counsel addicts. Go be a nurse instead. Counseling another's life needs understanding, not book smarts. If you haven't lived it, how can you teach it? I am being judged by someone who isn't even close to having their own shit together.

The world was my puppet. I knew in my heart I was much bigger than my life. I knew I would be someone famous that helped many people. I was intelligent enough to never let people know they were the star of my show for my entertainment. It is scary what a smile can hide. I was smarter than all those trying to help me. Except one day I got a new psychotherapist who looked me in the eyes and said, "You're lying". I knew at that moment she understood me and had been there. That psychotherapist truly helped me and emptied some of the pain load. Finally, I was able to carry less baggage.

Truly, that was when I had made the decision to take my hell and turn into healing for others. I wanted to be a psychologist because I knew I could help 1000's of women and children survive what I had been through. My dream of helping the world heal their pain had begun. My heart went out to everyone what was hurting on this earth. At that point my intuition heightened. I began to see into people and I could see their pain inside them. I could see what their problems were and how they could heal themselves. If I see someone was hurting, I was drawn to them immediately and tried to help them.

My foster-mother was an amazing role model for me. She taught me how to empower myself as a woman and gave me so much self-esteem. She gave me a great gift by teaching me that everything that had happened to me was not my fault and I was NOT the one who was sick. God gave me an angel, a wonderful teacher and one of the greatest gifts of my life. I will be eternally grateful to her for everything she taught me. She continues to be a part of my life and a wonderful second mother to me.

At 17 years old I was finally able to return home. Almost two years of being away from home and it was a few months before the end of my junior year in high school. When I returned I began right where I had left off full speed ahead.

One night at a party I had taken some LSD and was having so much fun with my friends. A local man asked me if I wanted to go back to his house to get some more drugs. I knew him and did not feel any threat from him. We got to his house and he gave me more LSD. I am not sure how much he fed me. We got in the car with me thinking we were going back to the party. He had other plans for me. We drove an hour from civilization deep into the woods. I was 115 lbs. (52kg) and he was 350 lbs. (158kg). He was three times my size.

Completely trapped, I did not know where I was to even attempt to run away from him. You can't just start running through the woods here. It is endless. He began his selfish game of raping me. I fought, kicked, punched and screamed for days. He never stopped trying. My will and strength was the only thing that kept him from taking me over. He had kidnapped me for over three days. He was holding me hostage with sex as the ransom. If I wasn't so drugged up on LSD I am not sure I would have had that physical strength to keep fighting for so many days.

Finally, he gave up the nightmare he was dragging me through and brought me home. I sat in hell, bruised head to toe and my eyes were swollen shut from crying. Shame and guilt had flooded me and I could not tell anyone about it. Only three people on earth knew that happened. They were the kidnapper, my dear friend and I. I hope nobody has to experience that type of hell. Never give up the fight, you are stronger than you ever imagined.

Six months later I ended up in another 28 day drug treatment center located downtown of a huge city. I had just taken some LSD, looked through the window and seen my mother's face. I thought I was hallucinating. It was an interesting three hour drive with my mom and her friend from church. Truthfully, I had a so much fun in treatment. People from all over the country were in there. It was an adventure every day to learn of different people and myself.

When I was finished with treatment I was shipped off to my aunt and uncle's house in the big city three hours from my home. On to another new school that was triple the size of the last one. Again, I was alone and completely trapped by life. It did not take me long to find the right people to hang around.

One month into my senior year I turned 18 years old. I had planned on going back home and taking care of myself. I was finally 18 and a legal adult. I told my teachers I would be moving soon. Suddenly, a girl in my class walked up to me and said, "You cannot leave, I have been watching you and I want to get to know you." Out the door we went.

Immediately we were snorting cocaine and drinking. We took a hit of LSD and partied all over two major cities. I was partying with people I did not know at all. We were drinking in biker bars on the bad side of the city, piles of drugs and the very best LSD I had ever done. I had met 100's of people wandering through this adventure. After three days of this I returned back to my aunt and uncle's house. I walked in the door, my bags were packed and they were throwing me out. I told them I never meant for it to happen, it just did. I called some people from home. Three friends drove down and got me. I was truly free. So my adult life began and nobody was going to tell me how to live anymore. I FINALLY HAD FREEDOM!!!!

I moved in with this couple I was friends with, quit school and dove head first into a cocaine addiction. Couple months into my new found freedom, my roommate came home with a very large amount of crystal meth. A new drug I really had not experienced yet. It is nothing like the meth they do nowadays. All you needed was a little amount of it, then sleeping and eating was not a part of your vocabulary. Every day was a party. House was filled with friends coming to buy it and everyone was messed up on it.

At some point I know I had completely lost my mind. The habit of doing a little amount had turned into lines of 'crystal' the length of door-sized mirrors. Years later men told me that they had sex with me, and of course, I do not remember. They told me I would snort a huge line before starting sex, stop during sex to do more and then a big line after the grand finale. There were times when I did not sleep for two weeks and seriously, do not even ask me if I ate. I was paving the road to hell one 'line' at a time.

The party living in that house ended when my friend called my mother and told her I was killing myself. Word came back to me that my mom was going to court order me into drug treatment. So of course, I began to run again. Going from house to house, sleeping with men for drugs and a place to stay.

One night I was awakened at three in the morning by a friend of mine who asked me if I wanted to go to El Paso, Texas. This person followed me everywhere I went. Serenaded me when I went to sleep and when I woke. It drove my dad crazy. Because he would sit in the apple tree below my bedroom window and play his guitar while I slept. He told me I was a goddess and he followed me every step I took, serenading me. He wrote songs about me and he never left my side. I did not have the same feelings as him, but I couldn't get rid of him either.

So, I threw all of my things in a back pack and got the hell out of this state. The withdrawals were horrible but bearable with marijuana. Without saying a word, I disappeared without a trace and traveled to the other side of the country. I am just that kind of person, someone says let's go, I am gone. You never know what kind of adventure you can get yourself into. Sitting in the same place never gets you anywhere.

Once we arrived in El Paso it did not take me long to see that I had the wrong hair color and skin color to be there. We were living on the border of Mexico and USA. We began selling drugs for money and all the insanity had gotten out of control. Some jerk had paid us in counterfeit money. I knew I had to get out of there before I ended up in prison. So we went to different businesses and started cashing in this bad money. I got on a bus and headed to Galveston Island, Texas to stay with my favorite aunt for a couple months. Thank God I did because it was the last time I would ever see her alive. It was also the last time I would see my friend in El Paso. Eventually, I wanted to go home, so my family put me on a bus and I left Texas five months after I disappeared from home. It was the last time I seen my friend, he died of AIDS few years later from shooting drugs with a needle. It broke my heart.

Upon my return I became a full blown cocaine addict and dealer. I was dating two cocaine dealers to support my enormous habit. The cocaine was flowing like water in and out my door. Life was one big party again. My only goal was to stuff as much of that drug up my nose as possible and along with whatever other drugs I could get my hands on. I had officially found the way to kill the pain with cocaine. Believe me when you are addicted to that you will do ANYTHING to get it and you think of NOTHING else but getting more. I was in relationships with much older men who beat me. It did not matter. They were feeding my fix and I needed them. I had no respect for anyone or anything, especially myself. Just give me more so I do not have to feel life, the hell and the withdrawal.

Suddenly, one night I started having chest pains and my heart was racing. The left side of my body was completely numb. I called my friend and he told me I was having a heart attack. So I tried to cut back a little and a few days later it happened again. I stopped smoking marijuana thinking that would help. Two days after that I was taken to the emergency room by three of my friends. The nurses had me hooked up to these heart monitors and I really thought it was the end for me. I will never forget my dear, sweet friends in the waiting room. I could hear them crying and I could feel their thoughts. They thought I was going to die this time.

My heart had enough and it just gave up. I could not take any more of the drug abuse, never sleeping, and never eating. I was killing myself like I had always wanted to. I had never had the courage to commit suicide. I knew in my heart I would have survived it. I always felt I would just do it slowly with drugs. Then everyone could watch me spinning in hell slowly killing myself.

As I was getting ready to give up this life, a light entered my mind, the cries of my friends filled my ears and I prayed. These exact words I said out loud, "God! Fuck this! I am only 19 years old. I am not ready to die yet. I have too many people to piss off still. I promise you if you let me live I will never touch that shit again." Then, I felt this warm sensation overcome my entire body. Within 10 miraculous minutes my heart rate was normal. I pulled all the gadgets off me that I was hooked up to. I started to walk out of the hospital and a nurse tried to stop me. I looked at her and said, "I know what my problem is and I will never be back here."

Thank God for my beautiful friends who took care of me for over a month. Three of them took 8 hour shifts watching over me. They never left me alone during the withdrawals and the nightmares of me having to face my life. They were so afraid I was going to start using again, so they never left me. I had finally sobered up completely and had to face reality for the first time in many years. But as you can guess, having to face my own hell, sobriety did not last long.

~Between two evils, I always pick the one I never tried before." ~Mae West

~Bad attitude is like a flat tire, if you don't change it, you can't go anywhere.

~If you obey all the rules you miss all the fun." ~Katharine Hepburn

~Soul, in its self-realized state, is like a wild stallion: noble, free-spirited, unfettered and spontaneous, forever roaming the wondrous skies of heaven. Humans without spiritual awareness are like tamed workhorses: corralled, kept in reign by the mind and forever following the dictates of others. ~ Unknown

~Think of all the beauty still left around you and be happy. ~ Anne Frank

~Life is like a party. You invite a lot of people, some leave early, some stay all night, some laugh with you, some laugh at you, and some show up really late. But in the end, after the fun, only few will stay and help clean up the mess. And most of the times they aren't even the ones who made the mess. These people are your true friends in life. They are the only ones that matter.

~From every wound there is a scar and every scar tells a story. That story says, "I survived!"

~Reality check: when you need "advice" everyone is there to "help" you. But when you need "help", everyone just wants to give you advice.

~ I am not crazy. I am mentally restricted!!!

Chapter 3
Run Natalie, RUN!

Oh the twenties was an interesting, full speed journey of complete chaos. When I was 20 years old my parents decided to get a divorce and I totally supported it. They had been putting each other through hell for way too long. I had been completely sober for about 6 months and said hell with it. I started drinking again.

Although, I never touched drugs again for another 20 years after that point, I just drank hideous amounts of alcohol instead. I am always the last one standing wondering why the hell nobody can last as long as me partying. It was 1990 and life was about to make a huge change for me in who I was.

Life is a teacher who tests our limits but doesn't answer our questions because our assignment is to find faith and strength in order to learn its lessons. Unhappiness is not knowing what you want and killing yourself to get it. I was drinking triple, seeing double and if I did not remember it, then it never happened. I should have become an actress because you couldn't see the pain behind my smile or the tears behind my laughter. I could stand in front of you and you would not see the hell inside me.

I flew through a few quick relationships and then finally settled down at 20 years old in another relationship. He was sweet and gentle. We had a great time together and spent about two years partying and enjoying our life. I started working at a local bar and coming home really late at night. Then about 100 construction workers, building a highway tunnel, arrived in town for the next two years. I was getting a lot of attention and I cannot say I did not enjoy it. I was hot, fun and twenty one. I started going to the bar to drink at 7 p.m. and party all night with the construction workers until 1 a.m. Then we would go ride around with the truck drivers until they got off work at 7 a.m., open the bars and drink until about 10-11 a.m. It was so much fun. I was going full speed ahead about 15-16 hours a day of drinking. I was beginning to lose interest and it began taking a toll on my relationship. I moved out.

    I was 22 years old and free again. I had long blonde hair down to my ass and I walked 10 miles a day. I was hot and wore nothing but skin tight leopard print dresses, or very short mini skirt. Normally, I was dressed head to toe in some hot, sexy leather outfit. I was already the talk of the town. Why not give them something to talk about. I became an awesome pool player and I would go shoot pool every night for $20 and a free drink for every game I played. I NEVER lost. My opponent had no chance. Not dressed the way I was. Just bend over and they couldn't shoot anything.

    Now, I had a power that got me whatever I wanted and I had to just stand there. I always drank for free and make $100's a night teasing men and kicking their asses in pool games. I fell madly in love with one of the construction workers and we were a match made in sin. We knew we had to part one day, so we just enjoyed every second we had.

    I also decided to start hanging with the bikers. I love riding a Harley. That is freedom with the wind in your hair. I have spent a week in Sturgis partying too. I can't miss a good party. That was one wild and crazy week on intense partying.

    At 23 years old I was asked to do a documentary about abortion rights pertaining to my experience when I was 15 years old. I accepted the offer. That shot me into 15 minutes of fame. I was in a few famous magazines. I did an interview with 20/20 news show that was primetime popular. I was on MTV and different newspapers around the world. It was quite the experience. But nobody who knew me seen any of it and I was thankful for that. Not that I have anything to hide but I know they all would have judged me the wrong way.

However, the construction of the tunnels started to end and so did my friend with benefits. Then another wave of construction workers came in building businesses. One night I was standing at the pool table and I had seen this guy walk in the bar. Instantly, I could feel his eyes on me and a strong energy between us. He walked up and put his money up on the pool table to shoot against me. I had control of table, I broke and never stopped. I shot every ball in and he never got one single shot.

Later, I found out his brother had transferred him up to this job to meet me. I was set up and did not even know it. He immediately started working hard on me. Eventually, after a week I gave in. We started a drunken sex relationship. After a few months I started going to his town two hours away for the weekend. The women hated me there. I would walk into a bar and you could hear the claws come out. Jealously! I hated it. I was a good person. I was being judged on my looks, not who I was as a person. Just because I was hot, did not mean I was some dumb blonde bitch.

One day a local woman came into the bar that I worked at and said she met my aunt from my real father. I had never met any of the Newman family. She asked me if it was alright with me if my aunt writes me a letter. I said yes. The next week the woman came in again with a letter from my aunt. It said that they always loved me and never forgot about me. They wanted to meet me. I agreed to meet them but I was not ready to meet my father yet. My mother and I went together. We met them for lunch and I fell in love with their loving energy. They had never forgotten about me in the last 22 years. It was a fabulous beginning to a beautiful relationship. Now I call her my earth angel because she always prayed for me the entire time I was out of their lives.

After a year of seeing the pool player, I moved down to his town. I left my home and friends to go to a place where I knew nobody, again. Within a month the hell began. He took my car and we lived out in the country. So I was stranded.

He would take the phone so I could not call anyone. I had nobody to call anyways. I did not know anyone. He imprisoned me into a hell I did not see coming. He would come home drunk 2-3 days a week and beat the shit out of me. He would come in the middle of the night, grab me out of bed and bang my head against every piece of furniture in the room.

After a year of being enslaved, I finally got myself a job in a town twenty miles away. I could get out of the house and had a good reason to go somewhere. I met some wild, crazy, fun people at that job and we partied a lot. He had been accusing me of it every day I had sat in that house and took his abuse for damn year. Of course, I started cheating.

The physical abuse only showed under my clothes. He was careful not to hit my face because I was working in public. However, under my clothes I was bruised head to toe. Sometimes for days I could barely walk. He had me so mentally abused I thought I was nothing. He told me the only way I could leave him would be in a body bag. Honestly, he was not joking.

With perfect timing my mother called me and asked me if I wanted to go with her to Florida for her work convention. I needed a vacation from life. My driver's license had been stolen by one of my friends and I ran into a lot of problems because of the name on my license. My step father had never adopted me and I was still carrying his name. I had to change my name to what I was born with, Natalie Newman. I got my new I.D. and we were off to the south. We had a fabulous, crazy, and fun time. Going home was the bad part.

His beatings were so bad because I worked in another town and he couldn't control my every move. It wasn't worth working anymore. I was so completely abused at this point I was a robot. There were many times he would come home drunk and rape me. You don't talk about those things because people did not believe it. Nobody believed a boyfriend could rape a girlfriend. But, no means NO! If they do not listen then they are violating your rights as a human being.

At this time I was drowning in depression and extremely suicidal. I just wanted out of this situation and something had to change. I got a phone call from a friend that was with the construction crew and he was going to fly in to spend Thanksgiving with me. I got in my car to get him and the blizzard began. I got to the airport after driving for hours in deep snow and the flight had been cancelled. I was spinning in my mind and I went to the pay phone dialed a number I had never dialed before.

Magically, my earth angel answered the phone. I was in shock! I had never called them. They were celebrating Thanksgiving with the entire Newman family at their home. I was invited and drove there. I walked in the door and the house was packed with people. It was all my family I had never met before. My aunt whipped me around the room and introduced me to everyone. They were all so beautiful to me. Then we came to the last person and she apologized to me that she hadn't told me my father was there. I was also introduced to my new younger sister.

Face to face with my father for the first time at 24 years old. I could not even breathe. It was all too overwhelming to me. My mother had made the decision for me to never see my father. She chose to take away my rights as a child to judge for myself. Everything I thought about him was far from the truth. He did love me and want to see me the entire time we were apart. The Newman's' were such nice people and I did not want to bring my hell upon them. I felt I did not deserve them. Although, I did promise I would come to celebrate Christmas Eve with them.

I attended the Christmas gathering with the Newman's and it was such a beautiful moment in my life. I had gotten really good at living a double life so nobody knew how I was really living. I was too embarrassed to tell anyone and feared he would kill me. My mother called me soon after that and told me that my family was afraid for my life. I played it off like everything was okay. The only person I was fooling was myself. I just kept running full speed ahead.

Out of the blue I got a phone call and was asked to go to

Hollywood to be on a talk show. The subject was the documentary I had done couple years before. I took my mother and we ran off to California. I was treated like a celebrity. Limos and a beautiful hotel room in the old Hollywood. It was my second time there but first time as an adult. We were walking down Hollywood Blvd and people were asking if they could get their picture taken with me. They thought I was a celebrity for real. I ate it up like chocolate. I had my own dressing room that had a gold star with my name on the door. I also had my own hair and make-up people. The talk show taping went well and the host was a famous celebrity. I have to say that moment changed something inside me. I tasted a moment of what the movie stars live. We stayed an extra week to visit my uncle in Oceanside, CA and then flew back to hell.

I started looking for a job and got one at the local liquor store. It was Heaven on earth to someone trying to drink their life away. That is when I started meeting people who lived there. I had been there for almost two years and had no friends. I never imagined it would save my life to get that job. I met a really wild woman and a really crazy guy. We started hanging out and partying hard. I would hide my car places so the Abuser could not find me.

Eventually, I started sleeping with the wild dude. I have never met a man to this day who brought the absolute crazy out in me. Believe me I am crazy as hell too. We started going to rock concerts 3-4 days a week. Every day we were partying like rock stars. Most people hated being around the both of us because we were so completely obnoxious together. There was no limit to insane fun with the two of us. We were sleeping together and he helped me feel secure again. He saved me and made me feel like a good person again. He helped me to start building strength within myself again. He made me laugh.

My crazy girlfriend came to my house one day and she packed my belongings. She was going to get me out before the Abuser killed me. It was winter in Minnesota and I was now living in my car. I could not stay at anybody's house because he would come there and I would be running out the back door. So I house hopped and found a job in another town 20 miles away so I could be out of the area. I was working 90 hours a week, partying like a rock star seven days a week and never sleeping. I was running full speed ahead. I was living life to the fullest because I had plenty of time to sleep when I was dead. I was going through men like diapers. Just shit all over them and throw them out.

Men used women and I was going to use them instead. I was destruction on wheels. I was looking for Mr. Right and I was not going to stop until I found him. I thought that someone must be able to save me. I could not seem to do it myself. I just kept getting myself into one mess after another.

However, I loved the thrill and adventure sex brought me. It was the perfect way to take my pain out on others. Men are players, but so was I and I was playing the best of them. I would just seek out my next victim and go in for the kill. The thrill of the kill and scoring was absolutely empowering. The attention made me feel like I was someone special for a minute. I sucked their powerful, passionate energy out and absorbed it within. Taking them in and digesting the blissful rush sex stirred up between us. I was a fabulous lover and it was the only thing I was good at. I had the control and I used them to rise within myself. Especially, after I spent a lifetime of people telling me I was a piece of dirt for a human.

One night I was drinking in a bar and I ran into a nice guy I had met a few times. He was a little shy but so very sweet by telling me how much he liked me. He was the nicest man I have ever met in my life. This man was the complete opposite of the Abuser. Immediately, I attached myself to him. I could not believe I had a good man like this. I had just spent years being beat and screamed at.

Next, I moved into his house and we decided to get married after six months of being together. He told me he could not have children but that was perfect. I did not like children at all. I had already raised my brother and sisters. I never wanted one. I accepted his proposal because he was such a nice guy to me. Although, I really knew he was not the right one. He was too quiet. Our wedding day was the first day of summer in 1997. I was 27 years old and had no idea who the heck I was. As I put on my wedding dress I began to cry. My mother asked why. I told her that I did not love him and it was not fair to marry him. She forcefully told me that I was just having pre-wedding nervousness.

I went down that isle and I married the nicest man I have ever met knowing in my heart I did not love him. For our honeymoon we had a crazy, fun time in Jamaica for a week. Oh I want a house there some day. Furthermore, right before we got married, he told me I had to quit my job because it would be bad for our taxes. He was rich! He paid for me to have eye surgery because my retina was half detached from the abuse to the head I had taken. I had only half my vision in one eye. They had to do surgery on both my eyes.

After I healed from surgery I started shopping and partying again. I would shop for hours and buy nothing. I was spending money like wild and he never complained once. It was just another way to cover the pain. Addiction to shopping and spending money was a thrill at first. Money only impresses lazy girls, a man who has money should just be a bonus to your life, not an upgrade to use someone.

However, my relationship was boring me and I needed to have a man that was a little more exciting. Six months after the wedding I went back to my hometown because my sister was having her third baby. I ran into one of my ex's and Naughty Natalie came out to play that night. I got pregnant with another man's child.

Now, I had really screwed up. My husband was wonderful about it. He told me he would raise the baby as his own. The father of the baby had other plans. He refused to let another man raise his child. So I left a sweet millionaire to go live deep in the woods back in my hometown. I never wanted to return to that place I grew up. I only went there for a good time not a long time. Now I was returning to a place of hell for me

I hope to God my ex-husband can forgive me for the hell I put him through. I shattered his heart and I really hope someday he can find a woman that can love him the way he needs. She will be a very lucky woman to have him.

I was sober for nine beautiful months being pregnant. I gave birth to my beautiful baby girl four days before I turned 29 years old. Nothing in life mattered but her. I had never loved anything so much in my entire life. She was now the most important thing. I wanted the madness of my family tree to stop with me. I vowed not to carry on the family sickness and lies. I would make sure that my daughter never had to go through hell like I did. I found out the hard way that money does not buy love or happiness. I tried it and I am not that shallow. Family should always come first.

The first 9 months of my daughter's life, I spent every second with her. One day the father came home and told me he did not want to do this anymore. He said I could stay until I found a place. I was in shock. I could not believe I had just given up a life of luxury to be kicked out on the streets with my baby. I got a job and a small trailer house on a beach next to a lake. We were all alone, no money and ready to start a new chapter in our lives.

A month after being single I ran into someone I had a crush on for many years. He was friends with both my little sisters. There was always a very hot energy between us. I was sitting in a bar with a friend of mine that was moving back to Colorado. The phone rang and my friend told me he had called to say he was on his way to the bar. He walked in the door and said "Natalie, I've wanted to fuck you since I was 8 years old." He was 7 years younger than I was. I told my friend to keep me away because I did not trust myself. Two weeks later we ran into each other again. We had sex and he moved in. He never left again. Why take time to heal in between? I just moved on to the next one. We were crazy about each other and he loved my baby girl.

One day, we had to go to my grandparents' house for some party. I can remember losing my mind with fear that my grandfather would look at my daughter with his sick mind.

It was torture enough that this man had been a part of my life continuously all this time. I could not heal from the hell. I was faced with it over and over again.

Every time I had to look at him for the last 21 years, I got sick. Now, I had to change my daughter's diaper in their house. I felt like I was going to vomit. I had someone stand guard to make sure he did not walk in and see her. It is the most nauseating fear to think he would hurt my baby, even if it was with his sick thoughts. I would not let it happen. From that moment on my moments with him became less and less. I had control of him being around my children and I did not trust him.

The three of us moved into a new apartment and things started to change. Life had twists and turns around every corner. After about a month, my boyfriend started acting crazy when he drank. He would drink and start breaking things. I should have seen the signs at that time of what was to come in the future. I already knew I would not be able to put up with this behavior. I had gotten myself out of a relationship that almost killed me. I was not going to do it again.

Every time the ex drank he got stupid. I was annoyed with his behavior and it was two weeks until my 30th birthday. I was going to celebrate it with style WITHOUT him. That man just acted like an ass whenever it was something important. Life is all about ass. Either you are covering it, laughing it off, kicking it, kissing it, busting it, trying to get a piece of it, behaving like one or you live with one.

So, I talked a bunch of crazy people into going to Las Vegas with me and I needed a good party. There was a vanload of us from my hometown. Also, I had two friends flying in from Colorado and two from Florida. I was ready for the party of the century and my soul was screaming to fly wild with freedom. I had twelve people taking this adventure with me. If they only knew what they had gotten themselves, into before leaving, I'm not sure they would have gone.

~A woman brought you into this world, you have no right disrespecting one. ~Tupac

~The truth is you don't know what is going to happen tomorrow. Life is a crazy ride and nothing is guaranteed. ~Eminem

~Sometimes the worst pasts create the best futures. ~ Unknown

~Giving up doesn't always mean you are weak. Sometimes it means that you are strong enough to let go.

~Strong people know how to keep their life in order. Even with tears in their eyes they still manage to say "I'm okay" with a smile.

~She is clothed in strength and dignity, and she laughs without fear of the future.

~You will meet two kinds of people in your life: Those who bring you up and those who tear you down. But in the end you will thank them both.

~If you could read my mind, I am pretty sure you'd be traumatized for life.

Chapter 4

Behind Closed Doors

Without humor- Life sucks! Without courage- Life is hard! Without love- Life is hopeless! Without friends- Life is IMPOSSIBLE.

So two days before my 30th birthday we flew off to Las Vegas with alias names. My alias was Nadia. Now let me tell you a little something about me. When Natalie Newman decides to have a party, I only invite the wildest, funniest, and craziest party people I can find. If you drink too much, cuss too much and have questionable morals, you're everything I ever wanted in a friend. I love wild and crazy fun. I love to put them all together and watch the show. I suck the craziness right out of people. I love to watch them have so much fun that nobody will forget me or that moment. When they let their hair down and find freedom, it is such a pleasure to for me to watch.

I am the instigator of wild and crazy fun. I allow them to do whatever they want or what they would not do anywhere else. I never judge them. I will be cheering them on. Something gets freed inside them and that is the way I live. I live in freedom and do not care what others think. I love to have fun and it is my favorite thing to do on earth. I love to surround myself with people who make me laugh, because laughter is the best medicine on earth. Warning: my sense of humor could hurt your feelings. I suggest you get over it. Never underestimate the importance of having fun. I put the FUN in disFUNctional.

Children laugh an average of 400 times a day but adults

laugh an average of 15 times a day, somewhere along the way we have lost 385 laughs per day. Regain this, laughing is good for you.

So we landed in Vegas and first night stayed in a casino. Then next morning we had to be out of the motel and had four hours to kill before we could check into our condominium. Hmmm! What to do in Vegas? Get a twelve person stretch limo, a carload of alcohol and let the adventure begin. Oh dear God! We never slept or stopped drinking for the next five days. Everyone was in every direction and completely out of control. We covered the entire city.

We partied like ROCKSTARS! On my birthday I got my very first tattoo. Also, we went to my favorite place to eat in Vegas and everyone there watched us, including the staff. There were people from other countries videotaping us. We were out of control having so much fun nobody wanted to stop us. They just sat back and enjoyed the comedy show in astonishment. Two people came close to an emergency room vacation. We came close to missing our airplanes because we were wasted and lost track of time. That was the WILDEST five days of my life to this day. Every person there said it changed their lives forever. We put the Hangover movie to shame. Twelve years later they still will not go back to Vegas with me. I cannot tell you anything else about that trip because what you see in Vegas stays in Vegas!!!

However, when I returned home, the party was completely over. I was so exhausted. I had been flying so high having fun that I crashed like a jet from the sky. Then the depression set in about turning 30. I had never dreamed of being this old. I had no desire to grow up. I did not want to be 'old'. It killed me to say I was 30. I wanted to be young and free forever. I never wanted to be a mother either. Now I had a child to be responsible for. I had to find a way to pull through this for her. It was time for me to be a mother now. I slowly pulled myself through a few issues to heal a little bit and move on. Once again, something carried me through it.

My intuition at this time was getting stronger. I began to really be able to see into people and I could see what was wrong with them. I could see better than I wanted admit. I could feel the pain radiating off people. I had the urge to stop each one of them and help them. I never did do this, except to my friends, but it was a lot to get used to. I also never talked about it to other people because I felt they would not believe me. I just thought I was crazy.

A few months after my birthday, my eleven month old niece died. The death of a baby is the most difficult pain I have ever experienced. The amount of pain is unimaginable. You can break my heart over and over, but please dear God, don't take one of my children before me. I watched my dear sister and her husband go through this. It was difficult to add onto my own pain of losing that beautiful angel.

The only advice I gave to my sister was not to push her husband away because he is the only person on earth who understood what she was feeling. I told her she was not all alone and he is lost too. We all survived it but it never leaves your heart. I can always feel her around me. I got another tattoo of a cherub angel blowing kisses on my leg. I wanted to have her walking with me forever and she is.

Furthermore, out of respect for the father of my children and my children, I will not go into detail about what went on behind closed doors of this perfect American family. We played a game well and everybody thought we had the perfect relationship and home life. We loved each other so very much. However, we kept running from our destructive pain.

Once again, things started to escalate in my relationship and I was ready to run. Then I got pregnant. That kept us together and we were so excited it changed everything for us. It was such a difficult time for me because I felt so much guilt for having a baby. I did not want to hurt my sister. My beautiful baby girl was born one year after my niece's death. I had been so scared about how I was going to have enough love for another child. When I looked at my beautiful new daughter I fell in love all over again. Daddy would never put her down and he was so in love with his little girl. Our relationship was doing fantastic and we bought an old 1896 Victorian house that needed complete remodeling. We began work day and night on that house. Friends and family came together and helped us through it all.

Finally, after working for many months, we moved into the first floor of our new home. Then we had a house warming party and 1st birthday party for our baby. Almost 100 people came and most just to see the house because it was so unique. However, someone had been sick and unknowingly passed onto my baby Respiratory Syncytial Virus or RSV. It is a respiratory virus in small children.

The next day she turned blue, made two trips to the emergency room and then an ambulance ride to the next city. She was placed in pediatric intensive care unit and hooked up to a bunch of machines. I felt like I was living in a nightmare. I have never been so scared in my life, as to watch my baby fighting for hers. Thank God she survived it and five days later she got to come back home. I hope I never have to experience that with my children again.

At this point in life I became a compulsive house cleaner. I followed behind my children picking up everything they put down. Every little thing had to be perfect because I did not want others to judge me and say anything about how dirty my floors were. I cleaned day and night. It was just another addiction I had found to cover the pain. Maybe if the house was spotless, then people would think my life was. I still continued to party about two days a week. Most of the time I did it was because the violence in my house was becoming more common.

We just couldn't get it right. We tried to do the family thing the best that we could, but we still had our pain we kept putting on each other. Both of us were cheating on each other. It was a vicious circle of you hurt me, now I hurt you. Yet, everybody believed we had the perfect life together. We loved each other very much, had two beautiful children, beautiful new house, he had a great job and we had everything everybody dreamed of. When it was good it was very good but when it was bad it was so very bad. We just smiled through it and lied.

I started working for a company that does in-home parties. I would go to someone's house and they would have a party with their friends to come and buy my products. I was partying for a living and loved it. I worked my butt off the first year and I received an award for "Highest New Consultants Sales" in five states. I was up against Chicago, Minneapolis, Milwaukee and small town Natalie beat them all.

Because of my high sales I earned a free seven day cruise to the Caribbean with red carpet accommodations. The ex and I had an amazing trip. Although, he pulled the Titanic drama and was going to jump off the end of the boat looking for sympathy or something. Out of complete embarrassment I just told everyone let him do it. I did not even care if he jumps and he won't because he was just looking for attention. I just went back to the cabin where we were drinking and was so angry that he had to destroy even the best moments because of his pain.

Next, I stopped doing the home parties and started college to follow my dreams of helping people. I was going to be a psychologist like I always wanted to. We made the decision to put our house for sale because after five long years of remodeling, we had finally finished. We had such a beautiful home, but it was our goal when we started to get out to the woods.

Also, I had gotten myself into a few very dangerous situations with one of the men I had been cheating with. At that point I realized I was playing a very dangerous game because of my pain. I looked at my ex and told him I was sorry, but I was fighting a war inside me and I did know how to stop it. He understood me completely. I stopped cheating on him. Yet, it was not enough to stop doing what we were doing to each other. It had become mutual to sell the house, split the profits and part ways.

Few months later I found out I was pregnant again. I went to tell him about it at his brother's house he was remodeling. I walked in and felt sick immediately. There was a girl there and instantly I knew she was sleeping with my man. Always trust your instincts. I did not say anything and walked out of the door. That girl slammed the door behind me the second I walked out. No way did I want to have this child with this man and stay with him longer. I knew I would be on my own raising two children by myself.

I finally told him I was pregnant and we both made the decision we didn't want to involve another child in our mess. So, I went to the abortion clinic to get an ultrasound to see how far I was and make an appointment. I found out I had two weeks to have the abortion. I got dressed and someone said that I had a phone call. It was the ex and he told me my sister had just started labor with her first baby.

So, I went to the hospital and helped her give birth. My other sister was there and my brother in law. When that beautiful angel came out, I looked at my sister who had lost her baby, we both cried with complete joy of this beautiful moment and the deep cutting pain we were holding inside. I realized at that second God had put me there to witness the birth of that child. I had never told my sisters at that time I was pregnant and wanted an abortion. I went home, the ex looked at me and said, "We are going to have another baby aren't we?" I answered him with sincerity that I could not have an abortion after witnessing the miracle of life.

Few weeks later, we found out by accident that we were having a baby boy. Our excitement was alive again. We were going to have a son. Everything was wonderful once more. The entire pregnancy I could not wait to meet him. I quit school so I could stay home and breast feed him full-time. I had done this for both my daughters until they were ten months and my children never got sick. So I wanted to do what is best for my baby and I would take care of myself later. I decided to return to college when I was done. On Valentine's Day in 2005 I went into labor. I smiled the entire time. I was walking around cleaning and acting completely normal. Daddy was bouncing off the walls because I refused to go to the hospital.

After six hours of being in labor in the comfort of my home, I let him take me in. We got to the hospital, they broke my water and gave me an epidural. Why feel the pain if you do not have to? The labor went perfect. When his head and shoulders came out the doctor told me to grab him. I pulled him out, put that beautiful little boy on my chest and watched him take his first breath. I cried so hard because he was perfect. I was so grateful God had intervened and stopped me from having that abortion. I was so in love. I never put him down.

When my son was born I was 35 years old. I refused to leave the hospital without having my tubes tied. There was no way in hell I was having another child. I knew at that moment I had to change everything. I did not want to raise three children the way that it was in our home. I started to change myself. I stopped drinking and cheating. The ex did not. We started looking for homes in the country to buy when life was good between us. We found a house and I fell in love with the land. I felt my heart belonged there instantly. But again, things began to escalate in the house and this time I knew it was not me. I had been sober for over a year and working hard on myself to be a better mother and girlfriend. I just wanted to make our family work. We had the perfect life and it was worth trying to save.

So I went to a psychotherapist to get some help because he had continuously blamed me for everything, I believed him and got help. First thing I told her was my life history and she told me I was doing fine surviving everything I had. She wondered why I even needed her, but she kept seeing me for a few more sessions. I basically thought I needed help, but the answers were inside me and I had to find them.

Once again we decided to just go separate ways and our house finally sold. It was the moment of reality when we should have ended it. We got excited again and decided to buy the home we had looked at a year before that I loved. We felt if we got out of town and into the country, we might be able to make things work. We loved each other no doubt and something just kept us together every time we went to part.

When we moved out into the woods my heart felt home again. I had the peace with nature. I was always exploring the forests. Life was wonderful. We had three beautiful children, good family and friends living close to us, beautiful piece of land, ready to build my dream house, a hardworking man and a fabulous income. We were truly living the American dream and holding deep inside our "behind closed doors" secret.

Things started to get out of control again. He was spending a lot of time drinking and hanging out in the garage all hours of the night. I had been working hard to be a good person so we could make this relationship work. I turned 37 and in November of 2006 my dad died a few days after Thanksgiving. It was complete shock. He had a brain aneurysm. It was instant death and thankfully he did not suffer one minute. The six of us children went through another terrible loss. Losing a parent is a crushing blow to the heart.

This loss drained me right back into the bottle and depression. I drank and drank wishing to wash the pain away. I always had fun partying. Up to this point, I had never drank in front of my children. I always waited until after they went to sleep.

Also, it is my choice and I feel my children have seen enough of it with everyone else in their life. I had lived a lifetime of hell because of the choices my family had made because of drinking. This was the moment when I felt I could go against my beliefs and drink in front of them. I was so depressed. The pain of my life had become the most unbearable load to carry. I knew I had to get out of this mess. On Christmas the ex asked me to marry him. I would not accept the ring. We had been together eight years and I knew I did not want to live the rest of my life like this. If it got better I would marry him, but not now.

My drinking had gotten out of control and one day I ended up having to call a friend for the first time ever to come get me. It was 2 p.m. and I was in a bar. I could barely stand up and fell out of the truck when I got home. My children were in the house. I had drank a month straight every second I could. They still had not seen it and I did not want them to. I stayed in the garage and drank another liter of vodka. It was rock bottom once again.

That is when I made the decision to quit drinking. Take the pain killer away and then you start to feel the pain again. This depression took me so far down into hell, I felt I would never get out again. I couldn't live through this anymore. I had shut myself off from the world and could barely get out of bed. I was literally dying and I could feel it. The depression was eating me from the inside out. Life was dark and I could feel the pain killing me. I couldn't even eat. But I did find a way to take care of my children the best I could.

After about four months the only thing I wished for was death. I would pray to God to just take me and please end this hell. I had lived through enough and I could not take one more second of pain. An incident broke out with my ex and this time my babies witnessed it. We had hid this from them also. It killed me to see their faces and fear. What had I done to my children? I had failed. I never wanted them to have the life I lived. I wanted the opposite of my life for my children. He yelled at me to get the hell out and never come back. To his shock I walked out the door this time. I went to stay with a friend's father. I walked away from my family feeling like a complete failure in every way.

I could see the good man that was inside him. He did nothing to change or make things better. The ex was afraid to face his demons, but I wanted change. I was tired of the constant battle and I had given him eight years of my life. Some things just do not work no matter how hard you try. I know I hurt him so much and pray he can forgive me. We were both just so messed up together. I look back now at all the signs I was given to leave and all the opportunities I was given to get out.

Yet, I stayed because of a hundred different fears. What goes on behind closed doors nobody ever knows. Just because it looks perfect does not mean it is. But you do not have to keep the secret forever. Nobody believed me when I told them the truth about our life. They honestly thought I was a liar. I had a good man and who was a fabulous father. They had never seen the bad side of him.

Furthermore, I tried to help him and myself through it. My only true wish for him is that one day he can face himself and heal the pain inside him. Then he can stop taking the pain out on everyone around him. He really is a great father when he wants to be. I hope one day he can be that fantastic person that is screaming inside of him to get out.

~Never have I dealt with anything more difficult than my own soul, which sometimes helps me and sometimes opposes me.
~Imam Al-Ghazali

~And so we know and rely on the love God has for us. God is love. Whoever lives in love lives in God, and God in Him. ~ John 4:16 Bible

~I don't suffer from insanity, I enjoy every minute of it.

~There are only two ways to live your life: One is as though nothing is a miracle. The other is as if everything is. That's a quote by Albert Einstein.

~ Don't wait for miracles, your whole life is a miracle.

~Therefore I tell you, do not worry about your life, what you will eat or drink; or about your body, what you will wear. Is not life more important than food, and the body more important than clothes? Look at the birds of the air; they do not sow or reap or store away in barns, and yet your heavenly Father feeds them. Are you not much more valuable than they? Who of you by worrying can add a single hour to his life? ~Matthew 6:25-34 The Bible

~Dear anyone considering suicide: Please don't give up. You are needed. You are wanted. You are important. You are loved. You are beautiful. ~ Natalie Newman

~Always remember who you are and you'll always know where you're going.

Chapter 5

The Divine Intervention of Natalie Newman

On March 11th 2007, my life changed completely forever. After I had left my home to get away from the abuse, I was trying to find out who I was and where the hell I was going. I had no idea where or how I was going to get there. All I knew was I had to decide if I would try to keep my children, how I would survive and if I even wanted to stay alive.

Unfortunately, I felt death was the only answer. I felt I had nothing to give anybody. I felt everyone would be so much better if I was dead and out of their lives completely. I felt I was a horrible mother exposing my children to this horrible suicidal depression and abuse I was living with.

At this moment they had no mother. I could not seem to escape the horror of abuse and failure. There was no reason to live anymore. I had failed in life on earth. I imagined my children and everyone happy because I was gone. I dreamed they all beautifully healed from the pain of losing me and everyone was content with life. They were finally free from watching me dying in deep depression.

I was staying at a parent's house of a lifetime friend who was like a brother to me. It was only a mile from my home, I was close to my children, free from the mental and physical abuse. I began to help his father clean and paint the kitchen of their house. I had to do something creative to get through it.

Next, my dear friend was on his way to a city three hours away to visit a friend for the night. He was in a bad mood that day and I was doing my best to avoid him. He walked through the kitchen while I was painting and did not say anything. He went to shower before he left. He came out of the bathroom with intensity in his eyes. He said to me, "You have to come with me. They were in the bathroom telling me you have to come with me." He was completely serious. I looked at him confused and said, "WHO was talking to you in the shower?" He said to me, "The spirits and they told me you have to come with me, so get ready to go now." I looked at him in disbelief. I thought he had lost his mind. I did not want to go anywhere with him and his anger. However, I got dressed and we left. I did not say one word to him the entire three hour ride there.

My friend and I got to a church parking lot near the home we were going to. He called to see if his friends were home yet. They were still 15 minutes away. As we sat waiting, he turned and looked at me. He said, "This dude's girlfriend is a psychic." I said, "oh really, what did she tell you?" He just stared straight ahead and said, "Everything she said was right." Not another word about it. I was a little curious. I had never seen a psychic before. Yet, I chose to sit in the car and wait for him. I was in no mood to socialize with people I did not know and have some dumb psychic fill my head full of shit. I wanted to just wait for him so we could go home. Ten minutes I sat alone in the car swimming in my depressive pool of self-pity. I was wishing I wasn't there at that moment and I could just leave this world filled with pain.

Suddenly, a woman the same size as me comes running out the house, jumps in the driver's seat, puts the keys in the ignition and says, "Where do you want to go?" I just looked at her with complete confusion. She looked right into my eyes and said to me "I knew you were coming, I have been waiting and preparing for you for a long time."

Next, I swallowed hard and my mind raced with the thought of maybe I had done too many drugs in my lifetime. I thought I was hallucinating. She took my hand and said to me "You believe in that fairytale love. I have read 1000's and 1000's of people and you are the only one who still believes in the fairytale romance. Don't worry honey, you will have it, but you have to get out of where you are now. He will never change enough to be your fairytale love. Let go and everything will work out in you favor." I was frozen in shock. What the hell was going on? Who the HELL was this woman?

She asked me if I wanted to come into the house with her. I agreed only because I really needed to calm down, look at things from a different perspective and with a more open mind. She seemed to have some guidance for me. My instincts said go with her. So we went into the house. I felt like I was walking out of my body, walking in some sort of dream with this woman guiding me through. We sat down and I was spinning off this earth with shock. Suddenly, she started talking at about 100 miles an hour. Not once during this time did I ever speak one word. I sat there straight faced, while this unknown human being began to tell me everything about my past and everything about my present and everything about my future. I swore to God someone had slipped me some LSD. I could not believe the words coming out of her mouth.

First, she started with my past. The connection with the father of my children in past lives and why it is the way it is right now. He had killed me in many, many lifetimes and took my children from me. It was a reasonable explanation for his abuse towards me and what was happening at the present moment with him and I. She told me "You have always been a tortured soul and you need to find the strength in your soul to walk away. If you do not walk away you will end up dying." Honestly, I was already dead in every way, except physical. She reassured me of my physical health at that present moment. She told me, "Physically, the depression and pain is literally killing you from the inside out. Depression does kill and you aren't far away from death with your physical self, unless you change now."

She told me my children's entire journey in this life and past lives. Explained their souls, told me what and who they were here for. She ripped through my entire history of this life, from birth to now. Word for word, like a book, she recited my life to me. I had never met this woman and I know about 50% of what she said I NEVER TOLD ANYBODY. She talked about my relationship with my mother and our connection together which explained so much about the relationship we have had to this present moment.

That psychic told me her and I were sisters in Egypt in a past life during the time of the pyramids. Totally explains my obsession to go stand next to those pyramids. It is my dream and I will do it. I will read or watch anything about those times in Egyptian history. Next, she went on to my last life here as a soul and told me I was 14 year old Jewish girl killed in a Nazi concentration camp during World War II. This completely answered my question about my infatuation with Hitler and Nazi Germany. I could never understand that one. Other kids would be out playing and as a young child and I wanted to look at pictures of World War II Germany.

Next, it was the life before that one I died very young because I drown on the Titanic. The other sick obsession I had was the mystery of the Titanic. Let me tell you. I LOVE WATER. I love its power and beauty. But, to be in it or on it, I have extreme panic attacks. I hate boats and all I can think about is sinking when I am in one.

When I go swimming very rarely do I go past my stomach. Once that water hits my chest I have panic attacks and I cannot go in farther. I did learn to swim very well and if I am completely familiar with the area then I am fine. But 90% of the time you will never see me in the water or on it. I will be looking at it from the beach. She also told me I had never lived this long in previous lives. I was always killed. It is understandable that my entire life I never dreamed of living past 25. Now I could see why I went insane and crashed hard when I turned 30.

She moved on to tell me about my three Guardian Angels that were surrounding me. One was a man who always played tricks on me. Here I always thought I was losing my mind. I would put something somewhere and it would disappear for days and return or end up some place else. She told me he is the one doing it. Next Guardian Angel was my grandmother from my very first lifetime and that she rocks me when I cry. Damn, when I cry really hard, I uncontrollably rock back and forth. I do not even notice it until I have been doing it for a long time and then I wonder why the hell I rock every time I cry. To this present day, today, I still rock when I cry hard because she is still with me now.

The third Guardian Angel around me was a 17- 18 year old boy. This young man chose to watch over me as a gift to my birth father. He wanted to repay him for being such a good friend. I did call my father and ask him if anyone had died in his life at 17-18 years old. He hesitated for a moment and said, "My best friend died at 18 and it took me a very long time to get over it." I told him, "Well he is here watching over me for you because you were such a great friend to him." I felt it click in his head over the phone, he believed me. How would I have known to ask him that question out of the sky? There was no way possible for me to know that unless what she said was real. My father knew that.

She explained every problem I had, why I had it and what I needed to do to survive it. She went back to the fairytale love explaining to me that there was only three men on this earth that could handle me, make me happy, accept me completely for who I am, and love me the way I dreamed of. Furthermore, if I left the one I was with now, I would know who #1 was by my next birthday. My birthday was in October and 7 months away. She told me so many things that I could write an entire book on that night and also so much got lost because too much was said.

Last, but not least, she told me this is my last life on earth. I have come here to accomplish everything as a soul and never return. Honestly, I think I was so damn grateful to hear that because I really could not wait to get out of "here" my entire life. Onward, she told me that I was here to help save the world, teach people to pray, to help save Mother

Earth, fight for world peace, help women and children all over the world.

At that point I think I got sick to my stomach. I had lost complete control of all of my emotions. I began to drift in and out of consciousness. I was not on this earth or inside myself. My brain was overwhelmed and she could see it. She said "I will stop. It is too much huh?" Yes it was. I had no idea what to believe at that point. I just knew it had to stop. I was laying personally scattered all over her floor in a trillion pieces.

I only asked her two questions the entire three and half hours she talked non-stop to me. I said, "Why me, why would God choose a pile of shit like me? I am nothing and I am not a good person at all." She smiled at me with great compassion. Calmly, she told me, "Natalie, if you need someone to help you and understand you, are you going go to the local church and talk to the lady in a pretty dress, with a pearl necklace with a perfect life? FUCK NO! That woman is not going to understand you. What you need is someone who has been through what you have and understands your hell. People need you because you understand them."

At that moment I knew what she was talking about. My entire body got warm and a tingle went up through all of it. I had felt that way about everyone trying to dig in my head who had only read it in a damn book. My powerful passion to help others had just been confirmed by this woman. I knew I had lived through all this hell to help others who had less strength than me. Surviving all this hell was for a reason. I could see and understand very clearly.

The last question I asked her was, "How the hell am I going to teach the world how to pray, do all these things to help create world peace, plus help woman and children all over the world? That is an overwhelming responsibility for one human being. I can't save myself so how I am going to do my part in saving the damn world? Seriously? WTF?"

She looked at me with a slight smile and said to me, "The

world is going to come to you. Don't worry about those things now. Do what you have to do to survive and get out of the life you're in at the moment. You have freewill to decide if you want to do it or not." All I could think was "How in the hell was the world going to find me? I live in the middle of nowhere, eight miles from the nearest civilization. I am in the woods two hours from Canada for God sakes."

My friend could see I mentally had enough and we decided to go back home. This woman had just completely dissected me in three and half hours, I was exhausted and could not take one more word. We got to the door to walk out and she said to me, "Go back home to your children. You don't want child abandonment and lose them. End that relationship if you choose. Trust that everything will work out. You will get your children, your home and the fairytale love. Don't worry! It is going to happen. I live up there by you and as soon as the snow melts I will be back up there to work with you. Just survive until I get there."

I got in the car and sat down. I really couldn't breathe and I had no emotion. My friend looked at me and very sweetly said, "Are you okay?" I replied, "I am okay, thank you for making me come down here, you literally saved my life." Smiling, he said back, "I told you she was right." I burst uncontrollably into hard crying, an intense rush of pain bolted through my body, but also relief flowed out of me with volcanic action. I cried the whole entire three hour ride home.

She was right about everything. I was in disbelief of what had just happened to me. It was truly an intervention by God to save my life. I was free! Everything was answered but it was all so unbelievable to swallow at this moment. I was off this earth for days after that trying to sort my way through everything she said and understand it. Every day I am still working on understanding everything she said.

Please people, listen to your instincts. Even through your pain, everyday life and anger, hear what is being said to you. You may not understand why you need to do something at that very moment, but do it. I thank God every day my friend forced me to go with him and listened to the crazy voices in his head.

My current life best friend (who is like a brother to me) and my sister from my past life came together with the help of many angels and saved my life that night. DIVINE TIMING! I was mentally, spiritually, emotionally already dead. Physically my body was ready to give in if I didn't do it myself first and commit suicide. My life sentence was up.

I will never forget that moment. The angels came down and guided my friend to get me to this woman. Angels told her every possible thing about me and guided her words to save my life. Truly, a moment created ONLY by God. My faith was completely restored. Discomfort is the call to set yourself free. You must go through the worst to arrive at your best. Although, she never told me the path ahead would be so damn difficult.

My weirdness will make me stronger. My dark side will keep me whole. My vulnerability will connect me to the rest of our suffering world. My creativity will set me free. There's nothing wrong with me.

~Sometimes we have to lose something precious in order to gain something priceless.

~You'll never find the right person if you never let go of the wrong one.

~When your ex says, "You'll never find anyone like me." Reply back with "That's the point."

~You can spend minutes, hours, days, weeks or even months over analyzing a situation, trying to put the pieces back together, justifying what could've, would've happened OR you can just leave the pieces on the floor and move the fuck on. ~Tupac

~The 3 C's of life- Choices, Chances, Changes. You must make a Choice to take a Chance or your life will never Change.

~Nobody can hurt you without your permission.

~And then one day she decided to do something different with her life, and that made all the difference... Choose life!

~Just went the caterpillar thought the world was over, it became a butterfly.

Chapter 6

The Search for Natalie Newman; An Ending and Beginning of a Life

After being away from my family for two weeks I returned home. Only to find that there was no point in staying. It was probably the most horrible two weeks of my life. He called me drunk the 2nd Friday night after my return, got a motel for the weekend and told me I had no right to know which room he was in. I told him it was over. I called for help. I called the women's shelter in town. They called the sheriff for me and it was enough to keep me safe until I could put an order of protection against him. I had to stand my ground to keep my children and myself safe. When God shuts a door I won't keep banging on it! I had to trust that whatever was now behind me was not meant for me to keep.

He returned home on Sunday, April 1st. It may have been April Fool's Day but I was in no mood for joking. He walked in and sat in the living room with the children. I told him he had to leave, it was over. He got a violent look in his eyes and I could see I was in for a beating. He told me to get the fuck out and never come back again. For the first time in my life I said, "NO, you are leaving." He refused.

So I got in my truck and drove to the neighbor's house to use the phone. I called the sheriff's department and told them to get him out of the house. I calmly smoked a cigarette and exhaled my entire life away with each breath. When I got into my truck to return home, I knew from that moment on my life would never be the same. I prepared for battle and walked in the door of our house. I again told him, "You have to leave." He laughed at me and started to look crazy again.

I looked out the window and the cars started coming up the driveway. I smiled and said, "No, you really have to go." He started to come towards me. I again smiled and said, "Sorry! You're gone." Then I opened the door to 2 sheriff's deputies, 1 state trooper, and 1 city cop. I exhaled the hell of the entrapment I had been living. I told him, "I am done and it is time for you to go now." Every officer on duty at that moment was sent out to my house with 4 vehicles. He has a history and those officers were not taking any chances with him. One deputy escorted him to the bedroom to pack his belongings. One stood outside and one at the front door. One deputy stood in front of me at the entrance of my bedroom door. I looked him straight in the eyes with disbelief in what I was doing.

Then the deputy asked me, "What is going on Natalie?" I exploded out to him, "No man will ever beat me, yell at me, or call me names again. I am tired of the abuse and being treated like shit. Get him the hell out of here because I don't want to look at him one more second." Then he was escorted off the property in between the officers. I was free! I felt overwhelming joy and deep sadness at the same time. I felt so terrible my children had to see that, but it was better than watching me die.

So, then the journey to find Natalie Newman began at that very second. The next day was Monday so I went and got an order for protection against him. The judge approved one complete year of protection for me. However, he really never believed he had to abide by any laws his entire life, so of course he didn't uphold it. He spied on me and drove by constantly. He told everyone he was going to kill me. The officers couldn't do anything because nobody actually seen it. I guess you have to get hurt before they can prove anything. Please everyone, put up a camera, get your proof and protect yourself against stalkers. Do not leave yourself vulnerable without witness. Ask God for protection and stand your ground.

I went through about 3 days of horrible gut thrashing pain as I watched the last eight years of my life come to an end, including my life of being abused. I promised my children at that moment they would never have to live in my home with a man who yells or hurts me. They will have a safe and peaceful home if I had to be alone until they all graduated from school.

Furthermore, I went through the most ungodly depression wondering what I had done. Had I made the right choice? How the hell was I going to pay for a house and feed my children? It was one second at a time and most seconds were a nightmare. I could not see how I was going to survive this.

The depression finally got to the point that I had written letters to each of my children, their father, all my friends and family. I apologized for not being able to keep fighting through the pain, for ending my hell and my constant failure in this life. Suicide was the only way I could get the hell to end. I had it all planned out how and when I would do it. I found a way to do everything so my children would not be the ones coming home and finding me. I was completely ready and I was content with my decision.

One day before I was going to kill myself, my neighbor friend came over and said to me, "She said you're not doing well, here is her number. Call her as soon as you can." I was shocked. How the hell did that psychic know anything I was feeling? So I called her. She had seen I was doing bad and prayed for me. We talked for about an hour and she helped me change my mind. She once again kept me alive. It's me who is my own worst enemy. It is me who beats my own self up, it is me who creates the monsters within and it is me who strips my confidence.

After that day I was constantly surrounded by family and friends. People I had not talked to in years. I had a guy tell me that he had asked my dad before he died if he could have my hand in marriage if I lever left the asshole ex. He told me my dad laughed and said, "If she becomes single I wish you the best of luck catching that one and if you DO catch her I will approve." I never had any idea that other people even thought about me at all, let alone like that. My world opened in so many different directions, I began to heal and that psychic was on my door step in about 2 weeks.

The psychic walked up my steps and asked if I had a drink. I came back with a half-gallon of vodka and said, "Hell yeah I do." We drank that and headed to the bar by 1:00 in the afternoon. It was complete insanity. Every person in that bar I knew personally and we were having a great time. At 4:00 she said to me, "In three hours you will be yourself again." All my surrounding friends all said at one time, "Oh shit, that isn't good. We're all in trouble." Natalie was coming back to life again. The psychic and I were both like two peas in a pod. It was crazy fun and we were politely asked to leave the bar because everyone was completely out of control having fun and we started it. Ooops!

Lesson in life: A wise man sat in the audience and cracked a joke. Everyone laughed like crazy. After a moment he says the same joke again. This time less people laughed. Then a moment later he told the joke again and again and again. When there was no laughter in the crowd he smiled and said, "You cannot laugh at the same joke over and over again. Why do you keep crying over the same thing over and over again?"

Crying is not a sign of weakness. It is a sign that you have been strong for too long. If you want to fly, you have to give up the shit that is weighing you down. At any given moment you have the power to say "This is NOT how my story is going to end." I knew I had to do better for myself in every way.

So, I applied for a job as a server in a beautiful resort on the lake. Immediately I got an interview and they hired me on the spot. My schedule was perfect: Monday-Friday, 7:00 in the morning to 2:00. For a job in a restaurant that is a miracle beginning shift. God heard my prayers. However, little did I know at that moment why God put me there at that place. They had people who came on visas to work there from other countries.

Within a month I volunteered my home for a going away party for an intern from India. He had been here in USA with an 18 month intern visa. A dude from Jamaica and the one from India came out to my house one day to see if it was a good place to have his party. They fell in love with the place, wrote in the dirt on the back of my truck "I LOVE FOREIGNERS!" and the party was planned for the next weekend.

The night of that party was unbelievable. I had people with tents, huge party-sized BBQ grill, tons of food, an enormous bonfire, over 100 American people and 30 foreigners from countries I had never even heard of. I never spent one dollar. I do not even count these people as the number of foreign people at my house because I cannot remember them all. It was crazy fun. People had driven hours to get there. The world had come together at my house. Colors, borders and prejudism did not exist here, we were all one. Just laughter and peace!

The world had come to me because of a party at my house. She was right! I celebrated this magical moment with all these people dancing and singing. It was inspiring! It was a huge success. To this day they still talk about that party. I also began many beautiful lifetime friendships from that night. Another moment in my history I will never forget.

I started having parties in my garage at least once a week when my children were gone. I found fun and freedom again. Men were coming at me from every angle. I was under attack everyday by some man. It was raining beautiful men from everywhere. However, not one was over 25 years old. Men my age would not even come near me. Well, I acted and looked like I was 25. Men my age told me they could never keep up and were not even going to try. I had the pick of many, many hot men. I survived through life and found the way to live again.

One of the Colombians, who was 19 years old, started flirting with me every day. This continued for a couple weeks daily and finally I just gave in to him. I was single. He was young and sexy as hell, why not? He helped me to find power, self-confidence and a heck of a lot of fun. It was an amazing summer with alot of partying, learning of other cultures and wonderful foreign cooked food. My children got to experience so much culture and spend time with them also. We had 2 from India, 3 from Colombia, 1 from Jamaica, and 1 from Turkey.

Two of the beautiful Colombians showed me the most beautiful loving relationship on earth and that true love is real. My sweet sister from India taught me about celibacy and waiting for her life partner. Everything she did evolved around this life partner she was preparing herself for and whom she had never met. I corrupted the hell out of that girl. I had her doing things that were very inappropriate in her country but okay in mine. She became a "little Natalie." Everyone was angry with me because this sweet girl was now wild and crazy. She did not even know the word Fuck when I met her. They each taught me how lives in their countries view sex, relationships, love, different religions and other cultures. It was an amazing summer with many, many beautiful new friends both foreign and American. I never stopped laughing the entire summer. I was on top of the world.

The psychic continued to work with me throughout the summer. She helped me with myself, my faith and my spirituality. She taught me many wondrous things that I still use today as a spiritual practice. Some moments were very difficult to deal with, but I was healing and flying high off life. Life was a magic carpet ride.

The psychic told me she had called in a great warrior spirit to protect me, his name was Darkface. Darkface is a protector of women and children. At this moment in time, I was still being harassed constantly by my ex. One night I had a dream. In this dream I seen my ex walking up toward my house, I went out the door and pleasantly said to him, "Don't do this, you know you do not belong here. Please leave." He jumped up at me with a knife to my throat, pulled me down the stairs into the yard. At that point something invisible started beating him. I ran to my house and watched the entire thing. He was beaten so bad that he was knocked out completely. It was over!

Then I sat there laughing and said out loud, "Great, now I have to call the police and how am I going to explain this? It is obvious I did not do that to him. I did not even have blood on my hands. How do I explain that something INVISIBLE did it to him?" The next morning I called the psychic and told her of my dream. She said, "That is Darkface. He is letting you know he's there to protect you and NOTHING will hurt you."

The battle had also begun for child visitation, child custody and child support. This was a complete nightmare. For one, in the state I live in, it takes at least two years to go through the court system to get any child support. They do not have enough people working for them so everyone else has to suffer. The one thing I realized for women in my position at the time was I truly understood why they run back to the abuser or they move on to the next bed to support themselves and their children. It is so frustrating and we have a system that does not work for us, but against us. It forces them to think there is no other way to survive and raise their children.

Please always remember, when you have God, you have help. Ask for help and God provide all your needs for you. You have to do the work, but God will open the doors for you to be able to take care of your babies. You do not have to go jump in bed with another abuser to feed them. The visitation for the children was settled immediately. We each had the children half of the time. So now I could be a mother half the time and heal myself the other half.

The middle of October I took the 3 Colombians down to the airport so they could return home and we spent a couple days in the city. We went out for dinner and my cell phone went off. I had gotten a message from a friend's friend. It said, "What are you doing??" I looked across the table at my Colombian boy toy, (who was going home the next morning) and I realized it was time to move on again. I sent the man a message back explaining where I was and what I was doing. He asked if the beautiful Colombian couple and I wanted to go out to dinner with him the next night. We agreed.

The next morning I brought my beautiful Colombian lover to the airport. It was a difficult good bye. That wonderful young man had made me feel more like a woman than any man I had ever met. I am so grateful for the incredible blessings he gave me. He helped to set Natalie Newman free. He made me feel confident and beautiful again.

I went back to the hotel. I sat in my car heartbroken and cried. I heard my name about five minutes later. It was the beautiful Colombian couple yelling at me out the window. "Hey Natalie, come on, let's go have fun day our last day together." We had a wonderful day together shopping at the Mall of America. The man picked us up and took us downtown for dinner. I couldn't help but feel this throbbing energy between him and I. He took us back to the hotel after our wonderful meal. He and I sat in his truck for four hours talking. I gave him a quick life story about myself. We decided to see each other again. I walked back to the hotel room and realized that he had been at my birthday party two weeks before that. My birthday? #1? Hmmmmm.....

About a month later he came up to go to his hunting shack a few miles from my house. He arrived at about 11:00 at night with beer. The plan was completely innocent to just have a few beers and hang out. I opened the door, we looked in each other's eyes, we hugged, he picked me up in his arms and carried me to my bedroom.

Hours later we both sat in disbelief asking what the hell just happened here. He said to me, "I have never picked up a girl before in my life. What the hell? I just came to drink a few beers with you." Honestly, I had never been through something so intensely powerful like that before and we all know I'm not no damn virgin.

We kept seeing each other and stopped being "players" because he was just like me. He always had a few on the side he could call if he "needed" anything. He was up for the next four weekends and we were having a fabulous time together. I kept healing and working very hard on myself so I would not carry my past in to my future relationship.

 But, I corrupted the hell out of that man. He was a police officer and I was a bad girl. I would do insane crazy shit to try to get us arrested. I would put my ass against his windshield while driving down the main street in his city where he was a police officer. I tried to get him arrested for indecent exposure, public nudity, you name it. That is why they call me Naughty. I can talk anyone into doing anything bad.

We spent the rest of the autumn falling in love, laughing our asses off and having fun. I just kept flying higher and higher. Also, at this moment, is really when I began to see the Angels and spirits around me. I was working double over-time on my spirituality, my healing, my sight and my hearing to open myself to what was around me.

Next, I had promised myself not to get attached to the next foreigners who were coming soon. It was too difficult to say goodbye and let them go. End of October we got three people from Peru that had one year intern visas. I was asked to wait on the Peruvian male when he came in the first morning. I started talking to him and realized I was only hurting myself by shutting these people out of my life. I took him shopping, showed him around the town, and then took him back to my house.

I then decided to show him some real American fun. We went to my lifetime friend's house and we shot off his cannon. Yes, I did say cannon. That thing blasted off and I yelled, "Welcome to the United States of America." BOOM! He was in complete shock. We went back to my home and he spoke on webcam with his family and they were so grateful to me for everything I helped him with. Still to this day he calls me his USA 'momma' and I have a wonderful connection to his family and him. One of the girls from Peru that came at the same time also, calls me momma, she just got married and I got to attend her beautiful wedding summer 2011 in the town that I live.

Thank God I did not cut myself off from such beautiful connections because I was afraid to hurt or lose someone. Lesson learned - when God takes something from your life, God replaces it with new and different blessings. You have to let go and open the new door.

The beginning of December I got very sick. I was out of work for over a week. The income I lost from not working took away from the Christmas fund and buying my children presents. It was the first Christmas without both of their parents. I was going to be a failure as a mother because I could not compete with the money their father had. My heart was broken and I could not tell anyone because I was filled with shame and guilt. I just prayed for God to help me so I could provide my children with a good Christmas. I just had to keep the faith that God would help me.

Two days before Christmas, one of the cooks from work came to my house and brought all three of my children a present. I cried tears of joy for the thought and the fact he did that for my children. Later that afternoon, a friend came from a city three hours away brought an expensive present for all three of my children and a lovely, much needed, bottle of vodka for me. That evening I had beautiful family time with the Newman's. On Christmas day the children went with their father and I had planned a Christmas party in the garage.

About fifty people came out for the party and at about 12:00 at night a friend walked up to me and said, "Natalie, could you come out here. We have something for you to see." Him and his beautiful wife walked me out to their truck and opened the door. I just burst into tears and shook so hard I almost dropped to my knees. There in the back of their truck, was hundreds of dollars worth of Christmas presents for my children. I just hugged them and cried and cried.

It was one of the most beautiful things that ever happened in my life. I will never forget that feeling. I will be eternally grateful to those people who showed me the true magic of Christmas. It showed me that my prayers are heard. It is now one of my dreams to be able to give to other families like that. Because I will never forget the feeling of true happiness it gave me. 2007 was a year of so many difficult endings with new magical beginnings. I found my freedom from abuse. I found laughter and many new friends. The world literally showed up on my doorstep and I began to heal everything about my past. I could see with my own two eyes God WAS real.

~Like a butterfly I am growing and changing and finding my true colors in life. I am finding my wings so I can fly and soon be on my way.

~Be Free! Fear is just an illusion that keeps you locked in a box and prisoner from your true freedom. You just need to spread your wings and set yourself free.

~Never put the key to your happiness in someone else's pocket.

~If you can't find the answer maybe it is time you change the question.

~To love oneself is the beginning of a lifelong romance. ~ Oscar Wilde

~Write bad things that are done to you in sand, but write the good things that happen to you on a piece of marble. ~ Arabic proverb

~ God always has something for you, a key for every problem, a light for every shadow, a relief for every sorrow & a plan for every tomorrow. ~Unknown

~Dear Past- Thank you for your lessons. Dear Future- I am ready. Dear God- Thank you for another chance.

Chapter 7

My Sweet Serbian Suicide

The beginning of 2008, was the moment when my thought process changed. I watched a movie about the future of what is to come in the future of this earth. About fifteen minutes into it I could not watch another minute. I went directly to the kitchen where the psychic was. I asked her, "So this is what you have been trying to tell me?" She said, "YES." I sat for a minute and thought really hard, trying to absorb it all. I looked at her and said to her with the most open feeling of compassion I had ever felt up to that point in my life, "I will not stand for this. I will not allow myself, my children, my family, my friends and their families and friends and every person on earth to live like this. I have seen with my eyes what is to come. I will now commit myself completely to God to do what I came here for. From this moment on, I give my life to God. I will find a way to accomplish the things I came to this life to do. I cannot see how I will do this, but I will ask for guidance. I will ask that God takes my hand and I will follow the footsteps of this journey chosen for me. I promise God to give my life to helping this world."

Next, I overflowed with a sense of fear of failing God and not being worthy to help anyone. Like a volcano the tears burst out of me. It was like a release and intense feeling of peace. So at that moment I gave my life completely to God and helping as many people on earth as I possibly could. We all have pain, we all have suffering, but every tear reminds me that I am alive. I knew I was a mess but I had to start working on healing myself again somehow. I had a big job to do and a promise to someone very important, God. After I was alone that night I made a promise that I would NOT stop until every human on this earth was fed, clothed, sheltered, and loved.

Soon after that moment, the relationship with the city man began to change. The psychic told me he was #1 of the three men. He ONLY came to this life to marry me. We had been married in 5 past lives and those were really the only good lives I had. If I could work through my unsatisfied behaviors and we got married, everything would be perfect. I would have had another daughter. I would finish my psychology degree and be a very, very successful psychologist. It would be the picture perfect, 'happily ever after' relationship. "THIS is the easy road." the psychic said.

In February the relationship became all phone calls and we were only seeing each other about once a month. We got along perfectly and spent most of our time together laughing our asses off. However, I thought I was in love and wanted him with me all of the time. I hated living apart and for some reason it made me feel sorry for those poor women whose husbands are away with the military and gone all of the time. I never wanted to live like that. I wanted my husband to live with me and I wanted more.

So of course I stomped my feet and demanded more of him. It was impossible for him to move here and make the kind of money he was making down in the city. I had already lived in the city twice and I refuse to go back to that life after living in peace in the woods. Needless to say, I destroyed it. I wasn't even close to being ready for a relationship. It had only been six months since I had ended the relationship with the children's father. I couldn't be patient. I couldn't live apart and I just started to spin out. I dumped him. Waved goodbye to the easy life and I let it go. I threw it all way. I didn't even know what the hell I wanted in life or who the hell I was. I knew one thing in my heart, I needed more than what he could give me.

Although, I am so grateful for the lessons he taught me. He showed me that someone could love me for exactly who I am. He was the first man to take me on a date. Can you believe I was 38 before I went on my first date? He made me feel special and it was the first time in my life somebody had given me that.

I picked up the million pieces of my heart scattered everywhere and started my journey down the "Hard Road". In the middle of March I began a very dark road that spun me into some real deep depression. Trying to dig deep to find out who the hell I am and where the hell I am going.

Once again, I felt like a complete failure in every way. I began to try to heal my past and work on becoming a better person. It was difficult to try to stay away from #1. He was persistent and always trying to talk to me. I remained stubborn and wanted more for myself. It was not him personally, he was wonderful to me, I just needed more than what he could give me. I needed to find Natalie Newman. I needed to heal all the pain from my entire life so that I could do what I needed to do for God and for myself.

Once again, I went to a deep dark hell and back every day. Some moments it lasted all day. Facing yourself and everything deep inside you is not an easy adventure. It was pure hell. I never went to a suicidal place in life again but damn there were many moments I just did not feel like I was worth existing to anyone or anything on this earth. I had fucked up my whole life and now I had to face it. I ran and ran and ran from it.

Now piece by piece I had to begin to face every horrible thing I had done and lived through because of others. I tore myself apart and I stuck my head into everything horrible about myself. It did get to a point that one friend said they were scared for me because it had gotten so dark in my life. That moment of absolute hell with those emotions began to end and I was given a break for the summer of 2008. That became one of my favorite times in my history to date.

Summer 2008 began with a wine tasting at work for the restaurant. One of the cooks picked me up and we rode together to work. We got smashed! We started to get ready to leave and the cook says "Hey, the new student is here from Serbia. Should we go kidnap him?" I had no idea where the hell Serbia was, but I said, "HELL YEAH!" We walked into the house for the foreigners and this beautiful 25 year old man walked out of the kitchen. Of course Naughty Natalie began to take over my brain. Thoughts began running in my head about all the things I really shouldn't do, but knew I was going to. He looked at us and said, "I do not speak English." All I could think was good, you don't need to honey. I am tired of listening to men anyways." The cook said to him, "Come with us."

Later another cook joined us and the four of us went to my house. We had to use a translation book to write down what we wanted to say to him. I translated to him that I promised to teach him English while he was here.

The Serbian did not drink but we started pounding down the vodka. We were already drunk from work but then we added 3 more liters of vodka on top of that. I was my normal, wild and crazy self the entire time. I jumped on my 4wheeler and took that Serb for a ride that I am sure he will never forget. Flying through the woods and getting air jumping off things. I was going to put the ATV in the garage because we were out of alcohol and going to the bar. I came in too fast, turned the corner and rolled it. Of course I jumped off in the beginning of it and I was fine. He just stood there watching everything I did. Actually, all three just looked at me in amazement and that is when that Serbian fell madly in love with me. He loved my wild and crazy attitude with life.

I began to spend two days a week with him teaching him English. Truly, he did not know but a few words of my language. I could not figure out how the hell he passed the English test they must take to get here on this visa. After a couple of weeks of having them dreamy, big, brown eyes constantly looking into mine, with his beautiful body next to me studying, I lost control and Naughty took over. I could not handle it anymore. We started sleeping together. He loved me for who I was and the crazier I got the more he loved me. I taught that young man a lot more than English, if you know what I mean.

He began to learn the language very fast just so he could express his feelings to me. He wanted me to understand him. He was an intelligent man who was going to school to be an international business lawyer. My sweet Serbian summer boy and I had an incredible time together. We grew a beautiful love and respect for each other. He was kind, gentle, compassionate, loving and called me "Queen". He never for a second stopped looking into my eyes. The psychic told me every one of my lifetimes he has loved me and helped me in some way. But we never got married in any life. Oh, he loved me so much.

It was the wildest and craziest summer I have ever had. The foreigners were 3 from Poland, 1 from Colombia, 3 from Jamaica (one was returning from last summer), 2 from Peru, and my Serbian. It was non-stop partying. Drinking, laughing and enjoying life to the fullest. From the Polish I learned the art of slamming straight vodka, boys never use mix. Just chase it with something else. I witnessed some of the craziest things with those people. It was a never ending movie of entertainment with them.

Forever, I will be laughing at those times we shared together. Well, what we remember of it. They were so much fun. When my children were home there was NO drinking at my house. But there was always a foreigner in my house at all times. I will forever be grateful to all of them for making me laugh continuously for the 4 months they were here. For all the happiness they brought into my life. How much I needed them at that point. They will never understand how eternally grateful I am to them.

The beginning of October I discovered they had given the job I was working and training for, to someone else. They told me I could not do the job properly because I had children. I told them where to go and walked out. Now, I had no job and my heart was about to be broken. The new one year interns had arrived at that exact moment. There was 2 from India, 1 from Jordan, 1 from the country Georgia, and 1 from Moldova.

My Serbian made me promise that I would be friends with the Jordanian after he left. He told me, "Natalie, he needs you and he needs your help, promise me you will help him." I promised him.

However, once again it was October and my heart was crushing with pain having to say good bye to such a fantastic man. He had loved me so beautifully in every way. I didn't want him to leave.

During the last week he told me I was not allowed to cry because he couldn't stand to see my blue eyes hurt or sad. It would kill him. So I didn't let him see me cry. I just hid it very well. I also knew by now how hard it is to get a visa from Serbia to USA. On my birthday I asked him to stay and he said he couldn't. He had obligations to his government and if he does not fulfill them he will never be able to return to his country and see his family. I felt like I was going to die with pain.

Next, the Serb made me download everything for video calls. I barely knew how to email. I was computer illiterate. He was persistent that he would be able to see his blue eyes after he left. I got a message from above and it said, "He will not marry for love, only convenience. He has to do what is right for his country and family. He will always love you the most."

Taking him to the airport and walking away from him was an ungodly pain I hoped I never had to experience again. It was over and I had to move on. Thank God for my amazing friends to take care of me. A new foreign family was waiting for me. I am so blessed.

After two weeks of endless crying and drinking, I went and

got the Jordanian and the Georgian. We had a beautiful day together in the city 20 minutes away. That winter brought me 1 from the country Georgia, 1 from Jordan, 1 from Peru, 1 from Poland, 1 from Ukraine, 1 from Philippians, 1 from Moldova, 2 from India, 3 from Thailand, 1 from Colombia, and 3 from Chile. All new beautiful brothers and sisters to keep me busy. I was connected to them in my heart immediately.

After three weeks, I finally heard from the Serbian. He sent me an email and it said, "I love you my Queen and I don't care if you marry or love someone else. I will be back next summer for my blue eyes I promise." So we had our first video call and decided to continue our relationship long distance. I quit drinking. It had been a long summer of straight vodka bottle after bottle with those crazy summer foreigners and my liver needed a break. I also did not trust myself to remain faithful. I did know how I was going to make it 8 months without sex. I had never gone more than three weeks since I was 15. Those three weeks was waiting for #1.

Well thankfully none of the new foreigners drank. So it was not difficult to stay sober. They became family to me and my brother from Jordan was at my home at least 3-4 days a week. He would make Turkish coffee and we would talk all hours of the night. We took care of each other and helped each other through some very, very difficult moments trying to save ourselves. I spent the winter running around helping the foreigners. They kept me busy and helped me survive through the hell. The man from Turkey, who came in 2007, got me started on FB and I started MySpace. That is when my internet history begins and when my worldly contacts really started evolving. This is when the world really began to open up to me.

Furthermore, I went into a deep depression for a long moment. I had to start healing my sexual self in order to be able to handle this life I was choosing. It was an ugly hell to go through. You know it was like when a heroin addict quits. I went through a withdrawal. Then I had to change everything I think about and how I think to stay clean. It is the same with any addiction. I had to step out of the temptations. Lock myself in the house out of fear of making a mistake.

There were moments I would just scream how unfair it was that I couldn't be touched. I felt God was punishing me because I did not have anyone to love me. I had to stop hurting myself and be the woman I knew I could be. I wanted to be a loving faithful wife to the right man who deserved me. Now I had to clean that hell out of my closet. I had to cleanse my soul of the toxic emotions and my addiction. The Serbian told me it was okay if I slept with other men. He did not care because that is not why he loved me.

However, I made the choice not to. I was determined to remain faithful or I was going to destroy every relationship in the future. It was extremely intense and dark to go through it. I now understood and respected those women whose man goes off to the military. I had lived through the one thing I never wanted to experience. However, I had healed my sexual self and succeeded. I proved to myself I could be faithful in a relationship for the first time in my entire life. A big, huge step for Natalie and also I had killed so much pain. It was internal death and rebirth of Natalie every day.

Also, at this time in life I started to really see the spirits and Angels with me. At first it was a scary experience but I calmed down. I began to see the blessing. I would see them in many different forms such as human, animals large or small, and small tiny light flashes. I was grateful to them for letting me see them. Proving they were real and around me. I began doing card readings on my friends and they were amazed by my accuracy. Tarot cards and oracle cards became a way of life. It also became a communication tool for the Angels to answer whatever question I had about myself or others.

Without warning I just took over the intuition to start researching skin care and food production. I began my path to natural healing and teaching myself continuously for a hobby. I began creating my body and face care. The entire learning process of how to heal people inside and out started taking form. Natural Natalie, my skin care line, was born.

June 2009 came faster than I had imagined. I waited for 8 months for my Serbian to return. He went to his interview for his visa to come back to me. During his interview the embassy told him he cannot apply for that visa more than once. He was DENIED! I remember the words coming out of his mouth, but that was it. All I could hear was DENIED. It was the only thing in my heart I truly had faith in. I had faith that God would return him to me. I was instantly the sickest I have ever been in my life. My body literally went into shock. Luckily, a friend showed up at that moment to come visit me. Instead, he had unknowingly come to take care of me while I try to survive through this painful hell.

~Every man must decide whether he will walk in the light of creative altruism or in the darkness of destructive selfishness. ~Martin Luther King, Jr.

~To keep our faces toward change, and behave like free spirits in the presence of fate, is strength undefeatable. ~Helen Keller

~Don't depend too much on anyone in this world because even your own shadow leaves you when you are in darkness. ~Ibn Taymiyyah.

~Nobody has it easy. Everybody has some kind of issues. You never know what a person is going through in their lives, so pause before you start judging, criticizing or mocking others. Everybody is fighting their own unique war. ~Unknown

~Remember that today's rain is what makes tomorrow's flowers grow.

~With our thoughts, we make our world. ~ Buddah

~Be humble for you are made of earth. Be noble for you are made of stars. ~ Serbian Proverb

~If you are having a hard time letting go, remember, if they wanted to stay they would still be there.

~ Sometimes even to live is an act of Courage.

Chapter 8

I am Surrounded by Angels I Call Friends

My internal self was spinning like a tornado. My entire body was shivering uncontrollably. Literally, I had gone into physical shock. My friend kept trying to take me to the hospital because my temperature was at 105 F (41 C). I was in a black out. I just lay in my bed and cried as the pain just kept destroying me. I kept vomiting and shaking with serious physical pain in my bed for over four hours. Every inch of my body was throbbing in extreme pain as I begged for it to stop. I do not remember much. However, I do remember the last two hours I kept praying non-stop, "Please God, stop this pain, it hurts so bad, please stop it, please stop it." I felt like my body had been run over by a bus literally.

Finally, I woke up from that nightmare six hours later, got out of bed and I heard voices in my dining room, so I went out. Sitting at my table was my brother, my friend, another dear friend and a childhood neighbor I had not seen for many years. I looked around with my eyes swelled shut from crying, feeling like I had just survived a war and realized God was taking care of me.

People I loved magically came together at my home to be there for me and did not even know it. I was never alone through the entire moment. I sat down at the table, they got silent, and I said, "I believe in magic. He's coming. I prayed every day and believed with all of my heart he was coming back to me. I won't stop now. Miracles do happen! I have FAITH." I think at that point my friends felt sorry for me and thought I was completely delusional.

　　Furthermore, I tried to get ahold of my Serbian. He did not answer anything. The next day I finally got ahold of his cousin. He told me my Serbian was popping pills and they were worried about him. I emailed him back and told him to tell my Serb to get his ass on webcam immediately. Few hours later he came on cam. My sweet man looked like hell. I told him he was still coming to be with me.

　　Then he told me it was impossible for him to get back here. I told him NO government is stronger than God. I told him every step to take to get here and how to take it. He did exactly what I told him. It all unfolded with the most unimaginable story. He said to me that it was not his government that did that. Only Angels could have gone into those people and did what happened. He seen the intuition I had and the miracles of God.

　　Ten days after he was denied, I picked him up at the airport. I was so grateful to God for allowing him back and testing my faith. If I would have lost hope he would never have come back to me. We had another beautiful summer together. His sweet friend from Serbia had also come several days before him. So that summer brought me 2 from Serbia, 3 from Colombia, 1 from Spain, 1 from Turkey, 2 from Moldova, 1 from Thailand, and 2 from Peru. Another wonderful group of beautiful people God sent to me.

　　Also, I had completely remodeled Natalie's Garage. I was going to have my first party of the summer and realized I did not have any furniture. So I looked around and found the wood I needed. I built benches into the wall, long benches for sitting, 3 tables and my own damn bar. I painted the entire place again and this time the way I wanted it. I had bubble machines, laser lights, disco lights, strobe lights, and a very nice stereo system. It was now a jammin club. I created my own place that people could be free and get crazy with me without leaving home. I now had complete control over who was in my party space.

I had started planning a Full Moon party in July. Strangely enough, I had people from all over the state calling and saying they were coming. People I had not seen in ten years called and said they were coming. I could not believe the blasts from the past saying they were driving 3 hours to see me that weekend. I was walking on top of clouds getting ready to have another great party.

Well, as you know what goes up, must come down. I got a phone call five days before the party saying my grandfather had finally died. My first thought was the son of bitch has destroyed my entire life to this point and now a great party. I wasn't canceling it. I told myself at fifteen I was going to have a wild party and dance for days with people I love when he died. Not one person in the entire family called me or my brother to tell us when the funeral was. I really had no desire to find out either. I never wanted to look at that human being again.

It magically happened that his funeral was the day I had planned the Full Moon party. Now you can see how God works in Natalie's life. My dream was to party and set that hell free inside of me. Everything I had imagined at fifteen had been put into place for that dream to happen. Life really is magic.

Sixty nine people were there to participate in this magical release of the hell inside me. At one point I looked around and realized people were there from almost every continent on earth. Friends from my entire life new and old had appeared in my garage to help me celebrate one of my biggest moments and they had no idea why they were there. Natalie Newman had a dream for twenty four years and that dream came true. It was the wildest party I have ever had.

The full moon kicked everyone into high gear and the entertainment was priceless. I want to apologize to the people who lost their clothes, engagement rings, cell phones, and started their relationships in the backseat of cars. I am so grateful to God for every crazy moment that happened that night. Oh I released! I peed my pants from laughing so hard.

I puked all over the front yard and just kept dancing and partying until the sun came up.

So did everyone there. Everyone was FULL MOON DRUNK and wild as hell. I loved it. I had the best time celebrating with those crazy people. What a fabulous moment. Anybody there will never forget that night. Both my Serbian and the psychic told me the next day, "Please Natalie, that was TOO crazy, don't do that again." Ooops! But those are my favorite parties to have. Nobody ever leaves my house without having a fantastic time. I make sure of it. I am the hostess with the mostest. I'm the person your mother didn't warn you about because no one knew this level of crazy existed.

My garage is like Las Vegas. But what you see in Vegas, stays in Vegas. What you see in Natalie's Garage, never happened. Everyone tells me when they walk through the doors they forget the entire world exists and they are free. People of all ages (that are old enough to drink), different countries, millionaires and homeless, police officers and convicts, crazy and the sane, all come together and nobody is better than the other. We all are equal. We dance in bubbles and laugh the entire time. I created the greatest entertainment at my own home. It keeps my heart and the hearts of people all over the world singing with great memories.

Even my children and their friends love my garage. My oldest daughter has her birthday party in my garage every year. Those children have so much fun dancing in there. Of course there is no alcohol for them. But, they love it and cannot wait until the next year to come back. It is what they look forward to all year.

It was another great summer coming to come to an end. Fabulous people and amazing memories I will hold inside me forever. I enjoyed spending what little time I could with my Serb. I was finally free of my grandfather forever. I never had to look at him and feel disgusted again. I began to heal that part of myself instantly. I had been faithful to a man I loved for over a year and I was getting ready to say goodbye to him again. My birthday is always the final party of the year before I shut it down for the winter.

This was the big 39th birthday bash. It was another wild and crazy success. I went to bed with two Serbians and woke up with two Colombians. Now that is how a Rock Star parties. I think I have slept with almost every foreigner that has come to my house. No, I did not have sex with them. Please don't get the wrong idea. A lot of my friends sleep with me male and female. After a party there were always many people covering every inch of my house. I never cared, they needed a place to sleep and I had room for them. I share everything I have.

Finally, the time of saying goodbye had come again. I kept in mind this time that he would marry not for love but tradition. Besides, I am not sure his parents would be accepting of me for their precious son. I wasn't exactly the kind of woman you want to take home to your mom. His mother probably would have dropped dead if I walked in the door as his wife. I was 13 years older, I don't act like it and I already had three children.

However, the worse part of the situation was I am an American. They were a traditional Serbian family with big dreams for their son. Again, we decided to part ways, but keep in contact. It was a lot easier to let him go the second time. I was getting used to so many goodbyes with all these people leaving my life. But now I had a way to see them with webcam. It is just like being there, but you cannot touch them. Don't cry because it is over, smile because it happened.

Neither of us could let go when he returned to Serbia. We continued the communications but he was so busy that he could only talk to me about once every two weeks for a couple hours if I was lucky. I never knew when he was going to come online. If I missed him then I would risk the chance of not seeing him another week or two.

So by the computer I sat. Waiting and waiting for whenever he had the time. I had become online friends with family and friends of the foreigners that were here. It just continued to grow and grow. I had expanded my heart to almost every country on earth.

Many of my online friends have been through all of this with me. Most of you just did not know it. I was helping someone every waking moment of the day. Either there was someone at my house, on the phone or online. Every day I would talk to hundreds of people. People would just email or call me and ask for help for themselves or another. I was helping people with everything you could imagine in every country on earth. I was dealing with abuse of every form, loneliness, suicide, depression, addictions, relationships, family, visas, green cards, contracts and every other problem under the sun. Helping them was helping me. The worst part about being strong is that no one ever asks you if you're ok.

Now I was finding a way to deal with my own pain by helping another heal. I was teaching many people English and learning other languages. I have the connections to make one phone call and get what I need from many governments in this world so I can help another. I never abuse my power and only use it if an emergency. I also ran into another type of pain on the internet. I had some terrible lessons online. I ran into the ugly, the liars, and the disgusting.

However, I will speak of this experience in another chapter. Most of the time I was helping 10-20 people at the same time all day long. It was a lot of work to keep each person and their problems separate when you are helping so many at one moment. Try keeping all that under control. But I did it well. I could not stop helping others and they were helping me survive. I had spread myself across the world. The world was coming at me with full force.

December Of 2009 the Serbian asked me to come to Serbia and marry him in January. I did not have any money and neither did he. So we started to plan and save to make it happen. He said he could not live without his blue eyes and wanted us to be together forever. After that conversation in December our communications became less and less. My heart was in crushing pain. It was beginning to kill me emotionally and spiritually. The pain just kept growing because I knew in my heart I was going to have to live like this the rest of my life loving him. I started praying for my heart to stop hurting every day.

March 11, 2010 was the last time I had spoken to him. Ironically, that was the day of my Divine Intervention three years before. I had asked him if we were going to continue waiting for each other sexually. He replied with a yes. On March 26, I opened my Facebook of 5000 friends. My newsfeed is a 30 second turnover and it is impossible for me to see anything. Sorry to all my online friends, I try my best to keep up with all you beautiful people.

As I opened my FB that day my eyes caught a tagged picture of my Serbian's friend and cousin. With a big smile on my face I clicked it. Instead, it went to the next picture. That picture changed my life forever. It was my Serbian all cozy and happy with another woman. Plus he was cozy with her in the next four pictures. HE HAD ANOTHER WOMAN. That picture was dated two days before that moment and I am lucky if I can see two hours on my news feed. It was Divine Magic and a sign from God.

I immediately got on the phone and called him. I asked him who she was. He told me she was just a friend of his sister. He lied. I called him every name in the book. I started yelling at him for fucking up the last two years of my life with lies. I screamed at him for keeping me here under his thumb while he is out with someone else. I told him I could not believe that two weeks earlier he told me we were going to remain faithful. I hollered through the phone, "thank you for destroying my life. I don't ever want to speak to you again." The last thing I said to him was "FUCK YOU!" Tact is the ability to tell someone to go to hell in such a way they look forward to the trip to escape your brutal honesty.

One thing my friends will tell you about me is that I am a wonderful person, but DO NOT PISS HER OFF. My mind and my mouth are vicious weapons. I do not see anything but red. That is why I have tight control on my temper. It is dangerous. That Serbian boy got to find out how dangerous that day.

Karma is a bitch. I had cheated on many people who loved me. However, I stayed away from married men. I knew about karma and I never wanted that to happen to me once I was married. Now I had gotten it back in my face with someone I truly trusted, loved and was going to marry. I never believed he was capable of doing something like that to me. I had trusted him completely. That is why I could heal my sexual issues and myself. It was my love and trust for him that guided my healing. I couldn't believe it. I was totally shattered. I cried so damn hard for six hours and let it all out of me. I was alone again and I did not know who I was anymore. My dreams of our future were shattered in a million pieces for me to try to pick up and put myself back together again. I had prayed for the pain to end. I never dreamed it would end like that.

Furthermore, I have children and they have watched me hurt for two years in this relationship. I had to pull it together and stand up for them. I had to fight, let it go and have faith. I had God and I knew I could survive anything. I prayed to God to take the pain from my heart, help me to heal and survive this.

After about six hours of depressive heart wrenching hell, I finally get the nerve to open my laptop. I had an email from my favorite friend on earth from Ireland. This man is crazier than me, wild and fun. He made a point to send me music and make me laugh every day I had known him for two years. We met on MySpace and were like crazy magnets attracted instantly.

Mr. Ireland had helped me laugh all the way through the difficulty of being alone by filling my world with crazy fun. We drank beer and partied together on webcam. He was a mess when I met him. I helped him through some horrible hell that he needed to face. He was one of Dublin's best DJs. So we had a huge music connection also. I emailed him back immediately because I needed him and he was my best friend. I told him what happened with the Serbian and within fifteen minutes we were on video call.

It is one of the many favorite memories with my crazy Irish friend. We decided to get drunk to help me forget about it. So he ran to the store and came back online. He opened his first beer and said in his Irish accent, "Natalie, I bought me one of dem Viagra thingys. What ye think would happen if I took it?" I just started laughing hysterically. I told him, "Don't do it. What if your mom comes home? I am not sure I want to experience this with you."

Next, he laughed, popped the pill and said, "Awww my mum ain't comin. We can make a documentary about this. You can record everything and we will make a video on YouTube about what Viagra does." At that very moment his mother walked in the door. I started laughing so hard I peed my pants. A half hour after I prayed for help, I was getting it. Six and a half hours after my heart had been shattered I was uncontrollably laughing. Laughter and friends are the best medicine.

At first he said something rude to his mother and then he had to confess why he was angry. He told her that he was sorry he yelled but he had just taken a Viagra and did not want to sit with HER all night. All three of us laughed for many hours. It was non-stop comedy. His mother and I handed him one joke after another.

Seriously, I lost track of how many times I peed my pants laughing that night, my stomach ached for days, my face was stuck with a permanent smile and it was the hardest I have ever laughed in my entire life. Oh, I loved this person so much. Actually, I think he gets the award for making Natalie Newman laugh the most and the hardest. Believe me, that takes a lot.

After that day thousands of people stepped up and helped me. I realized all the help and love I had given out was all coming back to me. When Natalie Newman loves the world, the world loves her back. They said the only way to get over a broken heart is to fall in love again. I was so truly blessed. I may not have a dollar to my name but I am filthy rich with life. I am a ZILLIONARE baby! I will survive anything.

~If u can find a path with no obstacles, it probably doesn't lead anywhere.

~Happiness is always at your door, you just have to let it in.

~At some point you have to realize that some people can stay in your heart but not in your life.

~It's not that life has been easy, perfect or exactly as expected. I just choose to be happy and grateful no matter how it all turns out.

~It's easy to stand with the crowd. It takes courage to stand alone.

~It is better to light one small candle than to curse the darkness. ~Chinese Proverb

~You couldn't handle me even if I came with instructions.

~ My strength did not come from lifting weights. It came from lifting myself up when I was knocked down.

~ Love is the light that dissolves all walls between souls, families and nations.- Paramahansa Yogananda

Chapter 9

Along Came the Swede Who Injected His Seed of Addiction Inside Me

I had remained locked up in my home for over a year learning, growing and healing myself. I had been prepared by angels to handle this relationship to end. I had spent the entire three years living alone working extremely hard to become a better person every damn day. I never stopped. After about three months, I had completely died and came alive once more a much better Natalie. Again, I had the greatest friends all over this earth to help me through. I was eternally grateful to my Serbian Summer boy for helping me through everything that was possible for him to help with. He had guided me to become a very strong woman and heal the very worst parts of me. He loved me so beautifully and I finally had learned to trust a man.

I hope one day see his face again to thank him for everything I received because of how he loved me. He helped me become so independent and strong. Sex had become meaningless without love. He gave me the gift of self-acceptance and self-esteem by loving me for exactly who I was. He was a beautiful soul mate that brought my soul to a much higher level. I could never be angry at him for what happened. I know God will do what is best for me. I see the entire journey as a blessing every step of the way. I am a much better person because he was a part of my life. So now it was time to move on to the next door God had waiting for me to open. After I wrote this chapter I called my sweet Serbian and said I was sorry for my behavior the last time we spoke. I also thanked him for everything he gave me to become who I am. I wanted him to know I was ok. I wanted him to be free of the guilt he was carrying for what he had done to me.

Before summer started I had to open another online profile because I was now over the friend limit. Within two months it grew to the limit again. Now I had 10,000 people watching what I say and do just on one social network. I realized the responsibility I had with it. I vowed to keep everything positive or post something I had learned. My private life would have to be kept out. It was too big to be sharing everything. I began to realize the time was coming for me to move on to the next level of my higher self. The wheels began turning inside. I had to find a way to fulfill my commitment to God. I had to save my children, myself and my house.

On June 14th, I was on MySpace, when it was still cool. I was awaiting a response email from my friend in Ireland. I realized I did not have any friends in Sweden. I am Irish, Norwegian, German and Swedish. So I was playing around with the friend finder and typed in Sweden. I scrolled through about 200 people. I couldn't connect with anyone. Nobody gave me a good energy.

Then suddenly I came across a pic of a man looking down from a side view and you could not really see his face. But he had a Palestinian scarf around his neck. I had thousands of Palestinian friends online and my heart is with them in their suffering they have to survive every day to be alive. He got to me and I went to his profile. He had a band on his music list I only knew of a few people on earth who had heard them. I sent him a request.

Few hours later he sent me an email back. It said he was not trying to be cynical, but why I do I want to be his friend. I emailed back to him that I had 1000's of friends all over the world and nobody from Sweden. I was Swedish and I wanted to learn of my family heritage of Sweden. Then I wrote if he didn't want to be my friend it wasn't a problem. I felt it was his loss, not mine and he just thought I was just a dumb, blonde bimbo from USA. He accepted my request and hour later we started emailing each other. He had come to MySpace to delete his profile and I had intercepted him with my friend request.

Twelve hours later we were chatting online. The first sentence he sent me, my entire body started flying and I felt like I was being sucked into my laptop. I had one of my friends with me and I could not hear one word she said. The only thing I could focus on was him. I was hypnotized and dizzy because of him. This man had huge magnetic energy and I just thought to myself, "THIS ONE IS GOING TO HURT LIKE HELL." I could feel the pain this was going to cause me.

I wrote him and said, "Listen I do not want a damn relationship. I just got screwed over and cheated on by a man in another country. The last thing I want was another man or a long distance relationship. Do not ask me to marry you, because I hear it 20-30 times a day. Do NOT fall in love with me because I am tired of friends doing that. Then I lose them because I do not love them back. Forget it! I will be your friend and nothing else." He agreed with me completely. The last thing he wanted was a relationship also.

Day three he sent me an email and said he could not believe it, but he missed me already. That was not good. The truth was I really missed him too. I was drawn in by his energy, but the last thing I wanted was another damn broken heart or long distance relationship. I had just healed from the last one.

On the third day we had our first video call. His cam was blurry so I really couldn't see his face well. His profile pics were also very difficult to see what he really looked like. However, the seed was injected. The addiction had begun. We became junkies to each other. We had no idea how deadly and Divine that addiction was about to become. We were nonstop every waking moment we could talk to each other. We were still claiming to be friends but something huge was growing inside us. Literally, he took my breath away every time I talked to him. Our paths in life were completely parallel at the moment. So many ways we were at the same level even though I am ten years older than him.

At this moment in life I was completely done with men. I had seriously thought about trying something new like women and trying that way. I was not successful with men so maybe my love wasn't one. I was so tired of being fucked over by men. As much as I tried to run from it, I was falling in love at lightning fast speed. Funny how someone can come into your life and everything else gets erased.

The summer foreign babies had come and I never even took the time to meet them. They had been here over a month already. So I arranged a party, got a limousine and went to get my babies. We rocked the limo and when they got into my garage, they went crazy. We were drinking, dancing, having a great time and all four Turks carried me around the garage on their shoulders yelling "We love you Natalie. You're the best." There were 6 from Turkey, 2 from Peru, 1 from Ecuador, and 3 beautiful girls from Romania. I fell in love with them all immediately. I always feel there is no mistake when I meet each one of them. We had wild and crazy fun. The limo picked the foreigners up at 3:00 am. to return them to their housing.

Everyone else cleared out by five in the morning. Except one guy and I hadn't had sex for 9 months for the 2nd time in two years. I just thought to myself, "What are you thinking Natalie? You are not in a relationship. So why are you acting like it?" So, I helped myself to a little action and a good time. I walked out of the garage and I just said to myself out loud, "SHE SHOOTS! SHE SCORES! HA!" Then I get into my house, opened my bedroom door and I hear this South American voice in the dark. "Oh Natalie, I have been waiting for you." I thought for one second and said to myself, "You only live once Natalie." I dove right in with that beautiful 20 year old South American. I think you can figure out the rest of the story.

The next day I had to face myself. Not in shame, because I never regret ANYTHING. I knew I needed to make a decision. I had changed my sexual belief that sex without love was meaningless. Not that meaningless sex is bad. You have to know what you are doing and not have any expectations. It just wasn't for me anymore. I had been in a relationship for two years and I knew what I wanted. I wanted a faithful relationship, but I also wanted to just experience life for a moment. I did not want to be tied down again, especially with someone on the other side of the world.

However, I felt guilt. I felt like I had cheated on somebody. I rarely felt guilt when I did cheat on someone and I had no reason to feel this. I was single. I had no idea who I was and where I was going again. I was just flowing through life. The Swede had already started disrespecting me from the beginning.

Sometimes he would be gone for 2-5 days while I sat and waited. I had already lived like that once. I had no patience for it. He would come back and say, "ooops sorry". Then whatever excuse he had for disappearing. It was continuous. I was in no mood to put up with a man who does not respect me and my time. I had thousands of men from all over the world trying to marry me. I had my pick of who ever from where ever I wanted. Men were trying to fly me all over the world. Yet, I was sucked in by this one human. I was insanely addicted to that Swede.

I had another party with the foreigners about two weeks later. This party we added another one of my best friends on earth from Jordan. We had helped each other survive life for 3 years on webcam almost every day. He had moved to USA. My first "online only" friend came to visit my home. Again we had another rockin wild party. It was a fabulous time.

However, I had to stop and think about life after my sweet Jordanian left me. I realized I was carrying guilt and I had to tell my Swede what I was doing and tell him the truth. Of course he had been missing for days again. But when we finally got on cam I told him what I had been doing sexually. He told me he had been at some girl's house to have sex with her. He stopped and questioned himself about why he had talked about me the entire night and now he was going to do this with another girl? He did not do it. He realized he had already committed himself to me. I told him I felt no regret but Naughty just took over and went a little crazy. He was cool with it. We talked it out and I realized that SEX WITHOUT LOVE IS MEANINGLESS. I wanted and needed more. So now I was back in another long, damn distance committed relationship. I was walking the edge of another sharp knife. I dove head first into another long distance pool of pain, loneliness, and sexless heartache. Let the next roller coaster ride begin again. Put on your safety belts people, because this is going to be a wild, fast and bumpy ride.

After four months of learning and loving, we became closer and closer. We were best friends. Although, we were hurting the hell out of each other because of our huge power struggle and bad behaviors in relationships. He was everything I had dreamed of. Sadly, we also spent half the time arguing. I could not live with him and I could not live without him. It was heaven and hell all at the same time. By this point in my life I was tired of hell. I just wanted a relationship with someone who wanted peace, love and happiness every second of their life or it was not worth my time.

Yet, we could not stop this growing force of intense love happening between us. We were crazy in love with each other. We were also destroying each other every day and trying to change ourselves.

Next, we decided we needed to figure out why the hell we can't stop falling farther in love or stay away from each other. He decided to come to USA. I was not going to make myself vulnerable and go into his world alone. I had to have the control and be safe. I am a woman who has learned her lesson in abuse more than once. That is leaving yourself vulnerable going to another country without knowing anyone or what you are getting yourself into.

Within six days I was going to the airport to get the man of my dreams. I showed up late as usual. (You want me to be on time, tell me to be there half hour earlier and I will be on time.) He was standing outside the airport and I jumped out of the car before it even came to a stop. I ran as fast as I could and jumped up into his arms. I hugged him as tight as my arms could squeeze. It was the longest 40 minute ride home. The entire ride I had to keep my hand on his shoulder. I had to touch him.

When we finally got to my house and I showed him to the shower. He had traveled 36 hours and I wanted him to be comfortable. I ran out to my friend who had been watching my children when I went to airport. I looked at her and shook my head. I told her with my head down low that he was too beautiful for me. He goes against all my rules. I cannot be with a man who is beautiful enough to be on a magazine cover. I cannot put myself through that hell. I understand it. I had to learn life being beautiful and sexy. It is a blessing and a curse at the same time.

Girls see over 400 advertisements a day showing them how they should look. 3 out of 4 girls feel depressed, guilty and shameful after just three minutes of looking through a fashion magazine. Men, if you can't look like Calvin Klein models don't expect us to look like Victoria's Secret angels. Remember you're beautiful; it is society that is fucked. Too many women don't realize just how beautiful they are, just the way they are. Saying I am imperfect is actually saying I'm perfect, because everyone is perfect in their imperfect ways.

~Your damned if your too thin and you're damned if your too heavy. According to the press I have been both. It is impossible to try to satisfy everyone and I suggest we stop

trying. – Jennifer Aniston

Nobody ever takes beautiful people seriously. They see your beauty and never what's inside. You are instantly judged by everyone who looks at you. Either they look at you like your their next dessert or they hate you with jealousy. Constantly living life as a targeted piece of ass for another is no picnic. People have all the wrong intentions with you. They instantly think you are stupid because you're beautiful and treat you like you're an idiot. They selfishly want you for their own needs and desires. Nobody understands the word NO. Going out with friends just ends up with sick perverts harassing you. I have had hundreds of stalkers and it is like living in a prison every day. I have to live with my house lights off to this present moment. If the lights are on, the stalkers drive right in.

People do not care if you are in a relationship. All they see is your hot. They still annoyingly try to get in your pants. You cannot become friends with the opposite sex because they eventually fall in love and you have to walk away. It breaks my heart every time it happens. I know that I cannot help men anymore. They see my face and they do not take me seriously. They do not respect when I am in a relationship with another person. That is disrespectful to want to take me from someone I love and selfishly thinking they can be better for me.

You have a responsibility as a beautiful person to never put yourself in certain situations that are normal for others. It is much more difficult to trust people because they always have the wrong intentions. All my life I have done my best to remember I am more than my looks. I always felt ugly because of what was inside of me. As I age, I have to love myself more and more every day. I do not want to lose who I am because my looks don't work for me anymore.

However, beauty gets you whatever you want on this earth. It is a great feeling when you walk into a room and ALL eyes are on you. It is a thrilling power and sometimes it gets you places other people could never go. The truth is you are much more than your looks. Find yourself, because being you is beautiful enough. You are not your looks. God made you perfectly.

Sometimes women wear makeup because they feel bad about themselves. It is less about concealing their facial imperfections and more about hiding their inner scars and fragility. A lot of women don't want others to see who they truly are. Makeup isn't always a mask that covers the face, it's a mask that protects the heart. ~Unknown

Top 10 Countries with the Most Beautiful Women

1) Brazil
2) Russia
3) Slovakia
4) Sweden
5) Venezuela
6) Colombia
7) Ukraine
8) Lebanon
9) Angola
10) USA- With a reputation as the most obese in the world. With so much obesity, Americans are obsessed with beauty enhancers. Fake bodies in Miami and Los Angeles are flawless.

Furthermore, my friend calmed me down. She told me I was crazy because I was beautiful and I definitely deserved someone who was beautiful too. Finally, the Swede came out of the shower and we went into my bedroom. I could not breathe. My head started spinning. Our bodies came together and my feet lifted off this earth. I had never felt a feeling like that before. I had always felt Hell was on this earth. However, at that moment I witnessed that Heaven is truly on earth. Our bodies just uncontrollably start swaying and dancing the minute we touched. Absolutely no control!

Together we were literally floating on a cloud somewhere

in the sky. We would kiss and wake up two hours later trying to figure out where we went. We get lost in each other completely. We had to learn the hard way not to get close to each other because it was dangerous. It did not matter where we were. Our souls just danced constantly, intertwining with beauty and bliss.

One day we were in the grocery store standing in front of the ice cream. Our bodies found each other and we started dancing. I opened my eyes and looked over to the left. There was my dear friend and she said to me, "Oh it is you, Natalie. I was just looking over and thinking those two people are so in love." That is the truth. When you see us you will say WOW those two are in love. We can't hide it. It is so unbelievably powerful, anyone near us feels it. My best friend came and told me that we were so beautiful to watch.

Also, the psychic told me that my Swede and I were twin flames. Twin flames are the "one" everyone is looking for. When a soul is born it splits into two becoming one female and one male. They live their first lives together and their last. Twin Flames are in each other's lives as spirit guides every life they spend on earth. While one is human, the other guides them. Their last life they are here to balance the karma of their souls and serve humanity.

The psychic told me he was a warrior spirit and a perpetrator. I was a tortured soul and a victim. We had opposite lessons in life. He had come into every one of my lifetimes because he loved me so much. He has to touch me, even if it was for a minute. He was born my son and died shortly after, just to touch me. He did something each one of my lives and hurt me because he had to touch me for a moment. I could feel this now that he loved me so much. I loved him that much too. Everything was incredibly perfect with us. Match made in heaven when we were together physically.

Furthermore, my entire house fell apart while he was here. I never let him see me stress out. I just handled it the best I could. He got to see the real life here and my experience with handling situations that arise. Truly, he got to see the handyman in the house and how I operate. I could not believe he loved me after that disaster. I made a promise to him to love him unconditionally for eternity. I felt he was the man I dreamed of. It was a magical three weeks.

But as the story of my life goes, I had to put him on an airplane and say goodbye. Now half of me had left to the other side of the earth. I knew the feeling I dreamed of really existed with someone on this earth. Yet, he was gone into the air and back to being a dream again. I could not understand how God would bring me the man of my dreams and then take him back. Oh God please help me. Here comes the pain again.

Immediately after he left I opened my home to a homeless woman and two small children. Seriously, I could have been that person with no home and babies. I had to help her. One of the children was extremely Autistic. I learned a lot about energies from him. Those children feel everything. If I was angry then he would get angry. I had to pay attention how I held emotions and what type of emotions I gave out. When you give out positive energy it goes out several feet. When you give out negative energy it triples. So when you hold that bad feeling in everyone around you feels it. You only fool yourself thinking nobody knows how you feel.

However, it is something you should always remember. I was so connected with that child. My friend said to me, "Now you can see your connection to children and how intense it is." They stayed with me for a very educational two months.

December of 2010 I had a long phone conversation with my psychic friend. She told me that she did not have any confidence in my Swede to change. She did not like him. She also told me that the spirits had told her the she and I were going to get into a huge argument and our friendship would end. I told her I had hoped it wasn't because of me. It was the last real conversation I had with her. She walked away from me for reasons I do not understand. My teacher, my best friend and the person I had relied on for everything spiritual for over three years. She was my strength and my rock. It was over. I was crushed with pain. Now, I was completely on my own. I was left out in the big bad world to try to find my own way. Yes, I had the tools to survive. But I did not know if I had the power to do it without her.

~A person who follows the crowd will usually go no further than the crowd. The person who walks alone is likely to find themselves in places noone has been before. ~ Albert Einstein

~Old age comes at a bad time. You finally know everything just in time to forget it!

~The grass is always greener on the other side because it is fertilized with bullshit.

~You have brains in your head. You have feet in your shoes. You can steer yourself in any direction you choose. ~ Dr. Seuss

~ I'm not like anyone else. I don't need to follow anyone else's lead. I am all I will ever really need to be. I am just simply me and simply unique.

~If we all understood that everyone has their own battles to fight, insecurities to face, love to contend and goals to attain, the world would be a gentler place.

~Stop thinking about all the reasons something may not work and start thinking about all the reasons it might.

~Cancel my subscription, I don't need your issues.

~Dear God, thank you for being there when nobody else was.

Chapter 10
It Takes a Strong Man to Handle a Broken Woman

I spent most of winter 2010 completely snowed in for days. The longest was ten days. I was always prepared and had whatever I needed to survive. We never went without anything. Plus, I really did not care one bit. All of our needs were met. The peace and serenity was amazing. Only the people who loved me still got in, but for the most part I was isolated the entire winter. People would drop me off at the end of my driveway after they had brought me to the grocery store. Some would tell me they thought I was such a strong person for surviving life like this. I would look at them and say, "I Love It! I am so lucky to have had these experiences because of it. One day it will be completely different. I will miss these days when life changes to being easy like everyone else."

Then I would just fill up my sled and start up my very long, snowed in driveway laughing. I always smile. I think it is funny. I know in my heart it is all just a moment to teach me something. I do not get anything for free. I have had to survive in extreme living at times. I learned so much about different ways to do things and survival. I believe that God is teaching me how to survive the future of our planet. Nobody knows the future, but question is, are you prepared for anything to happen? I am! I can cook a whole chicken, mashed potatoes, and gravy on a woodstove. I also cook my coffee on it every morning. It is like camping in the house in winter and tastes better for some reason too.

I certainly learned of my own personal strength in every

way. I learned who my real friends are. I learned the hardest lesson ever and that was to ask for help when I need it. It is one of my SOUL'S biggest lessons. If I could have had the courage to ask for help, then I would not have gotten myself into so many shitty situations on every level all of my life. My friends get so damn angry with me because I NEVER ask for help. Yet, I am helping everyone on earth. I can't take their time for free either. We live a life of bartering out here. I am a single woman with little money. If I need help that involves a man then I will bake them something or help them by listening to their problems. The man who does my firewood says he should be paying me $500 an hour for all the counseling I give him. My friends and I barter everything. I need this and you have that. If I need a ride, they will get repaid in some form from me. Even if I just buy someone flowers for doing it.

February 2011 came in with a big bad bang. It began with finding out my best friend from Ireland had been murdered. He was stabbed in an argument with a friend who was drunk. He died on the floor of his mother's home. I cannot tell you about that pain. Oh it was like someone ripped my heart out of my chest. That man had made me laugh every day for over three years. Moments when I wanted to die, he made me pee my pants laughing. It was a huge blow to my heart and my life. He was so damn special to me. I could not imagine life without him. Then next day I found out my niece went to the emergency because she went blind. Then find out she had a large brain tumor. It did not stop for days. Every day for a week was something so terribly horrible. I was in shock at the pain that was being thrown at me every day.

Then, I began to absorb all of this pain from others. My heart just kept getting broken every time I thought it couldn't get any worse. My dear Swede was on video cam with me for almost every phone call I got. I did my very best to just stay centered and completely filled with faith. I prayed and I prayed and I prayed. I prayed for everyone and their pain. I know I was filled to the rim with hurt. However, it was the families of these people that had the real pain. Everything happens for a reason. But sometimes it is just shocking how much can happen in a moment. One day you are on the top of the world and BOOM. You wonder if there is an end to hell. Thankfully, there always is an end.

After the storm, the new beginnings happen next. My crazy Irish friend's soul immediately started hanging around me. Sometimes we danced. Sometimes he whispers things to me, but he shows up for about 15-20 minutes a couple times a week. I made a promise to him when he was alive that I would help his sister. It was always his wish that his niece and sister could have a better life. His sister and I are now connected and just waiting for money to get her here to see me. I feel we are like sisters and I love her too. Endings create new beginnings and I will fulfill my promise to him.

Also, my beautiful niece had a successful removal of the tumor. I told my sister she would get her sight back soon. God needs her to listen right now. She will be an inspiration and a teacher to many people. I know in my heart she will be just fine. She handles it better than everyone else does. Life finally started to calm down after a couple of weeks.

Furthermore, every inch of my body was in the worst pain I have ever felt. It had started in November 2010 and slowly got worse until I could barely walk. It was like severe arthritis. It made it difficult to sit and talk to someone. I felt like everything in life had fallen apart. I was still trying to put it all back together after the tornado. A friend of mine took me to the emergency room one night. I felt like my heart was going to blow up. My entire body was shaking with needle sharp pain. They tested me for everything. I was in absolute perfect health, except low on vitamin D. They thought I had Lyme's Disease. The doctor gave me one type of medication for a week to try to treat it.

Then they found I did not have that strain of the Lyme's disease. They thought maybe another type instead. So they gave me an extremely heavy dose of medication to kill it. I had to drink 4 bottles of water before I could take it twice a day. It made me vomit every time. I would be sick for hours twice a day. On the tenth day of taking these meds, the doctor called and said I did not have Lyme's at all. I had something else, but they were not sure. Seventeen days of horrible medications I took for nothing. I took them only because a Doctor told me to take them and still no explanation for the pain.

Another place that got hit hard was my relationship. Oh my man went to hell and back with me. I handled it well, but that was an enormous amount of bad shit at lightning speed. We began holding the mirror up to each other. Every day was an intense therapy session with a therapist who has guided me every lifetime. We were working extremely hard on ourselves, each other and the past pain of our lives. We were continually challenging each other every day to be better people. A constant power and ego struggle within ourselves. We faced every horrible bad relationship behavior we had. We even had to deal with friendship behaviors because we were also best friends. We worked so hard. We talked about writing a book about our relationship climb to the top.

It is amazing when you have two people who know each other that well without knowing how. Then you use it against each other to force the other to look at themselves. It was the most confusing war I have ever fought within myself and with another. Our higher selves were growing at extreme speeds. Our connection is unreal. We know what the other is thinking. It doesn't work well when you try to argue with the other. It sucked having to face the shitty parts of yourself every day.

However, we were madly in love with each other and were grateful for every lesson we had. Each bad moment rose us up to a higher level of ourselves and our love. Life had become an intense therapy session controlled by God. Every day I worked hard on my positive energy, how I spoke to others, how I listened to others, emotions, every reaction and action I performed through every moment of the day. I had dissected myself in every way about everything. I wanted it all healed. I was going to be 42 and my life will be half over. My ass is not going to cry for the second half of my life. Forget it! I wanted to heal this and be a better person. My Swede was right along with me and doing it himself. So it got very deep on a regular basis. There is no other man on earth who could help me through it. There was no other person on earth who could have got him through it either.

In June my financial situation continued to get worse and worse. We had survived another winter without any problems but money problems were the focus now. I did not fear. God has taken care of me for 5 years. I learned to be grateful for my needs only and anything extra is a blessing.

I was walking across my yard to my garage one day. I heard my Irish friend's voice in my head. "Natalie, luck isn't always so obvious. Sometimes you have to look closer, deep within and you will find it." I instantly went down on my knees. With my hands I parted the clover. There standing alone was a four-leafed clover. That is how life is at my home. Magic! My friends say I have the greatest weather in Minnesota too. The sun shines at my house and it is raining all around me. This is not a joke!

Everything I pray for just happens. Sometimes I feel like I just wave a magic wand and POOF! Here it is! Not always the way I expected it to happen. But I always laugh at the final outcome. God has the greatest humor. Life opened around me in so many directions. My heart continued to open. I had taken control over my own life without the help of anyone but my man. I had worked hard healing myself.

On the 14th of June four butterflies came to me. The most beautiful babies I have ever seen. It was the one year anniversary of meeting my Swede. I let them go but one would not leave me. He is the cover of this book. I posted that picture with the butterfly on my face to Facebook. A spiritualist FB peep commented on it. I had just become friends with this woman and I did not know her personally. She posted, "Get ready to unfold your wings and fly precious." I commented back to her, "Thank you. I have never been more ready. The question is, is the world ready?" She answered back, "The world has been waiting for this joyous occasion to celebrate with you. No coincidence that the butterfly and your doors match. Open the doors as the butterfly has opened its wings. My words are from spirit and they like to speak through me." It was an amazing moment in every aspect of my life.

    I always talk to everything outside. One of my friends told me I remind her of Snow White talking to all the animals and singing to nature. But, that woman lived with seven men. I hadn't touched one for nine months again. But yes, I do love nature. When you talk to nature it talks back to you. When you send nature love, you receive double the love in return. I tell everything around me thank you every day. Without every plant I couldn't breathe.

    That butterfly stayed on me for two days. Inside and outside of my house he hung on to me. Most of the time he was on my face. I became like a butterfly magnet. I would go somewhere and they would all fly around me. I began to just hold out my arm or just pick them right up. I had a butterfly with me outside and inside my house at all times. I have no explanation for it. Just sweet beautiful angels coming to visit. Also, butterflies have always signified new beginnings to me. They make the greatest transformations of any creature. People started talking about this butterfly and I all over the world. It was crazy. So many people were sad when he died and so was I.

    However, they kept coming. My yard had literally thousands of butterflies everywhere. Life was like magic. I am Natalie in Wonderland! Curious and ready for what is behind the next door of my adventurous ride through life. Every moment good or bad had a meaning to it. I became grateful for everything and every second. Life may hand me my ass, but God never said it would be easy. Just said it would be worth it. My life has been worth every second I have lived.

    On July 1st, two weeks after the butterfly visited, my Swede came back to visit me for four weeks. We had been apart for over nine months. Everyone thinks we are crazy. We are just crazy in love. First couple days he was here I was busy being a bride's maid in a wedding for my sweet sista who was 22 yrs old. We went full speed ahead for two weeks straight. The second busy weekend was our hometown traditional reunion weekend when hundreds come back home to celebrate. The Swede got to meet people in my life that have known me from birth and all of their wild stories of their adventures with me. It was so much fun.

I also had the brand new foreigners out for the first time while he was here. We had a great party with them in my garage and they were so much fun to meet. There was one from Romania, 3 from Ecuador and 2 from Peru. So my Swede got to experience the foreign side of my life and the beautiful people God brings my world. It was a magical experience. My man really got to see my life in the public eye. The last time he was here we never left my home.

Another situation he had to witness was my stalkers. It is one thing to tell him about what I have to deal with, but he got to finally witness it first-hand. My lights always off and doors always locked. Men will just walk into my house without knocking. Thinking they have a right to do whatever and I don't even know them. Someone parked at the end of my driveway at 12 at night. He walked up and started knocking on my bedroom window.

Few days later, someone was walking around my house looking in all the windows. My daughters were woken up by someone knocking on the living room windows one night. I usually have myself locked up in the house. I honestly did not know how long or how many were doing this to me. At first I was horrified and would not let my man do anything. He was going home to Sweden and I had to stay here to face it alone. It happened so many times when he was here, I finally gave in. He did stop one of them. Sadly, I had to face my fear of guns, learn how to shoot and now keep one loaded in my home because of idiots. I have been living like this for years. I am ready for it to end.

My Swede also got to experience my butterflies. He said to me there are 10's of thousands of them here, not just thousands. You would walk and it was like magic. They would fly up at your feet by the hundreds each step you took. You could not look anywhere without seeing a butterfly. I even went to the gas station one day when a butterfly landed on my back and went it into the store with me.

One night we were in my garage together listening to music. My Swede said he had to go be alone because he wasn't feeling right. He returned to the garage one hour later and he lost his mind. He started screaming at me about how horrible I was to bring him to this country and treat him like shit. I waited on him hand and foot while he was here so this was out of the blue craziness. He yelled at the top of his lungs at me for 8 long, miserable hours. He even went into my home, continued to scream at me and woke up my children at 6:00 a.m. This was one of the most horrible moments I had ever experienced with him and his verbal abuse. I was shocked and it changed so many feelings inside me for him.

However, during his visit, the Swede and I made the decision to be together forever. We got married to each other before God and prayed for a love so strong nothing could destroy it. We committed ourselves to each other for eternity. I made a commitment to him in the presence of God to stand beside him through everything good and bad. We would face it all together. We prayed to several Archangels to help us through our process to be together again and heal our pasts. Being with him was heaven on earth and my heart was home next to him.

So back to Sweden he went again. We knew before he arrived that he would have to return back to Sweden. We also knew we were not ready to be together yet. He has a son that he must also worry about. This adds to slowing the process down of unity. There are things that need to be worked out so his son can come spend time here with us. It was easier this time to say goodbye to him. The feeling was more like get your ass home and let's gets to work. We knew what we wanted and what we had to do to achieve it.

Before we started our life together in the future, we wanted all of our old bad relationship behaviors gone. We did not want to destroy our relationship. Again, we started to work on ourselves. We both dove in head first again. This time it was different. It was more hurtful and egotistical then ever. I was running and he was running. Our lessons were so hard. We were constantly challenging each other in every way. However, we were still incredibly in love with each other. I kept asking myself why do I have to suffer so greatly to love someone. I could feel every emotion he had on my side of the earth and he could feel mine. It added to our pain and doubled it.

One day in the beginning of August I was looking out the window at nature. A butterfly came to me and a voice in my head said, "Butterflies and Bullshit. That is the name of your book." So that was it. I was writing a book. That is how I would get my message out. The whole world had taught me and now it was time to share it all with the world. I wasn't given this knowledge to keep it. I could write hundreds of books with what I know. But writing only one book would leave 90% of my life out. There is just too much. I had no idea how to write a book. I write constantly as a healing process. However, I am not an author. Hell, I did not even graduate from high school. So pardon any mistakes you may have noticed while reading this book. I just typed this story out on my laptop.

Next, I did a guided meditation to my future self. Your soul knows where you are going so who better to talk to. I went into meditation. Future Natalie came in, she took my hand and walked me through a door. There I was doing a book signing. Natalie looked at me and said "The world loves you. You did it. You are a success and you have helped millions and millions of people." Funny thing is that my children were behind me and the Swede was not there. This meditation was so real. I had seen it with my own two eyes and I could feel it.

Sadly, my Swede and I fell completely apart. That day was August 28, 2011. The day the chapter Bullshit was born. Everything in my life was a mess. We had learned so much and challenged each other way too much. I was moving on to a new chapter in my spiritual self. I could not survive or live in the pain anymore. I felt he had cheated on my heart by hurting me continuously every day. I ended it with him in my heart but, never got to tell him. My phone and internet got shut off. Everything happens for a reason. I had enough of our painful journey. I was so filled with hurt I did not care if I ever seen him again.

I went out and celebrated a little too much. I had sex with someone else. I was single, although, my heart and mind were not. I was filled with pain and went back to an old addictive way of handling things. Like an alcoholic that has been sober for four years and gets drunk. I hurt and I wanted to get it out.

Next, I went to work on writing this book. Within ten days I had written twelve chapters on paper. Not on a laptop. I wrote all of them on paper while dancing in my garage. Dancing is my form of meditation. I let the music flow through and so does my intuition. I need music to survive. I cannot live without it for a day. I could not write one sentence without music for this entire book.

Finances have been cut off, electric is moments from being shut off still and now I need money or my house will go into foreclosure. I have one month to save my home and keep my children. All I have is faith in God at the moment. When life has you on your knees, you are in the perfect position to pray.

However, I am a much better person through this journey. Many people laughed at me and said I was a loser for living like this. I know in my heart it was meant to be this way. I had to be cut off from the world to heal myself completely. I worked day and night on myself. Every waking moment I analyzed everything about myself. I have faith it is time for a new beginning of life. Some days you just have to be your own hero. I am one tough soul and nothing will take me down. I do not have fear. I know God loves to watch me squirm and wait until the last second to show me the magic. I put it in the hands of my creator and I have faith that God loves me. I wrote the story of my life and I know Natalie Newman. She did not come here to lose.

When it's complete chaos that is when the biggest miracles happen. I have one more huge mistake to face in my life. It will not be an easy thing to deal with. But I have to make my entire life honest and clean. It will be the hardest challenge I will have to face in yet. It will affect the lives of many. I know in my heart I have the greatest support group to help me through. I just pray every day for a positive outcome.

What an amazing experience my life has been. I have three beautiful children, my home, and the most amazing friends around the world. My lessons were difficult. Learning was a gift, even if pain was my teacher. You have three choices in life, Give in, Give up or Give it your all. Giving up is the easiest thing to do, but holding it all together when everyone expects you to fall apart, that is true strength. I believe that two people are connected at the heart and it doesn't matter what you are put through, who you are or where you live, there are no barriers when two people are destined to be together. Without my Swede I would never have gone to the depths of hell to dig it out. The result of my work is higher values, higher love and higher spiritual self. There are no short cuts to getting any place worth going

I will get through no matter what happens to me. Each step I take I trust is a step closer to my dreams. For every set back God had a major comeback. If you think you're trapped in a situation it's only because you forgot how to use your imagination. Life had no remote, you have to get up and change it yourself. If you're going through something hard and wonder where God is. Remember the teacher is always quiet during the test. I believe it was all a test of my faith. I am ready for whatever comes next. I promised to share the Divine Knowledge that the Angels and God guided me to receive.

So where Natalie Newman goes, next nobody knows. But you can guarantee I ain't done yet. Life is mine for the taking and I am going to go take it. My life will continue the wild ride filled with challenges and I will just face them. I will just keep celebrating life for everything it offers me. I will just keep it young and crazy.

I have always been crazy, that's what keeps me from going insane. I am like Natalie in Wonderland and life is one fabulous trip. Tomorrow I will be done with this moment of life and moving one to the next. I know where ever I go, is where God wants me to be. So I will just go with the flow. I believe what's next with complete faith in my heart and soul. Let go of your past so you have a free hand to open the door to your future. Life is full of fun, if you learn to play with difficulties. You know the rest of my journey will be another great story. I have to heal my heart of the hell my Swede put me through. I have to find a way to pay all these bills and keep my house or I am going to lose everything. I have nothing but my faith.

Right now, being without him feels better than being with him. Too much fear and pain surrounding him. Oh my poor heart is so broken. In shock! I know I tried my very best. I know I loved him the best I could. I just can't believe it. I had finally found my dream man, but he was fighting a war inside that is bigger than my love for him. It destroyed us. Sometimes it is not about the happy ending. Sometimes it's about the story. I don't just ride the crazy train anymore. I am driving the fucking thing.

She was beautiful, but not like those girls in the magazines. She was beautiful for the way she thought. She was beautiful for that sparkle in her eyes when she talked about something she loved. She was beautiful for her ability to make others smile, even when she was so sad. No, she wasn't beautiful for something as temporary as her looks. She was beautiful deep down in her soul.

~There will come a time when you believe everything is finished. That will be the beginning." ~ Louis L'Amour

~People usually say, 'THE SKY IS THE LIMIT'.
I believe, 'THE SKY IS JUST THE BEGINNING.' ~ Author Unknown

~Happiness is like a butterfly, which when pursued, is always beyond your grasp, but if you will sit down quietly, may alight upon you. ~~Nathaniel Hawthorne

~Never be afraid of the scars life has left you with. A scar means the hurt is over, the wound is closed, you endured the pain and God has healed you

~Invariably, sudden disappointments, a bit of "bad" news, or a flock of butterflies gathering in your stomach, are all omens that a fabulous adventure is fast approaching.

~When you realize how perfect everything is you will tilt your head back and laugh at the sky. ~ Siddhartha Gautama Buddha

~You can't start a new chapter in your life if you keep re-reading the last one.

~ I haven't got an attitude problem, you just have a problem with my attitude.

While I was writing the end of the book I had to clean out a desk because it needed to go to a different room in my house. What I found was shocking. I came across an old school folder from 1984-1985. I was 14-15 years old at that time. I thought this folder was long gone and forgot it even existed. But the best part about it was, it was filled with about 50 poems I had written. It was interesting to see who I was then and who I am now. I would love to share some of them with you. It is surprising how I thought back almost 30 years ago and how I think now. Not much has changed I just healed myself and found more faith. I always had a dream to be free of pain and help others.

The first one was written about myself at 15 years old. It is about killing myself with drugs and how I looked at what I had done to myself.

Why?

by Natalie Newman- 1985

I turned and looked away. I couldn't face you.

You just laid there. I didn't know what to do

I gave you my flower. I put it between your hands.

I couldn't take this. I couldn't understand.

We were friends, for many years

We shared so much, laughter, dreams and tears.

I looked upon you, with all the memories.

You looked so beautiful, just like a fantasy

Then the tears began to roll, as I sat and looked.

Why did you start? Why did you get hooked?

That was the wrong way out. Why did you use drugs?

I could have helped you. I could have talked to you and given you a hug.

Now you're not here. I can't love you anymore.

You won't be here to talk to, or to do things like before.

I looked up to the sky. I wanted to run and hide.

Why didn't you come to me? Why suicide?

Someday I'll be with you. But for now you're in my heart.

You were so young. Your life was only at its start

As they took you away, I turned my head to above.

And I thanked God for your life and all of your love.

The next one was a prayer I had written at 14 years old.

Dear God,

Help me please to stand strong. To face the world at its worst.

To help me complete the race of life, even if I don't finish in first.

Glide along beside me. As I walk a lonely road.

Be happy and love me, cause life's a very heavy load.

Please guide and direct me. On my most dangerous ride

Cause I need you my friend. I need you by my side.

This next poem was written at 14 years old.

Just You and Me
by Natalie Newman- 1984

Why is life so cruel? Why is it so mean?

Pictures show it so beautiful. But that's the only way they see.

They show it with loves songs, beautiful friendships and friends that love you.

Everything seems so perfect. But only in a picture can you see it so untrue.

You go on so unhappy, wanting to cry.

You need somebody. Somebody to stand by.

To lead you on, to make you smile.

Someone hold you and make life worthwhile.

But these people seem so far away. So very hard to find.

It seems like none loves you and everyone's so unkind.

We all know life's so cruel, but that's the way it must be.

We have to hang on to each other. Just you and me.

Another one from 14 years old.

You, an Empty Space
by Natalie Newman-1984

You told me it was over. That we were through.

At first I couldn't believe. Now I realize it's true.

I still love you so very much. You don't seem to care.

When you left me all I could do is stare.

There's much I have to say to you. So many reasons why.

I still love you. I can't say I don't, that's a lie.

I know you won't come back, but I like to pretend you will.

It makes me want to go on. It sort-of gives me a thrill.

I still have dreams of you. I keep them inside.

I thought I could give you up. Now I can't decide.

Why? Why do I hold onto you?

I loved you so much. I just can't face the fact we're through.

You left me with nothing, but a memory of you face.

And the time we spent together. There's just and empty space.

This was from 15 years old.

Life

by Natalie Newman-1985

I reached for a dream. But the dream was too high.

I yearned for happiness. But all I do is cry.

Life is quickly passing. And dragging me along.

I am waiting to be loved. But time is passing on.

All I have is sadness. All locked up inside.

I need to get away. I need somewhere to hide.

I always wear a smile, but inside I want to cry.

I act like things are great, but the tears will never dry.

The Streets

by Natalie Newman-1985

The streets are misty in the morning light.

It's time to make a move to change my life.

I gotta make my dreams come true.

Cause I know there's something more inside of me.

Cause I'm losing my mind living their life.

I won't get nowhere, if I don't break free.

I am not running away, but I just gotta try to live my life.

I hear the siren and I feel the heat.

A child cries alone, and dies without a fight.

And all these dead end streets keep telling me

I'm losing my chance the longer I wait.

They say you can't escape your destiny.

So I'm making my move, before it's too late.

Break out tonight. The doors within my reach and I don't need no key.

I got the power and I want the glory.

And now it's time to do or die.

I wanna make my dreams reality.

But something's got me caught in a bind.

They try to tear me down and keep me in.

So I have to break open the cage, if I wanna fly.

Please God help me.

Let Me Be

by Natalie Newman-1984

I'm sitting down thinking about losing my mind.

Cause I keep telling myself I'm only one of a kind.

My life is broken because my dreams are being shattered.

For so very long nothing else mattered.

But I'm living to lose and dying to win.

With those people around here, my patience wears thin.

Yeah, I'm trying to get away, get away from it all

and I'm not gonna crawl.

The dream never dies. That's why I write this.

I'm hearing cries in the night.

I can't wait another day. Tell me no lies.

I'm standing cold in the light.

I lose the dream and I'll go crazy.

I'm hearing cries in the night.

Time never waits, time never ends.

You thought it was gone but the fire goes on.

And I thought you knew me and I told you before.

That I'll never run free

I have enough pain and anger in my brain to last many lifetimes.

Yet, it still grows and the more that it shows, I won't have peace of mind.

The fires still burns, the fire to be free.

I have a dream and as strange as it seems, there is no embers glowing.

The fires gone out and there's no need to shout.

I'm gonna be me, get out of my way.

Why does no one seem to understand?

It's so hard to carry on when all your dreams have come undone.

I beg for freedom. Leave me be.

Just leave me alone.

Let me be who I want to be. Let me run free.

The River

by Natalie Newman-1984

The river floats on hopelessly, with not a destiny.

For this very reason, it resembles me.

We both drift on in loneliness.

As a force pulls us dreadfully on.

And we unwillingly enter tomorrow

Sensing it soon will be gone.

We go where the currents take us.

And take it one day at a time.

Since we have not a dream to reach for,

Nor can we pick a mountain to climb.

No purpose for being, nowhere to go.

These problems we both face each day.

So you can see we have so much in common.

And need someone or something to lead us the way.

A Piece of You

by Natalie Newman-1984

When a piece of you is taken, from deep inside you.

One that made you happy. A happy you never knew.

You feel left all alone with nowhere to run.

You feel you haven't a life. That there'll be no more fun.

Don't let that piece be taken forever. Move on, move forward.

Don't let anyone stop you. Just fly high like a bird.

Spread your wings, reach out be strong.

Cause you are great and that could never be wrong.

Happiness will come soon. Don't dwell on what's just been done

Cause there's so many more. He's not the only one!

The next two poems were written for my mystery dream man I used to fantasize about but never met. Well, 28 years later I finally found him. Never give up on your dreams. When you are ready the "right one" will come.

Him

by Natalie Newman-1984

We know not a single thing about one another.

But I just keep wanting you. Just wanting to be your lover.

You sit there with eyes inviting me in.

But my dreams run too far, much farther than sin.

Your body I want, so much to hold.

My fantasies are so beautiful, but could never be told.

Maybe someday I will get a hold of you.

But until then, I'll dream precious dreams and hope they'll come true.

If I am Dreaming

by Natalie Newman-1984

If I'm dreaming don't wake me. I don't want it to end.

It's all too good to be true. Please don't wake me my friend.

It's been so beautiful, us hand in hand.

Walking together alone, to wake I could not stand.

Being with you, looking into your eyes,

and feeling you close to me.

I hope this dream never dies.

I never want to move as I dream making love to you.

As we lay close to each other. It seems all too good to be true.

The feel of you, a feeling of love, that only we can see.

I cherish these moments together.

And if I'm dreaming please don't wake me.

~The only people who get somewhere interesting are those who get lost. ~ Natalie Newman- 1985

BUTTERFLIES
Conclusion to Part 1

~To make a wish come true, whisper it to a Butterfly. Upon these wings it will be taken to heaven and granted, for they are the messengers of the Great Spirit.

Life is a bunch of bullshit until you realize you don't have to keep standing in it. There is also a very beautiful side to life, even when it seems to be the very worse. From the day I was born, to this present moment, has been truly an act of God. I was given the gift of healing at lightning fast speed. I have an incredible mind that just lets things go immediately and move right on to the next door in life. However, no doors just open for you. You have to ask for it, believe it, work hard and earn it. My abilities and my faith in God got me to where I am today. I had many Angels and beautiful Spirits around me holding my hand when I could not stand up. Every horrible moment I had the most perfect people around me to get me through. They loved me and helped me laugh when my world fell apart.

Because of the intense drive to help myself I was able to take what I was given and turn it into something better. I was born into a family "secret "and a bunch of lies that went through generations. I ended that string of hell so my children could be safe. I had parents who tried to do their best with what they had. I forgive them for their mistakes and try my best to learn from them. Every day I strive to be a better mother. Childhood abuse led me to more abuse in my life and addictions of every kind. I was filled with suffering for 41 years. I used sex, alcohol and drugs to numb the pain.

Now I only drink on special occasions or whenever it is time to have a damn good party. I ran around for years thinking and acting like Samantha from Sex in the City. Men were just toys to me and sex was a game. I used others and allowed others to use me. I had no respect for them because I had no respect for myself. Today, I have only had sex a few times in the last four years. I have healed that pain and the painful behaviors I learned because of it.

I have learned to love myself. That was the hardest lesson because it is the most difficult thing to do. When my good friend met my Swede on webcam for the first time, she said to him, "You do not know how lucky you are to get Natalie. She is so beautiful inside and out. But she does not believe it. She is just starting to see it after all these years." That was something that stuck with me. I never felt beautiful because there was so much ugly inside me. I worked very hard to love me and that was the path to finding myself. I do love me and I love ALL of me. I am proud of who I have become and what I have survived. You might as well love yourself. It's the longest relationship you will have with anyone.

Today, I live in the "now" moment. I can only handle what is given to me at this very second. Nothing can be done with yesterday. Tomorrow never comes. Now, I stop and look around when life goes to hell. It is magic all around me. Yes it sucks, but it is worth it. I would not miss one second of life, good or bad, because it is all mine. I want to feel it all, dance with it, and learn from it. It is the process of my journey to my higher self and empowering Natalie every step of the way. You only have this moment. Grab it by the balls and take it. You weren't made to simply survive until you die. Live it up, embrace life. This entire planet exists for all God's creatures and that includes you. Don't wait to start living, begin right now, with your very next breath. There are many wonderful experiences waiting for you, so get going. The past is behind, learn from it. The future is ahead, prepare for it. The present is here, live it.

> ~People in life who are the happiest don't have the best of everything. They make the best of everything they have. ~old Irish proverb

My life has been an amazing journey to this point. I could honestly write another 100 books on my life story and the knowledge I have been taught. Every day I could write a book about the lessons and magic I see. I just tried to get some of the highlights the best I could without overwhelming people. There is so much more than this. The last five years have been a magical journey from suicidal depression to loving the Earth with a mission. I locked myself in my house for four years and worked every second on myself. If you want to walk a spiritual path you have to completely destroy yourself. But the result is the greatest prize on earth. I was given the tools and time to tear myself into a million pieces and put myself back together to create a better me. My life was a wild and crazy ride. I do not regret one single second of it. I regret NOTHING. My life was not a mistake. It is a story about survival. I experienced every kind of pain imaginable. I faced it and conquered it.

> ~Did you know the people that are usually the strongest are usually the most sensitive? Did you know the people who exhibit the most kindness are the first to get mistreated? Did you know the one who takes care of others all the time are usually the ones who need it the most? Did you know the 3 hardest things to say are "I love you," "I'm sorry," and "Help me?" Sometimes just because a person looks happy, you have to look past their genuine smile and see how much pain they may be in.

I know God believes in me, because I am worth it. God chose me to walk this life, because I was strong enough to live it. I know I have made a million mistakes. Most success is born on former failures. That is how I learn. Those mistakes gave me great knowledge and strength. Our greatest glory consists not in never failing, but rising every time we fail. If you don't go after what you want, you'll never have it. If you don't ask, the answer is always no. If you don't step forward, you'll always be in the same place. So I guess I will keep making mistakes.

Nobody can teach me who I am. You can describe parts of me, but who I am - and what I need - is something I have to find out myself. The world will just keep spinning and you're trapped in it. Maybe sometimes you have to stop waiting for someone to come along and fix what's wrong. Maybe you have to stop feeling sorry for yourself and realize that no one else has the answer. Maybe sometimes you just have to be your own hero.

~*The butterfly said to the sun, "They can't stop talking about my transformation. I can only do it once in my lifetime. If only they knew, they can do it at any time and in countless ways." - by Dodinsky*

I've made a million mistakes in my life. I've let people take advantage of me and I've accepted way less than I deserve. But I've learned from my bad choices. I know there are some things I can never get back and people who will never be sorry. There comes a time in life, when you walk away from all the drama and people who create it. You surround yourself with people who make you laugh, forget the bad, and focus on the good. So love the people who treat you right and pray for the ones who don't. Life is too short to be anything but happy. No one will ever live your life. No one will ever feel your joy. No one will ever expand in your heart, but you can. Your life is totally yours. Remember there is no normal. We are all going crazy trying to act normal. Life is not a problem to be solved, but a reality to be experienced. Falling down is a part of life, getting back up is living.

~*How far you go in life depends on you being tender with the young, compassionate with the aged, sympathetic with the striving and tolerant of the weak and the strong. Because someday in life you will have been all of these."* ~ George Washington Carver

I'll know better next time and I won't settle for anything less than I deserve. When you have come to the edge of all the light you know and are about to step off into the darkness of the unknown, faith is knowing that one of two things will happen: there will be something solid to stand on or you will be taught how to fly. Do not pray for easy lives. Pray to be stronger! Do not pray for tasks equal to your powers. Pray for powers equal to your tasks. Then the doing of your work shall not be a miracle, but you yourself shall be the miracle. Every day you shall wonder at yourself: At the richness of life which has come in you by the grace of God.

I fill myself with faith and I live with complete integrity. Living with integrity means: Not settling for less than what you know you deserve in your relationships. Asking for what you want and need from others. Speaking your truth, even though it might create conflict or tension. Behaving in ways that are in harmony with your personal values. Making choices based on what you believe, and not what others believe.

Why lie to make yourself look good? God knows the truth! Others will see the truth. Be true to yourself, and you won't have to worry what others think of you! Some things are worth FIGHTING FOR, some things are just NOT WORTH the fight, and everything else JUST SHAKE YOUR HEAD AND LAUGH. It doesn't matter anyway. It's not your job to like me - it's mine.

One major way I survived through life was by helping others. It has brought me the greatest joy on this earth. Helping people does not always have good results. Sometimes there are heartbreaks when people do not listen. But, you cannot help someone who does not want to help themself. However, the ones who rose up from hell and succeeded, make my heart sing. At times, the pure happiness that rises to my heart from seeing a miracle happen because I helped another, is indescribable.

When it happens I drop to my knees. I just scream with happiness and tears roll down my face out of pure gratefulness for God's magic. I can't stop helping people. I love to see people happy. I know what I do, does matter to people. I do make a difference in other people's lives. It is the greatest joy on earth to help another live life again. That is what life is all about. It is about sharing and caring. It is a great gift to give your help, compassion and time to another. It always comes back to me in the most beautiful ways.

Continuously, it grows and grows as thousands and thousands of people continue to fill me with so much love for helping them. I have to give it back. I take that loving happiness and send it out around the world to every human being on earth. My soul is here to help every living creature on earth have a better life. It is the adventure I chose when I came to this life. Making another person smile and helping them creates thousands of miracles that snowball from their happiness. Just because of taking one moment for another. It makes it all worth it. A good deed always pays itself forward. You will never comprehend how far your compassion will travel.

Faith sees the invisible and receives the impossible. My life's blessings are endless. First, I had more fun than you could ever fathom. I always make a point to make people feel good and have so much fun they will never forget me. I have three beautiful children and without them I would never have kept fighting. I have been a single mother for five years and it is the most empowering experience to handle it all on your own. I have my beautiful home and for the first time in my life I finally feel safe at home. I keep it a place of fun, love and peace. I allow only positive energy into my space.

Also, I had the most loving and supportive man. Without him pushing me every day I would never have healed myself or wrote this book. I have the most loving and funniest animals, that not only make me laugh every day, but they bring laughter to the hearts of many people. I have an incredible family that continues to amaze me with their strength. I have the most beautiful friends on this earth. They are crazy fun and I love crazy people. They understand me. I have a great relationship with Spirits, Angels, and God. I see my prayers that I speak into the wind manifest into reality. Every prayer gets answered in some way. I give whatever I can to help another and love the people of this earth. I know when you love life, life loves you back.

A flower starts deep under the dirt and has to fight against gravity in the darkness before finally breaking free and opening its bloom to the sun. You may feel like you're in darkness and everything around you is muddy. But keep pushing toward the Light and when the time is right, you will burst into blossom. If you want to make your dreams come true, the first thing you have to do is wake up. You don't see nature stress out because they have to change. WHY DO YOU? It is a normal process of life. In order to move forward you must open yourself to new experiences.

There is no failing, only results. Be courageous and push yourself to new heights. Besides, what is going to happen if you make a bad decision? You will learn from it. The more results you make, the faster you will reach your destination. God didn't give me a map of my life; so I'm a bit lost. He didn't bless me with a set of specific instructions; so I'm a bit dysfunctional. He didn't make me with a manual; so I'm kind of hard to understand. But what He did do is promise me light when I'm lost, a solution for every mistake, unconditional love and understanding. Just when you start to think you can't take anymore...a light shines through.

Ten great rules I live by:

1. Live with passion and love with fire.

2. Take risks. They are worth it.

3. Make sure each day is different from the one before.

4. Smile even when there is no reason to.

5. Live, love and give with compassion.

6. Your thoughts create your life.

7. Every day is a gift.

8. I am grateful.

9. Change is the only way forward.

10. Everything I need is within me

I would rather have one rose and a kind word from a friend while I am here, than a whole truck load when I am gone. I am grateful to every human being that has come into my life. I am so thankful to those who have loved me. For those who helped me and for those who made me laugh my ass off. I am grateful to the people who have hated me, who have been envious of me, who haven't been there for me, who have disrespected me and who have put me down. Without each person I would never have achieved becoming who I am today. I love you all. Be careful, you may just be the next chapter in my book. Thank you for being a part of my life. Remember everyone's life is a story. Some are just bestsellers!

Part 2
My Life Lessons

I learned about energies, forgiveness, acceptance, patience, letting go, healing, prayer, children, relationships of all kinds, many religions, love, family, many cultural differences, survival, miracles, manifestation, internet, Angels, Spirits, faith, people on every level, pain of every type, unconditional love, balance, expectations, actions with reactions, karma, death, afterlife, Mother Earth, fear, intuition, integrity, finding my souls' plan and walking it with a smile on my face. I mastered all of this to the best of my ability so far. You would need a lot of years of college to learn what I have. That is why I have written this book. So you do not have to suffer through life without understanding how simple it really all is.

~Do not be afraid of showing your affection. Be warm and tender, thoughtful and affectionate. Men are more helped by sympathy, than by service; love is more than money, and a kind word will give more pleasure than a present. ~John Lubbock

~Be the person who makes others feel special. Be known for kindness and sympathy. You will receive everything you give out and more. God gives great rewards for selflessness, loving and caring people. Everybody is themselves perfectly, being the best that they can be. Nobody has it easy. Everybody has issues. You never know what someone is going through. So, pause before you start criticizing or mocking another. Everybody is here fighting their own unique war. What makes anyone better than anyone? Help others, don't hurt.

~People are often unreasonable and self-centered. Forgive

them anyway
If you are kind, people may accuse you of ulterior motives. Be kind anyway
If you are honest, people may cheat you. Be honest anyway
If you find happiness, people may be jealous. Be happy anyway
The good you do today may be forgotten tomorrow. Do good anyway
Give the world the best you have and it may never be enough. Give your best anyway
For you see, in the end, it is between you and God. It was never between you and them anyway
~ Mother Teresa

I've learned that no matter how thin you slice it, there are always two sides.

I've learned that it's a lot easier to react than it is to think.

I've learned that it's taking me a long time to become the person I want to be.

I've learned that either you control your attitude or it controls you.

I've learned that maturity has more to do with the types of experiences you've had and what you've learned from them and less to do with how many birthdays you've celebrated.

I've learned that quantity is not as important as quality when it comes to best friends.

I've learned that it isn't enough to be forgiven by others, sometimes you have to learn to forgive yourself.

I've learned that no matter how bad your heart is broken, the world will not stop for your grief.

I've learned that background and circumstances might have influenced who you are, but we are responsible for who we become.

I've learned that you can't make someone love you, all you can do is be someone who can be loved.

I've learned that the word "love" can have many meanings.

I've learned that no matter how old or wise you think you are, life never stops teaching.

I've learned to never judge a person for who they WERE, but who they are trying to BECOME.

I've learned to never have expectations about anything or anyone but to just have faith and gratitude in your heart.

~It's okay to have butterflies in your stomach. Just get them to fly in formation. ~ Helen Keller

~Sometimes it's the weakest set of wings that ultimately flies stronger and farther.

~"How does one become a butterfly?" she asked. "You must want to fly so much that you are willing to give up being a caterpillar." ~Anonymous

~Like the butterfly I have the strength and hope to believe, in time, I will emerge from my cocoon…. TRANSFORMED!

~ Lovers don't finally meet somewhere. They're in each other all along. ~ Rumi

~Dear God, Thanks for this beautiful life and forgive me if I don't love it enough.

Chapter 1

Change Your Thoughts to Beautify Your Life

The biggest question people ask me is how they can change their thoughts to being positive, loving, honest, and faithful like me. They say "I want to think the way you do, Natalie." I tell them they can. It is about healing and changing your world around you and how you see it. I tell them to never have expectations, pass judgment, or react without really thinking. You need to dig into it before you react. Think before you speak! Do I choose to see what is good or do I choose to see what is wrong? 100% of the time when something is wrong, you created it. When you focus on the bad it will continue to get worse and worse. It is never about them. It is always about you and your judgment against another. Stop blaming others for everything and look at what you did to create this. Be excited with the miracle of life. Stay astounded by everything. God is always beside you and you're never alone. Today is a new day and dreams come alive again.

I was told by Archangel Metatron to begin detoxifying myself by not holding any negative thoughts, but only loving. When you stand for love, you will never fall down. Now this was a very enormous job I didn't think I could accomplish and every day I work very hard on it. I am consciously aware of things that hurt or anger me and why it did. I feel it for a moment. Then I surround it with love.

The biggest piece to healing myself was to understand expectations. My Swede was the biggest teacher in this lesson. When we meet someone, love someone, do something, pray for something, or someone speaks to us, we place an expectation on them of how we want them to behave or the way we want the outcome to be. We expect our loved ones to say and behave the way we want them to. We expect our lives to become a certain way. We expect our children to be perfect. We expect everyone to talk to us the way we want them to. We expect God to answer our prayers the way we want. We expect people to behave the way we want. We expect when we tell somebody to do something, they will do it. We expect them to do it exactly how we want them to and when. That is controlling another person or thing. CONTROL!!!!

So when they don't do it exactly the way we want or things do not work out the way we wanted, we blow with anger or hurt. We cannot control ourselves. Now you have caused yourself a lot of unnecessary negative energy. People only behave the way their soul knows how to behave. Do you want others to have expectations on you?

Here is a good example of expectations. I helped a beautiful woman a year ago. The angels told me she needed me immediately. I hadn't talked to her in years. I sent her an email, she called instantly, came to my house and I saved her from killing herself. She had an incredibly difficult situation with the father of her children who was keeping their daughter from her. He lived on the other side of the country.

I helped her get her emotional health back together and she moved across the country. Got an apartment near the father and they started working together beautifully sharing the children with their work schedules. She never showed anger and handled the entire thing like an angel. Everything began to work wonderful for them. They were working together harmoniously, began doing things as a family again and eventually started having sex again. It was a beautiful story of how two parents could put aside their anger and do what is best for their beautiful babies. Everything was perfect in her eyes. I told her every step she took to NOT have any expectations.

However, one day she called me extremely angry and hurt. All she could say is, "Why? Why, Natalie? Why? How could he do this to us?" She found out there was another woman. She was second best in the game. I let her get it all out and then put an end to it. I said to her, "Honey, you can stop blaming yourself because you did nothing wrong. You had a beautiful dream of doing what was best for your children. You wanted to have the family back together. You wanted to do what you felt was the best for everyone. It is ok! You only wanted to do what your heart was telling you. But, this is also ALL your fault. I told you not to have an expectation on anything. You placed and expectation on him wanting the same thing as you did. You placed an expectation on how he should behave. You placed an expectation on him to bring the family back together. So when he didn't do what you expected him to do, you got angry and filled with pain. It was all you and you created your own reality. He only behaved the way he knows how to for what is right for him. You can't blame him for the way he acted. That was his choice and that is what he wants. Why is he wrong for following his instincts based on who he is? You based expectations of who you are on him. That is not fair. Let him be himself and you be you. Forgive and let go. Just let it go."

Next, I told her, "You caused yourself so much unnecessary bullshit because of the huge pile of expectations you placed on him, that he doesn't even know about. Reverse the roles and how you would you feel if someone did that to you? Your mother placed expectations on you and you didn't behave the way she expected you to. She went against you with complete anger, when you did what your soul knew was best for you. Now you see it is the best decision of your life. Yet, you have to suffer because your mother wants you to do what she wants. That is what you just did to the father of your children." Her lights turned on in her mind. She completely got what I said. I teach with honesty and love. Sometimes people do not like what I say because it is truth.

Furthermore, I asked her this, "Do you want your beautiful daughters to grown up and marry a lazy man who relies on his parents to support him and wants to play video games all day?" She answered, "Absolutely not!" I replied to her, "Then why do you want that for yourself? You are the teacher and your children will grow up to have a man just like yours. Maybe God didn't answer your prayer for a reason. Maybe your job as a mother is to show them independence and self-respect. Then one day a great man will come to you who's a good example. Find that man that you want your children to marry and be that person you wish they could find for themselves. Set a good example. Trust in God's plan for you and live without expectations. Just do your best and God will take care of the rest for you. Forgive yourself for doing what you thought was right. And forgive him for doing what he though was right." That was the end of the conversation.

Honestly, we need to listen to the other without judgment when they speak. Either they are showing us who they really are or what we honestly don't want to hear. When a person speaks to us, we react instantly. If this reaction is negative, then you have some work to do inside. Normally, when we are reacting without listening to the entire conversation, it is never fair to the person speaking. Step out of it and listen.
Listening is the greatest wisdom we can give to ourselves and others. It is where you learn the most. Listen!

Helping people is another way I have learned about expectations. They have a path. They have an easy route or the difficult route. I tell them both. 75% of the time they choose the hard way. It breaks my heart to watch them. But, I have to remember they are not done banging their heads against the wall yet. They have not learned enough so they have a need to create more hell for themselves before they get it. I love them and I don't judge them for what they choose. All I say is "You were told! What you do with it is your choice, I still love you." I can't have any expectations on them how to behave. I wish the best for them, but they are not ready to be healthy yet. They cannot face the truth, even when they know it.

As I said earlier, my Swede was my greatest teacher of expectations. Through all our challenges when we were together and living 6,000 miles apart, I learned this lesson the hard way. What I learned was, I needed to never forget he loves me so much. In my relationships I will be fine as long and I remember he has the right to feel his own emotions about issues that anger or hurt him. I need to listen and know they are not my emotions.

How I react while he is expressing them is my problem. I need to listen with an open heart, not defensiveness. But with love, so he can express it the way he needs to. No, I don't always agree, but he feels it. I must accept that and without judgment work together to solve it. We continue to grow every day. Each day is a lesson, or challenge and some are intense.

It is difficult to see the mirror what that relationships show me of my own bad behavior. Things I do not want to hear that hurt and make me angry are what I need to hear the most. Those emotions only signal unnecessary suffering within myself. If I don't listen to the things he does not like, then how do I ask him to do the same for me? We are in this together. We need to act like it. Accepting it is a beautiful way to love another back. Just learn to step back, stay calm, and say "FUCK IT! I WILL GET THROUGH IT!" We will always come out above it. It is a lesson! I am being loved and guided through it by him. That is what relationships are about.

Listen and try to understand. If you don't understand what they are saying, it is your job to tell them. Allow them to explain! Know you will live through it. Try to make it the easiest you possibly can. Emotions come when we have fear in ourselves. Judging the other and how you react becomes our karma in it. That is the mirror he shows me of my own bad behaviors I need to change. Listen, love and understand! Then you can change it, fix it and love each other through every difficult moment. Love is the only answer to every single question you have about everything. When you ask yourself how are you going to do this or that? Love, trust and respect it. You have to fight for the good love. You have to heal each other and help each other through it, even if hurts like hell or pisses you off.

So, be grateful to them for saying it. Love them for loving you enough to care about you to say it. Mistakes are needed to learn. Challenges are thrown in your path to face them. Accept them with integrity. We are all here to learn and LOVE. Say thank you to them because you want to be a better person.

Another expectation I never placed on my Swede is what he will do with his life. If one day he said to me that he chooses to stay in Sweden, keep his life and stay with his son, I must accept that. If he moves to USA and says this is not what I want, I must accept that. I loved him and I wanted what was best for him. I can't be angry with him for what he wants. I will survive and my heart will hurt, but I love him enough to let him go and understand that he wants what he thinks is best for him. Why would I selfishly hang on to something that does not want me and wants different for himself? I can't! I will not destroy myself with pain and anger if he chooses that. I love him enough to let him be who he wants to be even if it does not include me.

Before you respond to anything you need to think. You need to respond with loving words. When you get angry or hurt, you have lost control and let the other take your power. Are you proud of your pain and anger? Are you proud of what you have to offer this universe with the way you behave? Who are you to reject the gifts that God gives you because you don't like it. You chose those lessons before you came to earth. Next, you curse and blame God for what you have to face. You obviously needed it and God was helping you. Do not do anything in this beautiful universe that you can't be proud of. That includes everything you do and say. When bullshit gets thrown in our path, it will open your heart to face the change and challenge. You can blame another or feel unlucky. When you approach everything with a negative reaction, you cut yourself off and close off your heart. You take the gift God sent you and throw it back in his face. These gifts are only given to you to help your soul along with the lessons it has come here to learn. Listen to yourself. You have so much to teach yourself about how you think. Look in the mirror staring back at you. It always changes.

How to make the biggest change in your life is to try to never judge, never expect, and really think hard before you react. Sometimes I take a 'time out' for days before I react to something. When I have thought it out and can handle it with integrity, only then am I ready to react to it. 100% of the time your judgments, expectations, and reactions are wrong if you do not find the truth in it. When you take that time out your thoughts will change to a more positive and loving mindset. Never react out of anger or pain. You will create an action that could affect things very badly. Don't create in your head what is not real. That is how you get out of the box and set yourself free. Allow others to be who they are. Everything and everyone is not a mistake.

We have 60,000 separate thoughts every day. Each day we choose the same thoughts over and over. You need to step back and ask yourself this question, "Are the thoughts going through my head actually true or did I create them to be something else?" When you constantly tell yourself that it is too difficult to deal with, or it will take me forever to do that, or I cannot heal that, or it is too impossible to do that, or I feel that person did wrong to me, then that is what you have created in your head.

Those thoughts almost 100% of the time are wrong. You need to reexamine it will a loving mind and you will see everything is just as it is and will be okay. When you surround it with a negative thought you will not find your way out of it. You are a human being and sometimes things make us angry or sad. Sometimes we don't want to think the right thing and choose the negative thought instead. Breathe in your thoughts and allow love for yourself to come. Then you will see all those negative thoughts were just that, negative. You are love and you need to react with love.

First thought that is negative, your neck gets tight, or you hold your breath, your heart rate goes up and you get anxious. That is where you need to stop. Breath in, breath out. Identify it! If possible, writing it out is best because you can look over it, see the truth in it and see how ridiculous is. Last, look back on the situation and how it would be if you would have reacted negatively. Choose to change those thoughts. We are much more critical of ourselves than others. When you change the way you think, your whole body will change. Stress, anger, fear, pain and worry cause 70-80% of heart disease. So if you want a heart attack, keep thinking negatively.

~Stress never changes anything, except yourself. –Erik Grondahl

~A ton of worry never paid off and ounce of debt. –Finnish Proverb

~The worst part is not in making a mistake but in trying to justify it instead of using it as a heaven-sent warning of our mindlessness or our ignorance. ~ Santiago Ramón y Calah

~Don't write a check from your mouth you can't cash with your ass.

~Life isn't happening to you, it is responding to you. –Rhonda Byrne

~Life is an echo. What you send out is what you get back. – Chinese Proverb

~Everything is a reflection of a choice you made. If you want different results, make different choices.

~We forget all too soon the things we thought we could never forget. -Joan Didion

~ The GREATEST illusion in this world is the illusion of separation.

Chapter 2

Numb and Dumb is how they want you!

When the pain ended so did my heavy drinking. The more I healed the less I drank. I can have fun without it. I drank almost every day of my life for 14 years before I got pregnant with my first child. I am a professional party animal. But, it just really has no purpose for me anymore. I am not saying I completely quit and won't go out 4-5 times a year with friends. I am not saying I will not have a one or two parties a year in my garage. I just see now how ugly it really is throughout my life and through the lives of everyone around me. Everyone is affected by alcohol in some way. Most people drink around their children showing them out of control behavior is a good thing. I will never be drunk and out of control in front of my children. They deserve a better me that is in control. Nobody makes good decisions when they are drunk. I want to be in control of myself and my life at all times. My life is already out of control enough as it is.

Drinking makes me do dumb things. Yes, it was fun almost every time. However, I am tired of waking up and saying. "Oh shit Natalie, did you really do that?" Most of the time it was because of how impressed I was at what I had done. With my psychic gifts and the angels around me giving me information for myself and for others I need to be clear to receive at all times. If you drink, you cannot help others. Your intuition is scrambled and you're not thinking clearly. Both good and bad energies can pass through you because you can't tell the difference when you are not in control and numb.

That is why people who shouldn't drink behave like complete assholes and crybabies. They don't have control of their life already. They are swallowing down pain and anger so deep they can't take it anymore. They get drunk and the bad energies take over. They say stupid things, get violent, rude, cry, have sex with anyone they can, and do things they will wish they hadn't. Then they can pile that on top of the fact they already feel like hell about themselves. They tell themselves they won't do that again.

As soon as they feel good, then they feel they can handle the drinking again. Maybe this time they behave and then justify it. In their mind they say, "Hey look at me, I learned this time and I really can handle my alcohol." Complete delusion! Maybe they do well a couple of times but the bullshit is still bubbling inside them because they can't face themselves. It is just a matter of time before that bad behavior returns. However, it is time for everyone to face themselves.

Do you know that the number one killer of adults in USA today is? It is not heart attacks, not cancer, not any disease, it is painkillers. The saddest thing to watch is that now my life is affected by more people popping pills then alcohol. We are now living in a country heavily medicated and sedated on painkillers that it is now killing them. I watched a woman die from pills and now I am watching many, many more in the process of doing it. It is growing at a fast and shocking rate.

In some cities in Florida there are pain clinics on every block. The newspapers are filled with hundreds of advertisements saying we prescribe opiates. They even prescribe drugs that are given to you before a major surgery. Oxy is synthetic heroin and Adderall is synthetic meth. These clinics only require you to walk in and pay them money for the visit. They will then prescribe you 1000's of pills a month and right there they will hand you the pills. They are the doctor and the pharmacist.

There are airplane companies that charter flights called the 'Oxy Express' flying people down and right back to get their pills. The plane hits the ground when they return home and now they are dealers selling to support their habit. Also, you can see more than one doctor because it is not monitored. These doctors are high paid drug dealers killing our country and our minds to make money.

The drug companies have won the war on drugs. They managed to take control and create the biggest drug addiction in this country yet. They have become the largest drug dealers this world has ever seen and they are getting rich off killing you. Some states 60-70% of the people incarcerated are because of prescription drugs. I have heard that they are cracking down on this, but we need to stand up as the people and stop believing the lies. We all support the government when they want to take down drug cartels. Yet with eyes wide shut, we sit back ignoring the biggest drug cartel, the pharmaceutical companies, and do nothing.

All these pill poppers who can't face themselves have doctors prescribing medications to them long after they need and create the addiction. People are going into as many different emergency rooms a day as they can claiming pain to get pills. In my state they will catch up to you after the 3rd pharmacy in a day and you will go to jail. Sadly, most states do not monitor it that well.

Painkillers are a highly addictive hell. Painkillers are a depressant that numbs you completely to everything. You have absolutely no intuition with those toxic chemicals running through your blood. They really should be called 'everything killers' because they kill everything in your life, not just pain. People walk around saying they are doing good and feeling good. Yet, they can't take a moment of reality without pills and lie about it. We joke about it by saying she needs a pill or just pop a pill, or she must be off her meds because she is a bitch today. Society accepts it as NORMAL.

When I was in drug treatment at fifteen years old, I watched two different women come in and go through withdrawals from painkillers. I told myself I would NEVER put myself through that. I have tried a few different types of pills during my life. Honestly, the minute those toxic chemicals go into my blood I went insane wanting to scratch myself from the inside out. My body does not want it and I hated that feeling.

Furthermore, it is numbing and killing our country literally. The numbers of people that pop pills overshadow those that drink alcohol. The drug companies are literally killing us physically and mentally with chemicals. We do not question it and we have no idea what chemicals are really in them. Our doctors are sent off on fabulous world vacations, given incentives, bonuses, prizes and a healthy paycheck. They already make a lot of money. Sadly, their job is not to help you anymore, but paid to medicate you. The drug companies pay them more that what they normally make. Every time you go to the doctor they will prescribe you something. The worst part of it is, we take it and don't question it. 99% of the time you can heal it naturally yourself or you do not even need it. But the doctors don't tell you that because they will not get paid.

Doctors should be ashamed of themselves for their greed. Doctors are fully aware they have created an addict. Now they have to continually up the dosage because the patient becomes immune to it. One doctor said, "What will we do when they are 70 years old?" Doctors and parents have our children addicted the minute they say ADHD, ADD, Autism, or uncontrollable. As I said, Adderall is synthetic meth. Now our children that we label with all these disorders, whom we can't control, are taking synthetic meth so we can control them and make our lives easier. Get them off of it immediately. You are making them numb and dumb because you can't handle them. You sat back doing nothing, made your child a drug addict and feel it is ok because a doctor did it. You allowed yourself and/or your children to become a drug addict and think it is okay because it is medication. You are no different than a heroin addict. What a shame!

The doctors will continue to make the prescription stronger and stronger. Once it has reached the highest dose they will lie to the patient, cut the amount in half and sell the other half on the street to turn a profit on it. They are also dealers pushing drugs on the street just like the illegal drug dealers. They are no better than the drug dealers we point our fingers at. Do you trust that illegal drug dealer on the street with your life? Next time you go to the doctor again, remember that is a drug dealer you trust with your life. I honestly trust the illegal dealer more than a doctor.

The worst thing I see today is our children who parents put on Adderall or synthetic meth. We are labeling and drugging our children for being CHILDREN. These children are told it is normal. So they feel good taking it and when their friends feel bad, they sell them some. For half the children it is ok and half it is illegal. This is a confusing game to them. Now your addicted children are drug dealers too. The teens tell me that all the kids are doing it. They are snorting, smoking, and popping these pills. All because the parent couldn't handle the monster they created and the doctor wants to make money. Wonderful way for Satan to creep in and destroy the minds of our future leaders. WAKE UP!

So how do we stop this? We educate ourselves about whatever we take and educate others. Strength in numbers! Only the people can change this. We need to stand up for ourselves. It will be impossible if everyone is addicted, numb and don't want change. First thing people have to do is heal the pain of facing themselves. Stop hiding and running from it like an alcoholic. Nobody wants to heal themselves. They just find a pill to make it better. Everyone is addicted to something so they can hide from themselves. Addictions can be drugs, alcohol, food, television, internet, porn, lying, shopping, sex, anorexia, bad relationships, religion (many people hid behind this one so they don't have to face the truth) and that is only to name a few. We find a way to hide it and get a high to cover it. You adapt your body so you don't have to face it. What you are hiding from is YOURSELF and that is the TRUTH.

USA sat back watching T.V. that provides all the mind numbing reality shows and fear spreading news with complete lies from the media. The media is the true terrorist. We are more interested in what the celebrities do, then paying attention to the fact that while you checked out from reality, the government took away every right you have. These mind controlling things are paid for by more lies called commercials. Commercials fill your head with unrealistic bullshit. Constant food commercials making you want extremely unhealthy foods that make you feel horrible, sick and cause disease. Lawyers that will promise to make you rich for suing anyone for anything because now the FDA has found the horrible side effects. But by the time you settle and pay them, you get nothing. You are the one that got screwed! Last but not least, they have a pill for every problem you are too damn lazy to fix or face yourself. People who do not watch television are not taking a bunch of pills. Your mind and the minds of our children watch this continuously every day. You fill your head with bullshit and enjoy it better than reality. MIND CONTROL! Turn off the television and ditch the pills.

Oh and let's not forget the big one that causes about 75% of your problems, the addiction to the drug caffeine. There is a coffee shop everywhere you look. Yes, caffeine is a DRUG and your all drug addicts. You cannot point the finger at a meth addict and think you are better when you also have a drug addiction yourself. For some reason because it is legal, then it is accepted. I drank a pot of coffee along with 5-6 Mountain Dews every day for 23 years from the minute I woke, until I went to sleep. I know about this addiction very well. I am fighting the battle with this drug and winning. I now have 1-2 cups of coffee throughout the day and about 2-3 mountain dews a week.

Caffeine takes every problem you have and makes much it worse. It skyrockets your anxiety levels, creates nervousness, intensifies stress, welcomes in worry, causes physical pain, excessive sweating, mood swings, enhances being unbalanced and sleeplessness. Then you sit back and wonder why you can't handle yourself or anything at all. Now you need a pill to deal with all of that. Here comes the anti-depression pills and anti-anxiety pills. Not to mention the headaches caffeine creates so you need a pill to get rid of that problem too. Caffeine DEHYDRATES you, so now you need something to cover the physical pain of dehydration. Caffeine is a stimulant which creates sleeplessness. So now you need a pill to help you sleep too. You need drugs to bring you up, some to level you out and then a pill to sleep. See how making a choice to quit caffeine could change your life completely? Get control of yourself and get off this shit controlling your life. Are you too lazy to care about yourself and be healthy. Then you wonder why you feel horrible.

Every time you get a headache, sharp pain or your child does not feel good, you run to the cupboard and get the ibuprofen. Once again stuffing unnecessary chemicals into our body and not allowing itself to speak to you. Now you are ignoring your body telling you something is wrong. You are ignoring the fact that a fever is the body's way of slowing you down so you can fight something. Yes, if things are at a dangerous level it is needed, but 90% of the time you need to let your body speak to you, tell you what it needs and let it heal properly. Yes, these over the counter painkillers are also dangerous. But we listen when they tell you to just take a pill to get rid of whatever is happening to you. Don't listen to yourself and don't face what your body needs. Just numb the pain. Real Brilliant!

Another fabulous pill popping scam is vitamins and supplements. Because you are too lazy to eat right, you must take a pill to make up for it. The levels that vitamins contain are toxic. You do not need 200-300% of anything every day. When we take calcium every day, most calcium supplements are actually creating the opposite effect we want. It is destroying our bones. You truly do not know what chemicals they have in that pill. I know people in the medical industry and they say that almost all multi- vitamins come out looking the same way they went in. They do not even dissolve. Just another money making scam. You fell for it and just hand them your cash. You do not need to take supplements every day. Certainly, they have great health benefits, but alternate them and only take them a 2-3 times a week. What you really need is to eat good food. Your body can get all the vitamins it needs if you change your diet and get off these pills because you only want to eat poison. Do your research on the supplements you put into your body please. I sell 100% plant powders on my website. Plants have the natural vitamins and minerals we need. I studied this for six years. There are plants that give you natural energy, natural anti-depressants and natural pain killers.

In the Chinese culture they believe that if you get sick it is the Doctors fault. The doctor should take care of you and catch any problems you have before they start making you sick. As humans we have sat back all drugged up and allowed them to control our minds. We allowed them to brainwash us into thinking that a pill will take care of everything in your life so the drug companies can get rich off your stupidity. Every pill has a side effect that will come later and then you will need a pill to fix that. It becomes a lifetime of covering up one problem after another. It is time for you to WAKE UP. It is time for you to face yourself and what you have done to yourself. It is time to get sober and FEEL your life again. Sure it may be painful, but that is why you have to face it. When you are numb you don't care or feel the real problems you must face.

The drug companies, insurance companies, and medical companies are all together in this. They hide the truth from you because making you sick and keeping you sick is a multi-trillion dollar business. BUSINESS is all it is. Food companies hold their hand in this also. Your food is poison. They are getting rich by making you sick and keeping you sick. You are letting them and do NOTHING about it. They don't want you to feel good or be healthy. They want you to keep buying pills and need medical care.

The 'Big Dogs' did this to you on purpose so you don't care or pay attention. You continue to think everything is ok because a doctor told you that you must do it. It is working because you are all addicts, sick and in denial. If I walked up to you and said, "Here eat this rat poisoning. It will make you feel better and heal your illness or mental health." I guarantee you would all say HELL NO. Yet, you do it every day by taking that pill and eating that horrible processed food containing poisonous chemicals. It is the same thing whether you want to believe it or not. You were just brainwashed into thinking because a doctor gave it to you, everything is okay. 300 tons of confiscated pills a year are being destroyed. Think about how much one pill weighs, then think about that enormous amount. Now you got to think about how many get consumed. Evil just moves in and takes their soul. A slave to chemicals created by man to get rich. Mind blowing to me that humans fell for it.

Take control and remember your mind is the root of all your problems. You can heal cancer and other diseases. You can also prevent it and I will teach you all of that in my next book 'Naturally Natalie'. I went through the incredible journey of healing my physical self naturally because I care about myself and you. I want you healthy and intelligent. I will teach you how to prevent illnesses and heal them, naturally without a doctor. I will tell you the truth about everything they don't want you to know. It is shocking! I will teach you how $1 a month will change your life, health and keep you disease free. I explain all this in great detail so you can better understand how everything is poison. Do you really think God left us here without ways to take care of ourselves? NO! You're brainwashed into believing that. There are natural ways to heal everything and it is time you knew how easy it is. Check out my web store on my website.

My website is – www.natalienewmansworld.com

~The American people don't believe anything until they see it on television.- President Richard Nixon

~If you want to understand a society, take a good look at the drugs it uses. And what can this tell you about the American culture? Well, look at the drugs we use. Except for the pharmaceutical poison, there are essentially only two drugs that the western civilization tolerates: Caffeine from Monday to Friday to energize you enough to make you a productive member of society, and alcohol from Friday to Monday to keep you too stupid to figure out the prison you live in. –Bill Hicks

~ Pharmaceutical industry does not create cures, they create customers.

~There is no way to scientifically test for "chemical imbalance". The same pharmaceutical company profiting from your suffering rely on doctors making a small fortune to say your "chemically imbalanced".

~The greatest medicine of all is to teach others NOT to need it.

~Symptoms are not enemies to be destroyed, but sacred messengers who encourage us to take better care of ourself.

~If you are sick, it's all in your head. You created your illness through your thoughts and emotions. Positive thoughts create a healthy body. ~ Natalie Newman

~CHILDHOOD IS NOT A MENTAL DISORDER!!!! ~ Natalie Newman

Chapter 3
You Wrote the Book of Your Life

One enormous thing that everyone must face, accept and realize is that you wrote your own book before you got here. You chose this entire life and every little thing around you. Blame yourself for where you are in it. This is what you wanted. Nobody did this to you. YOU did this! Your soul wanted this to become better. You have to come out of the box and see it is much bigger than you are here and now. Nothing or no one is a mistake. However, you're unnecessarily suffering by egotistical ways of living. The Buddhists believe you do the best in this life to make yourself better for the next lifetime. That is the truth.

I laugh at myself for the many horrible lessons I chose in this lifetime, which is my last lifetime. I say, "Natalie Newman are you serious? Holy shit! Why did you choose this painful lesson too and why so many at once? I never dreamed I would have to go through this also!" Then I accept everything that happens to me with integrity. I am in complete awe sometimes when I realize how much I pushed myself through this lifetime. I am astounded by how much I trusted myself with all these intense lessons. I came to this life to party, not to hear and deal with BULLSHIT!!!!

However, I must trust that God and I are in charge of this life I choose to walk. God puts in place absolutely everything my soul asked for. I chose this. God, along with the Universe, conspired together and created every second of it with complete perfection for my soul to learn and grow. I see the horrible messes I have at this present moment and I don't fear, stress or worry. I just tell everyone and myself, "Hey, I wrote this book. Do you really think I have come this far and fought this hard to fuck myself over now? Why would I do that to myself? I have to believe in my soul that I chose this, so I could become stronger and better."

How could I not believe in myself and believe that God is taking care of me? That is an insult to God. God created everything and I cannot refuse to trust in that. We created this lifetime together. Facing that fact is when you open your heart to love. God is complete perfection and do you really think that you are not made from God? Pure perfection is what you are. Your soul is perfectly you, doing what it came here to do. Stop creating the hell within. Trust and listen to yourself. Sit in silence and listen to what you have to say. Bad is put in your path for a reason. Good and bad is a part of life.

We create this horrible idea of what is and scare the shit out of ourselves. Why do we fear the darkness? It is exactly the same as daylight, but we cannot see anything. Everything is still the same. Do you fear your bedroom because the lights are off? We fear or create what might not be there and it really isn't. Our minds create anxiety and we freak out. My question to you, why you keep living in the darkness if you are so scared of it? Turn on the light. Open those wounds you buried so deep that are keeping you trapped in fear. You are never alone. Ask for help. The angels have been waiting to help you turn on the light.

When we are born, we just came out and we did not have to do anything at all. We did not have to worry about what we look like, if we were born handicapped or if we have both arms. We just trust in God we are perfectly our self. Babies do not hate, judge, or question. They are pure and society changes all that. Society and parents point fingers and portray negative energies onto us. They say. "OH my God, she has no leg, or she is poor, or he is ugly, or he is retarded." We get labeled for what we are not. We forget our purity and our faith in everything. Society tells us what to think and feel, but it is not real.   That is where we begin to lose our innocence.

When our innocence is leaving us, our ego begins to set in. E.G.O.=Edging Out God!!! An ego is just an idea we have pounded into our brains about who we are. Our parents are the root of this. You begin to believe you are your looks, you are what you do, what others think about you and what you have. You begin to feel that you are separate from everyone and everything. Separate from what you feel you need. Separate from other people and separate from God. Society and your surroundings took these ideas and place them in your head. This takes you away from the truth and who you really are.

You begin to develop at a young age that you are what others think and that is the farthest from the truth. We are raised in a materialistic society that tells us having a lot of "things" makes you better. We are all equal no matter what we drive, what color we are, or what street we live on. Materialism is a false sense of being. It is not who you are. You feel you are what you accomplish. You look at everyone else and feel you need more, to be more, buy more and do more. Then we feel we are better than everyone when we have it and we fall apart when we lose it.

You are not those things. You cannot be free until you let that ego go. Realize we are all in this together. We are all the same. Each one of us chose a different body, different country and different lifestyles for our soul to learn.

I read this story one time by a psychic who had done a past life reading on a blind woman. In the blind woman's last life she watched her mother be beaten for years and finally to the death. She chose this life to not see anything because it was so traumatic. Then when she walks down the street we say, "Oh my God, she is blind." So stop judging everyone for their handicaps. They chose it.

It is stabbing God in the back to say I am better than someone else. God loves everything, including you. Stop thinking with your ego that you deserve things and be things that you are not. Everyone is created equal and came to experience human life. Never forget that ever. Then your ego will dissolve. Your life will get easier and your heart will fill with love for all living things. You have to see yourself in everyone.

God loves you so much, but he also loves every single thing just as much as you. Who are you to think you are better? Because you live a materialistic life, you think you are? Let go of the soul killing ego! God, everyone and your soul will thank you. Ego is evil. Respect everyone for their journey. The sun shines on good and bad. Your mind says they don't deserve it. Who are you to play God and judge his work? When you think you are better than another, that is evil moving through you. That is moving you away from God and your higher self.

For every act of evil there are a million acts of kindness. Stop allowing your ego to sit in the negative energies of darkness. There is a lot wrong with everything on earth at this moment. There is a lot more to come. Please remember the world is fine without your worries and it is doing everything it is supposed to do without you adding more negative energy to the process. You are living in the darkness you fear already. Everything and everyone is needed to produce what is to come on earth. Everyone has a part in it, both good and bad. Trust in it!

The earth is full of empty souls that try to suck every ounce of faith and happiness out of us. Empty souls are the life suckers that refuse to change. They lie, steal, manipulate, and fill our lives with negative energy. They never do anything good for anyone. Their intentions are all bad. I get nauseated around them. I feel their presence. It raises my blood pressure and I feel the darkness. However, I do not fear them anymore. I smile back at them.

When empty souls die they don't have any faith or light. They don't go HOME. They just slip into another body of someone who sells their soul by wishing for something so bad and praying so hard to get it. When you pray or beg for something intensely, it opens up a channel for the angels to come in to help you. But what you need to know is, you also have to give thanks and close that opening back up. If you do not, you allow anything to come through to you. Give thanks for your help and allow God to do what is best for you.

Empty and evil souls are waiting and lurking around you just waiting for a victim body of someone vulnerable to their desires. This is what our earth will be cleansed of. These dark negative souls will be healed or removed from this earth over the next couple decades. We need to get rid of them to let the light shine, bring peace among the people and to our Mother Earth. Time for a house cleaning! Your Mother Earth is begging you to help. We are all here to be a part of this moment. Whether it is to be a great parent or support for our beautiful children and the future leaders of this planet. Or just by smiling at people and being kind. We are all here to spread our light to help this process. So take responsibility for your part of this. It is truthfully why you are here on earth at this moment.

Allow your soul to do what it came here to do. Every person, every word, every feeling was put in action for you to deal with. If we don't experience bad we will never understand what we want. Most times we run and hide from these bad situations. Then take it out on everyone around us because we can't face ourselves.

My life is a high speed train ride with people continuously coming in and out. Faces on all different levels, color, wealth, languages, ages, old and new souls. I love every one of them! Each person comes into my heart. What they do with that place in my heart, is up to them. Some abuse it, some walk all over it, some take it for granted and those I let go. Some are challenging and draining. But I help them and keep working with them until they finally get it. Some of them melt my heart with love because of their beautiful sunshine they bring to my life. Some are blessings that never stop giving.

They all matter to me. Whatever way they chose to treat my heart, I will still love them back. We are all trying our best. I shall not judge another's path or how long it takes them to get there. We all learn at our own speed. I only send loving energy back to them that will heal them instead of hurt them. I am grateful for each one no matter what they do to me because I needed it to learn. To become a better woman and to be the best I can be.

The darkness is needed to help the light and the light is here to help the darkness. Never forget we are all born PURE. Nobody was born bad. Their environment and parents created the monster. Somebody hurt them so much and they take it out on everyone else. THEY NEED LOVE! That is what the light and the good people teach them - LOVE! That heals them so they can be good again. Stop hating and love your enemies. Love the most evil and controlling people on earth, because they need it the most. Their behavior is a cry for help, but nobody is listening.

When nobody listens, it manifests into horrible negative energies allowing dark souls to enter the body. When love hits their heart, the light shines in. Their addictions and pain become less. They begin to heal and love back. LOVE your enemies, because it needs you to love them. Then they can stop and become good again. It is all up to you. Spread your love and hug the Earth, because we all need you.

The darkness challenges the light by pushing us through fears, pain, anger, jealousy, stress, etc. It challenges us to become better souls. To want more for ourselves and to know what we want in life. The darkness teaches us to overcome our fears and be stronger within our being. It challenges us to question and find the answers. This enhances our knowledge and our faith.

The dark teaches us to love what we have with everything we've got. Darkness teaches us the magic in life by pushing us to another step in being a higher person. Without each other we would never have gotten here. This moment on the planet, is the moment of the end of the world as we know it. 2012 is the END and it is the beginning of a new life. A new way of living is coming, by creating peace and love with complete unity on this planet.

Through the devastating and difficult times ahead on both a global and personal level, please remember, everything is put in place to push for a better future. Have faith in God's work and know you will be protected as long as you understand everything happens for reason. The greatest gift you can give this world is to love. When you love, your light will shine to everyone. The world will feel your love. Stop letting negative energy in. Learn and move on! Love the moment for what it teaches you or the gifts it brings. What you give is what you will receive back. Love provides us with all our needs. Positive brings positive.

Hold your faith and trust in God that you will be taken care of. When you feel fear just ask for help. Those who have faith will see this beautiful cleansing. So figure out what you want. Make a choice and get to work on your mind. Choose to stay negative or choose to awaken. Less than half of this Earth at this point will assume responsibility for their choices. Over half want to stay in negative ways of thinking. There is research all over the internet about this. It is my wish to help you choose the high road. I dream of seeing EVERY man, EVERY woman and EVERY child awaken to walk our Mother Earth the way we want it can be. IMAGINE PEACE ON EARTH. That will be Heaven!

When you learn to let go, the process of going forward to less structure, to a more open way to handling things like reactions and attachments, get easier. We can choose to disagree or infuse it in light and love. Our bodies feel the pain and when it hurts you look at it. Suffering is when you hang on to it long past it's time. We can change everything.

For the next couple of weeks pay attention. Watch what comes up with all your situations. When you feel a negative emotion, stop! Ask yourself, why would this piss me off? Why did that hurt me? Those are the answers to your fears. Face your fears and find something that works for you. Take responsibility and deal with yourself please. We need you on this Earth to feel better inside. The rest of the world would appreciate it. It is not all about you, we have to feel you too. We do just by standing next to you or being in the same room. We are all ONE!

Keep your thoughts positive. Look for the lesson before you fall completely apart. Let the tears come and let them water your soul. Feel the feeling, then step out of it and look at it with a positive outlook. Tell yourself, only you have control of everything. You cannot control another. You will begin to grow and open a new way of handling things. When you send positive out, you get positive results. Stop, look and listen before you THINK. Your reactions are a reflection of the emotions inside you. How you act and react defines your personality. I always call it my PERSONATALIE.

Try thinking before you react or act. Is it in alignment with how you want to be treated yourself? Integrity is treating others like you want to be treated yourself. Do you live with integrity? Do you treat others how you want to be treated? If not, then do not expect them to either. If you try this you will see things are so easy to handle when they come. You will stop having to learn your mistakes through pain. Stop worrying what others think. Create your own reality and live in it.

When you try to control everything that is when the lessons are the hardest. Go with the flow of it. Love yourself and live in the moment of it. Be grateful for the chaos. You are really just here for the ride my friend. Enjoy it. You will eventually lose the need to cling to people because you are needy. You will begin to move through life experiencing things lightly and begin dancing through it embracing it all as an experience. Remember, you have the right to learn at your own pace. It is your journey. We only move as fast as we are able to.

Sometimes when I pray hard for lessons, things start to move really fast. The world around me spins like a tornado with lessons. Then I have to ask God to please put on the brakes a little bit. Please allow me to slow down and process it. I ask for help because I am having a difficult time at the moment. Life will slow down for you. We learn at the speeds we choose. I happen to choose lightning speed. I get my ass handed to me in enormous amounts. However, look at what I have learned because of it and I can handle it. You are stronger than you could ever imagine.

People may think they are separate and all alone, but the truth is there is so much interconnection. I am connected to all living things. When you feel alone, allow time for connection and communion. If there are no people around for good company, then be with nature, a dog, cat, a tree or the ocean. Good company comes in many forms. You just need to OPEN your mind and ears.

Everyone is an aspiring human growing. People are what they think about all day long. We are all here to only be our self and nobody else. Trust in your own intuition. Society tells you not to trust it. Believe in yourself. Let go of your attachments to your outcomes. Everybody wants the world to change, but nobody wants to change. Find your truth inside yourself. The truth will set you free, but first it will piss you off. When you make a decision out of anger or frustration it is almost always a disaster.

Pay attention to the fact there is a lot of fear, arrogance, sadness, stress, hate, worry and guilt on this earth. Try not to get caught up in it and absorb someone else's garbage. Humans generate it out everywhere around us. It goes out to our Mother Earth, the plants, animals, and every living thing on this planet, straight out to the Universe, absorbs it all. So address the fear and experience life.

You know life is worth the struggle when you look back on what you lost. Realize what you have now is way better than before. What are you complaining about? Somebody on this planet has it far worse than you do. It's not that life is so short, it's that we wait so long to begin living. We are all going to die, but not all of us are going to 'live'. Also, everything you are running from is in your head. Running away from a problem only increases the distance to the solution. The easiest way to escape from the problem is solve it. Learn from it and find your freedom by letting it go.

Also, it's important that people should know what you stand for. It's equally important that they know what you won't stand for. Now smile, be proud you survived another day and love yourself for being the best you that you can. If you hold hate and anger in your heart, then you've been skipping out on God's most important gift to humans - LOVE. Love is the blood of the soul. God wants all beings to have healthy and strong souls, so God created a simple law to nourish the soul: the more you give love, the more you receive love. Please keep in mind laughter is God's medicine and if we want to form an addiction, this is the best way to medicate. Try to naturally heal yourself first. It does wonders for your soul and your age.

~It was possible that a miracle was not something that happened to you, but rather something that didn't. ~The Tenth Circle

As many times as you can each day sit for a moment and breathe in. Stop for a second and feel your heart. Take a moment to feel love and gratefulness in your heart. Really feel it. Let it travel freely through your entire body. Imagine if you could feel this all of the time. Take that love and spread it through the entire room. Love is surrounding you. Then send it through your home, across your neighborhood and then throughout your city. Let your love travel across your state, flood it across your country. Then explode in every direction across the entire earth. The entire earth is hugged by your love. It will all come back to you. Just close your eyes and imagine it. Spread your love around the world. It is that simple to make a big difference. We all feel it. Nothing is impossible, the word itself says I'm possible. The sky is not the limit. Your mind is. Believe and your half way there. The secret to having it all, is believing you already do.

I cheated on my fears, broke up with my doubts, got engaged to my faith and now I am marrying my dreams. You are far TOO SMART to be the only thing standing in your way. You know, I don't even try to fathom it, tomorrow is another day, who knows what it brings. But I do know it will bring all new life in many different forms. Something fabulous is out there calling your name. Stop and listen!

Imagine what would happen if everyone woke up today thinking of helping others instead of themselves. Likely, this would bring peace. This would be heaven. What is the point of being alive if you don't at least try to do something remarkable? Be anything, dream something, fear nothing and love everything. God has bigger plans for you than you have for yourself. If an egg is broken from outside force, a life ends. If an egg is broken from the inside, life begins. Great things always begin from within. The greatest battle is not physical but psychological.

~You did not cry or get angry about every new math lesson in school, did you? So why are you crying and angry about every life lesson?-Natalie Newman

~Give so much time to improving yourself that you have no time to criticize others.

~To be kind is more important than to be right. Many times what people need is NOT a brilliant mind that speaks but a special heart that listens.

~If you realized how powerful your thoughts are, you would never think a negative thought again.

~When everything seems to be going against you, remember that the airplane takes off against the wind, NOT with it. -Henry Ford

~No one saves us but ourselves. No one can and no one may. We ourselves must walk the path.- The Buddah

~As long as there is someone in the sky to protect me, there is NO ONE on earth that can break me.

~If you have food in your fridge, clothes on your back, roof over your head and a place to sleep, you are richer than 75% of the world.

If you have money in the bank, your wallet and some spare change, you are among the top 8% of the world's wealthy.

If you woke up today with more health than illness then you are more blessed than the million people who will not survive this week.

If you have never experienced the danger of battle, the agony of imprisonment, or torture or the horrible pangs of starvation, you are luckier than 500 million people alive and suffering.

If you can read this message you are more fortunate than the 3 billion people who can't read at all.

Chapter 4
I Can Learn, Let Go and Grow

~Forgiveness is the fragrance that the violet sheds on the heel that has crushed it. -Mark Twain

    One of the very first steps in living a happier life is learning to forgive. God forgives us, so who are you not to forgive? Without forgiveness you continue to allow yourself and others to suffer and be victimized over and over, forever. According to the Bible forgiveness is one of the spiritual duties of the Christian believer. Remove your ego from the situation and look at it again. Does the situation look different? You can say I forgive but not forget, is just another way of saying I will not forgive. It is a well learned lesson which will only make you stronger. With the healing power of forgiveness, I can overcome every mistake others or I made. I forgive myself. I forgive them.

    When you forgive yourself, you forgive everything. When you forgive everything, you forgive yourself. Now I know most of you are a little uncomfortable in your chair at the moment about this subject because we are all guilty of holding unforgiveness in our lives. Forgiveness is not saying what you did was right. It says, I refuse to hold on to the suffering it caused me to free myself. Holding unforgiveness in our hearts does not give us freedom or the ability to move on with our lives. It holds us trapped there at that lesson we need to learn. Unforgiveness, if not taken care of, is destructive and can cause pain, diseases or illnesses within us. It lives inside us, eating us alive until we deal with it. You're a victim to your own mind. Honestly, it does nothing good at all. It takes a strong person to say sorry, and an ever stronger person to forgive. When forgiveness seems impossible, know that your life is FOR-GIVING.

~*The weak can never forgive. Forgiveness is the attribute of the strong*~ Ghandi

When someone does something wrong to another or to ourselves we make the choice how to react to it. We have the right to feel the emotion it gives us. Whether it be pain, anger, or confusion. It is important to feel that emotion. Normally, when someone does badly to us we carry the negative emotion with us. We attach ourselves to the feeling it gave us. We feel we have the right to continue to be angry and/or hurt. We blame them and continue our anger or pain long after the situation has ended. We carry this around on our shoulders every day and fill our bodies with toxic negative energies.

~*"We attach our feelings to the moment when we were hurt, endowing it with immortality. And we let it assault us every time it comes to mind. It travels with us, sleeps with us, hovers over us while we make love, and broods over us while we die. Our hate does not even have the decency to die when those we hate die--for it is a parasite sucking OUR blood, not theirs. There is only one remedy for it. Forgiveness!* ~Lewis B. Smedes

Almost every time you hold unforgiveness it is because you're angry or hurt with their actions. Truthfully, it is a lesson they gave us we do not want to face. When you hold anger and hurt, it will keep attracting the same situations until you learn the lessons and let go of it. We don't want to look inside ourselves and ask "Why do I feel this emotion and what is it inside me that causes me to react to it this way?" You react because it is something you do not like. You need to look inside to see what you can do to fix it, learn from it and move on. It is so much easier to point the finger and hold these negative thoughts so we do not have to face ourselves. By holding unforgiveness, you acknowledge them as successful. You give to yourself to them by holding those emotions to them. If you or they didn't make a mistake, you would never learn.

Some never learn and stay swimming in negative energy of suffering forever. Most of the time it is not our fault and/or it is something we needed to learn. This reason we may not even understand until years later. Like my life of abuse, I had to forgive those who hurt me. I know in my heart they had a pain that caused them to act out with a form of abuse. They had to throw their pain onto everyone around them to get it out.

I can now look at the abuse as something I needed to go through so I could understand so many things in my life to get to where I am today. I am able to understand so many different kinds of pain and healing because of all of that abuse happening to me. I know it is not my fault they behaved like that.

However, it is my fault for staying in the situation and enabling it. Now because of that pain, I understand and help so many others survive what I have lived through. I chose this path and the things that happened to me in this life for a reason. I always ask God "WHY so many bad things happen to me?" I also have to remember, I came here to survive this and learn from it. It is about how you react to it and how long you want to hold on to the unforgiveness. Stop asking WHY ME? And start saying TRY ME! Forgive them and thank them for teaching you something. You will learn from it and grow into a stronger person for surviving it. I don't forgive people cause I'm weak. I forgive them cause I'm strong enough to understand people make mistakes. A little girl was asked what forgiveness is...She gave a beautiful answer..."It is the fragrance that flowers give when they are crushed."

~ *"I don't know if I continue even today, always liking myself. But what I learned to do many years ago was to forgive myself. It is very important for every human being to forgive herself or himself because if you live, you will make mistakes- it is inevitable. But once you do and you see the mistake, then you forgive yourself and say, 'well, if I'd known better I'd have done better,' that's all. So you say to people who you think you may have injured, 'I'm sorry,' and then you say to yourself, 'I'm sorry.' If we all hold on to the mistake, we can't see our own glory in the mirror because we have the mistake between our faces and the mirror; we can't see what we're capable of being. You can ask forgiveness of others, but in the end the real forgiveness is in one's own self. I think that young men and women are so caught by the way they see themselves. Now mind you. When a larger society sees them as unattractive, as threats, as too black or too white or too poor or too fat or too thin or too sexual or too asexual, that's rough. But you can overcome that. The real difficulty is to overcome how you think about yourself. If we don't have that we never grow, we never learn, and sure as hell we should never teach."* ~Maya Angelou quote

Some people hate their parents or cannot forgive them for the life they had. I lived that way in the relationship with my mother. All my life she put me in terribly painful moments. Yet, I understand in my heart that she only did the best that she could with who she was. I have to forgive her for all she put me through. I cannot wish healing for her if I cannot love her and forgive her for doing what she thought was right.

Furthermore, I know this woman whose relationship with her mother was a childhood of horrible abuse, with an adult life of rejection and verbal abuse. The mother of this woman is on her death bed as I speak. The daughter, who is a 60 year old woman, has lived and carried around the pain, hatred, and unforgiveness 60 years.

To me it is a dark way to live and has caused her so much horrifying suffering that has affected every part of her life. It had her in extremely abusive relationships and spun her into a deadly drug and alcohol addiction that is killing her.

As her mother lay there dying, the woman's only wish is for her to apologize. However, the mother continued to live in delusion that anything ever happened. She claimed she had a beautiful life. The woman is wished for something that will never happen. Her mother died and they never resolved the pain.

I spoke to the woman and told her that she needs to forgive her while she has the chance and understand she only did the best she could with what she was taught. Sadly, the battle is still went on and went right to the grave. If she just opened her heart to forgiveness, everyone could begin to heal while there are only moments left to do it.

But, instead this woman will have to continue to carry this pain and suffering long after her mother died. Ironically, the woman lived almost the same life her mother did and she also feels she did nothing wrong in her life. The chain of abuse continued into her own life. If she could forgive her mother she could heal her own faults and face them.

It is one of the saddest stories I have witnessed in a very long time. Stubbornness is not the answer. It will only continue the cycle into everyone else's life until the woman can heal it. I just pray for her to be able to heal it before it is too late. So she can heal her own life and face what she has done to others also.

I make mistakes and try to do the best I can with my own children. At some point in your life you have to be a responsible adult and assume responsibility for your own actions. You need to stop blaming your damn parents for everything mistake they made 20-40 years ago. I learn what I do not want to be from my own mother and moved forward. I cannot control anyone. All I could do is pray for her. I understand abuse and I understand her. We only know what we are shown.

It is my mother's choice and her freewill to decide how she wants to live. I have to forgive her for her choices. This is her journey, not mine. I do not put an attachment on how I believe the outcome should be. I know the outcome is what is best for her and me. I have learned so much from her path of how to walk mine in the opposite direction.

I also see what my life would have become if I would have

stayed in abusive relationships. I love her very much and I put it in God's hands choosing what is best for her to ease her pain. Holding unforgiveness only puts more negativity around the entire negative situation. I only want to send loving energy and healing energy to her. I can only love her and be there for her. I do not stress or worry because I know God is holding her close with loving arms.

Many children grew up without a parent or even both parents. They hold unforgivenss to them for not being there in their lives. When your father, mother or both leave your life, you need to be thankful. You need to trust that God did what was best for you and protected you from a life that could have been so much worse. God did you a favor whether you believe it or not and it was a blessing. So be grateful and forgive them. You chose it.

Forgiveness is not saying what that person did was correct. It is saying I do not want to carry around the bad emotions (pain, anger, guilt, and shame) because of your actions. It is saying I am letting this go so I can begin to heal and be at peace. The situation is then free inside me. When you forgive them and you forgive yourself, it magically heals. Some things take time and more work to fix. Once you have made that decision to forgive, then you have made the biggest and most difficult step to healing. You can be mature enough to forgive but you do not have to trust them.

Hanging on to negative energy only attracts more negative to the situation. It's not about who's right or who's wrong. There are more important things than that. That's why we have things like apologies and forgiveness. If you allow people to make more withdrawals than deposits in your life, you will be out of balance and in the negative. Know when to close the account. Be the CEO of your happiness, not the janitor of someone else's misery.

One of my lessons by a teacher of mine was to make a list of every man that has hurt me and a short description of how they hurt me. It took two days and the list ended up with over 100 men that had hurt me deeply in some way. Next, she told me to pray and forgive each one separately. I prayed for each one, what they had done to me, and to open my heart to forgiveness. So I can learn, let go and grow. Let the wind take this unforgiveness from within my soul in exchange for peace. Yeah, it took a long time but I did it. I died and I cried remembering each horrible moment I was hurt. Digging up the most painful memories of my life I felt were dead. I let go and forgave every one of them. I came alive with an amazing peace and feeling of fulfillment inside because I survived it. I learned from what they had done to me and became a better person through it all.

    Now I can be grateful for the horrible disasters I had to go through. Without them I would not be HERE and who I am today. That is total freedom. I needed them to challenge me to learn something. You cannot change another person but you can change how you react to it and how long you want to hang on to it.

    All of my life others judged me and called me terrible names. They spread horrible rumors and gossip about me. Most of them never speaking to me in person or it is someone who barely knows me. It seems they have nothing better to do with themselves. If you ever meet any of my "REAL" friends they will not say bad things about me because I am not who the liars say I am. I have remained hidden for over four years so whatever you hear is bullshit. Don't judge me by my past because I don't live there anymore.

    Dear Haters, Please be patient I have so much more for you to be mad at. Just be patient!

    My greatest humor in people who love to talk about me, are women. I do not know what it is about these ladies but, they thrive off telling lies about me. They love to talk about my parenting skills, my life, my love life, one of them told my daughter I am on meth and that is why I am so skinny.

    Well for one, I am running in every direction all day long. I raise three very busy children MYSELF. I carry, stack and split wood for a woodstove to heat my house 7-8 months a year every day. I get no sleep for 6 months because I have to wake up and fill the woodstove every three hours. I have to work and maintain an old house out in the country by MYSELF with no man to assist me with the heavy or difficult things. I have to cut about a soccer field of grass with a push lawn mower that takes about 3 days and in the summer I have to do it every week. I have many huge flower beds to maintain. Also I have a relationship with someone in a different country which is not always easy with 7 hour time difference. I help 100's of people from all over the world here where I live. I help 1000's online.

Also, I am praying for the world with every living thing on it. I live an extremely active life. I do all this and I never leave my house. I leave about once a week to get food. I do not talk to anyone in the town I live in. Nobody ever sees me. Yet, they tell everyone they know who I am and everything I am doing. I guess it is wrong not being fat and if you are thin you are on amphetamines for sure. SERIOUSLY? They continuously get a thrill off talking bad about me. They really just need to move on. Why don't people have better things to do? Real eyes, Realize, Real lies! Don't worry about what other people say behind your back, they are the people who are finding faults in your life instead of fixing the faults in their own life. Jealousy is the art of counting someone else's blessings, instead of their own.

~A teacher in New York was teaching her class about bullying and gave them the following exercise to perform: she had the children take a piece of paper and told them to crumple it up, stomp on it and really mess it up but do not rip it. Then she had them unfold the paper, smooth it out and look at how scarred and dirty it was. She then told them to tell the paper they're sorry. Now, even though they said they were sorry and tried to fix the paper, she pointed out all the scars they left behind. Those scars will never go away no matter how hard they tried to fix it. That is what happens when a child bullies another child--they may say they're sorry but the scars are there forever. The looks on the faces of the

children in the classroom told her the message hit home

~15 year old girl holds her 1 year old son; people call her a slut; but no one knows she was raped at 13. People call a girl fat; but no one knows she has a serious disease that causes her to be overweight. People call an old man ugly; no one knows he had a serious injury to his face while serving our country in Vietnam. ~ Unknown

~"I've always hated being gossiped about. When I heard that people were talking about me, I consoled myself with what my mother, Ruthie, used to say: 'Birds peck at the best fruit."~ Bette Davis

You don't like me? Then you can just have a seat with the other bitches waiting for me to give a fuck. I am so grateful to the people who have hated me, who have been envious of me, who haven't been there for me, who have disrespected me and who have put me down. Because they are the ones who have made me who I am today. I kept my head up and did not let them break me down when they wanted to. I do not care what anyone says. They have painfully tried to destroy me and kick me in the face with their hideous words. They do not understand that I always have had the ability to laugh at it. You have my full permission to gossip about me, I am fucking fascinating.

I was proud when they talked about me. I was always grateful they were talking about me instead of another who would be destroyed by their lies. With gossip, I knew they were thinking about me. I know I am deep in their heads and they take time out of their pathetic lives to talk about me. My name is spinning in their heads for one reason or another. Gossipers only talk if they are jealous of another in some way and want to make a person look bad. There must be something they are jealous of about me because they cannot stop thinking about me. Never hate people who are jealous of you, but respect their jealousy. They are the people who think you are better than them.

Judging a person is only judging yourself. They can just keep thinking about me, draw attention to me, and then they will see the truth behind your lies. Karma will come back in your face honey. How people treat you is their karma and how you react is yours. I do not need to say anything at all. I am not going to run around and try to correct it. Why? Why do I need to fix THEIR lies? I am not what I have DONE. I am what I have OVERCOME. I don't have time to hate those who hate me. I am too busy loving people who love me.

~*You have enemies? Good! That means you have stood up for something in your life.* ~*Winston Churchill*

My life! My problems! My mistakes! MY LESSONS! Mind your own problems before you talk about mine. The people who are my family and friends know the truth. That is all that matters to me. I have been blessed with an abundance of loving people in my life. So if I am such a bad person why do so many 1000's of people love me for who I am? Unless it involves my children, I could care less what they think. I have heard the most unimaginable things about myself. I am not saying I am perfect. I was wild and running free most my life. But what they say is never true. Usually the truth is a way better story.

Hell, I am telling the whole world about my worse moments. I am not ashamed or hiding anything. I know who I am. I have made many mistakes and I also learned from them. I learn so well I am thinking about making some more and I know I will. It is a learning process. I know I am a great woman, mother, girlfriend, friend, and that I try my very best every day. No matter what happens, be yourself. Life isn't about pleasing others. It is about making the best out of the life you were given. You are you and that is what you are here to be. I know where I am going. I love myself and my world is beautiful. So what do you have to say about that? THAT is the truth.

There are now seven billion people in the world. Why are you letting one of them bring you down? Never sacrifice who you are because someone has a problem with it. One of the greatest mental freedoms is really not caring what other people think of you. Words can be very powerful. Why not use them to lift people up instead of knock them down? They laugh at me because I am different. I laugh at them because they are all the same. If you didn't hear it with your own ears or see it with your own eyes, don't invent it with your small mind and spread it with your big mouth. Great people talk about ideas, average people talk about things and small people talk about others. If only closed minds came with closed mouths.

~Don't take anything personally. Nothing others do is because of you. What others say and do is a projection of their own reality, their own dream. When you are immune to the opinions and actions of others you won't be the victim of needless suffering.

It is better to have an enemy who says they honestly hate you, then to have a friend who secretly puts you down. I have to forgive them and understand they do not have better things to do than talk about Natalie Newman. I understand that they do not want others to look at them. I have to understand that there is something inside them that has to talk bad about others. I pity them for having to tell lies to feel better. I never talk bad about them in return, it is just not worth my time. I have so many beautiful things I would rather talk about instead. I understand I am not those things they said. Forgiveness lets it all go. It frees me from their prison of pain they are trying to create for me by trying to make me look bad. Allows me to feel sorry for them and wish healing to them. That is a negative energy they carry and spread to others. Bullying, gossiping, and stereotyping are evil ways to live. The truth always comes out. Rumors are carried by haters, spread by fools and accepted by idiots.

~Think before you speak= **T- Is it True?**

=**H- Is it Helpful?**

=**I-Is it Inspiring?**

=**N- Is it Necessary?**

=**K- Is it Kind?**

--If not then keep your mouth shut!

~ Don't ever use someone's past against them. You're just reminding them of the mistakes they made back then. If you watch their facial expression carefully, then you'll see the hurt in their eyes as they reminisce everything that happened. Never use emotion as a weapon, it strikes deeper than you can imagine. ~Unknown

    I also decided to pray to God to please guide all those that I have hurt in my life to find forgiveness in their hearts for my actions by my past pain filled behaviors. That is an important part of healing yourself and sending healing to others for what you have done to them. So very important if you want to choose a life without more pain is learning to let go of the guilt for things you have done to others. You made mistakes but you need to learn from them. You do not need to continue to beat yourself up with guilt forever. Forgive and let God heal it so you can feel peace in your heart. The most difficult person in life to forgive is yourself, but it is the most important one. You are the one that carries the emotion.

    I realized how many people's lives I turned upside down or broke their hearts. I know that if those horrible things I had lived through had never happened, I would never have done those painful things to them. As a child I did not know any better at all. I only knew what I was shown. As a young adult I had to begin to live with myself and deal with it. Sometimes I dealt with it all wrong. I can't change anything I did to others. I was messed up by the vicious cycle of abuse and the fact that I chose to run from it. That abuse unleashed by my grandfather, caused me 39 years of pain. That was pain that I took out on others and myself. It was not fair to any of us that it happened, but it did. As an adult I can only assume responsibility for my mistakes and be the best I can be today. I never want to hurt anyone again, ever. I hope those I hurt can understand that I put myself in some very bad situations because from a very young age I was taught in bad ways. I faced all of it and relived it. It hurt me so very deeply. I am sorry to each and every one of them. I am an explorer of pain, my life is pain and I help people in intense pain.

Today I am not that person and I try really hard to face it, heal it, and be better. I am better! I only strive to do what is right and to be love. I thank God I am who I am now and that I overcame it all after the horrible, torturing and ugly situations of abuse I lived through. I pray and I let it go. I cannot change it, except to ask for forgiveness to the many I have hurt and myself.

It is over and there is no more horrible abuse in my life for the last 6 years. I have no reason to continue to take anything out on anyone, especially myself. I am my own worse enemy. However, I am also my very best friend. I guided myself through it. I survived to heal it, fix it and tell the truth. I hid everything from everyone because at a young age I learned when you told the truth about bad things that everything would get worse. I learned that bad habit when I told the truth about my grandfather. Everyone would blame me and everything would be destroyed like my family. I kept everything inside. I told very little to anyone.

Instead, I just said, "Screw it! Let's go have fun and laugh. I will deal that shit some other day." That caused me alot of unneeded suffering by not facing it and running from it. Suffering is needed to figure out what you want. It never seemed to take long to know I didn't want to feel like that. I can't say I won't make any mistakes again. I know I am going to try damn hard to live with integrity and not repeat again.

Dear God,

Please forgive me for the pain I caused others with my bad behaviors. I acted out my pain that others inflicted on me in ways I am not proud of. I ask please, that every person and everything on Earth I hurt, find forgiveness in their heart for my mistakes because I truly did not know any better or loved myself enough to behave properly at that moment I hurt them. I would not have done wrong if I knew what was right. I am sorry to everyone I hurt. Please help me to forgive myself because if I would have known better I would have done better in the situation. I am trying my best. Thank you for hearing my prayer.

~ Natalie Newman

~Hatred paralyzes life; love releases it. Hatred confuses life; love harmonizes it. Hatred darkens life; love illumines it. ~Martin Luther King, Jr.

Usually, those who do something bad to us never felt anything. Some people are only in your life to go against you and challenge you. It is only you who carries this emotion. They carry on with their life. Take a moment of stillness and say I want peace, I want love and forgiveness for this person hurting me. We ALL make mistakes. We all make the wrong decisions. If these things did not happen, we would never learn anything. Because of break-ups and heartaches you learn what you want from a relationship or what you will do differently next time. Because of mistakes you learn what you don't want. So forgive yourself for everything you have done. Know in your heart at that moment you tried your best with what you had. Because you did! You should give yourself a pat on that back for that at least. YOU TRIED and YOU SURVIVED.

Forgiveness is a process we must do every day. It promotes healing and keeps negative energy out of our minds and bodies. Forgive yourself for being at variance with yourself, its part of the human experience. Become perfect in your imperfection and complete in your incompletion. Just repeat this. "I am strong because I've known weakness, I am compassionate because I have experienced suffering, I am alive because I am a fighter, I am wise because I've been foolish, I can laugh because I have known sadness. I can love because I have known loss." I know I have weathered the storm but still love to dance in the rain. What doesn't kill you will make you stronger!!!!!!! So forgive yourself and others. Always be kind, it may be an Angel standing before you!!!

~The most beautiful people we have known are those who have known defeat, known suffering, known struggle, known loss, and have found their way out of the depths. These persons have an appreciation, a sensitivity, and an understanding of life that fills them with compassion, gentleness, and a deep loving concern. Beautiful people do not just happen. ~Elizabeth Kubler Ross

~To hate another is to hate yourself. We all live within the one Universal Mind. What we think about another, we think about ourselves. If you have an enemy, forgive him now. Let all bitterness and resentment dissolve. You owe your fellow man love: Show him love, not hate. Show charity and goodwill toward others and it will return to enhance your own Life.....in many wonderful ways. ~Bryan Adams

HATER'S
A hater is someone who is jealous and envious and spends all their time trying to make you look small so they can look tall. They are very negative people to say the least. Nothing is ever good enough!

When you make your mark, you will always attract some haters...

That's why you have to be careful with whom you share your blessings and your dreams, because some folk can't handle seeing you blessed...

It's dangerous to be like somebody else... If God wanted you to be like somebody else, He would have given you what He gave them! Right?

You never know what people have gone through to get what they have...

The problem I have with haters is that they see my glory, but they don't know my story...

If the grass looks greener on the other side of the fence, you can rest assured that the water bill is higher there too!

We've all got some haters among us!

Some people envy you because you can:
a) Have a relationship with God
b) Light up a room when you walk in
c) Start your own business
d) Tell a man/woman to hit the curb (if he/she isn't about the right thing)
e) Raise your children without both parents being in the home

Haters can't stand to see you happy.
Haters will never want to see you succeed.
Most of our haters are people who are supposed to be on our side.

How do you handle your undercover haters?
You can handle these haters by:

1. Knowing who you are & who your true friends are

*(VERY IMPORTANT!!)

2. Having a purpose to your life: Purpose does not mean having a job. You can have a job and still be unfulfilled.

A purpose is having a clear sense of what God has called you to be.
Your purpose is not defined by what others think about you.

3. By remembering what you have is by divine prerogative and not human manipulation.

Fulfill your dreams! You only have one life to live...when its your time to leave this earth, you want to be able to say, 'I've lived my life and fulfilled my dreams, Now I'm ready to go HOME!

When God gives you favor, you can tell your haters, 'Don't look at me...Look at who is in charge of me...'

Don't worry about it, it's not your problem, it's theirs.
Just pray for them, that their life can be as fulfilled as yours!
Watch out for Haters...BUT most of all don't become a HATER!

'A woman's heart should be so hidden in Christ that a man should have to seek Him first to find her.'

Written by Maya Angelo

Chapter 5

Without the Darkness You Will Never Search for the Light

~Darkness cannot drive out darkness; only light can do that. Hate cannot drive out hate; only love can do that. Hate multiplies hate, violence multiplies violence, and toughness multiplies toughness in a descending spiral of destruction. The chain reaction of evil -- hate begetting hate, wars producing more wars -- must be broken, or we shall be plunged into the dark abyss of annihilation."~Martin Luther King, Jr.

You can't talk about life without talking about the negative side of life. At one point I feared the darkness. I have been hit by fallen angels, dark entities and witchcraft it in the most grueling ways. They want to stop me from finishing this book and helping you overcome fear, which is their control over everything. Most of us don't understand and/or fear the negative and dark sides of life. Yes, they do exist. Fact is 60% of humans are living in darkness and negativity. They are in many different forms of life and moments of our life. Negativity is a killer and the evil side just wants to assists you in going down the drain. Being awake and aware keeps them from entering our lives and stops them from taking over our soul. Darkness is needed to show us what we need to fix, push us forward to the light and happiness again, and teach the soul.

~Most people are searching for happiness outside of themselves. That's a fundamental mistake. Happiness is something that you are, and it comes from the way that you think. ~Dr. Wayne Dyer

The 1st thing we need to understand is the negativity we generate around ourselves. The hardest and deepest wounds we carry are losing THINGS. We say goodbye to every single thing in our lives every day. Sometimes it is just for a moment, or years or a lifetime. When you close your eyes to sleep you can guarantee that tomorrow nothing will be the same. You cannot go through life without sleeping because of your fear everything will be different or gone tomorrow. So why do you hang on to the things that have passed their time or need to end? It is the same. Everything will be new and different in every way. That is the magic of life. It is cleansed and renewed every day of our lives, but most of us never see it. What we have lost will be replaced with something else. Still, we swim in negative fear without seeing the beautiful blessing sent in its place. We walk around in our negative bubble crying over a loss when it is just a natural process of our journey.

The biggest negative energy we have is FEAR. Fear is the root of ALL evil. Fear is what makes evil survive. Fear is what controls all of our bad behaviors, addictions, the torturing hell we put ourselves and everyone around us through. Fear is something inside of OURSELVES we don't want to look at or overcome and heal. When we are filled with fear, our minds and bodies race in the wrong directions. It closes our minds to the answers we need to hear to fix this problem. Some of the worse behaviors that come from fear are judgment, rage, guilt, shame, anger, sadness, jealousy, blaming, unforgiveness and eventually the death of our soul.

~ *"I must not fear. Fear is the mind-killer. Fear is the little-death that brings total obliteration. I will face my fear. I will permit it to pass over me and through me. And when it has gone past I will turn the inner eye to see its path. Where the fear has gone there will be nothing. Only I will remain."* - Espavo

Judgment is an egotistical way of living in fear. Pointing the finger at another for whatever reason we don't want to look at ourselves or for others to look at our bad behavior. When instead, we should empathize with them and not assume anything. How can you judge another when you don't even know them or understand the truth? Judgments are 100% of the time WRONG. We need to process the situation, listen and find the truth about that situation. Only when we know the truth, can we then make a clear decision of how we feel about it. Gossip is a killer. We talk about others as if they have no feelings at all. We say the most horrible things never knowing the real truth and cause damaging pain to another.

    We have trained our brains to saying, "Holy shit, did you see what that person did?" Instead, we need to train our brains to the truth. What we should be saying is, "Holy shit, what pain or anger pushed this person to behave like this?" We judge the action when really we should realize we have been given a huge warning signal that something is wrong. Something is so wrong with that person that they have to let it out and act like that. That is your signal from God they need help and can't take it anymore. Open your heart and realize happy people do not behave like damn idiots. These people can't hold that emotion in forever. It is sad when it comes out and they can't tell someone. Instead, they blow the lid off their steaming pot. We sit back and judge them for that and not who they really are or why it really happened.

    As a child I learned in a very difficult way about how others judge and as an adult they are still saying the same thing never even knowing me as a person at all. Yes, I am still in the same body but all these years later I am not the same person. I was sexually molested by a pervert, in return the entire town pointed the finger AT ME. People calling me the most knife cutting names at 11 years old, words like slut, dirty and whore. What did I do? When I needed help and support they condemned me instead for something that was not my fault. With that seed planted you begin to become that person because they will not look at you any other way. It was hell on earth which caused me to turn to drugs and alcohol to drown it all out. All I really needed was love and someone to listen.

    The worst thing you can do to yourself is judge yourself though the eyes of others. To this day I am still facing this fear of what others think. I was afraid to face the fear of everyone else's opinion of me writing this book, being psychic, being a card reader, communicating with the dead, being a healer, talking to Angels, seeing Angels, praying, who I am now and who I will become in the future. I had fear of rejection and a fear of others thinking I was crazy. I had fear that nobody would believe me. Writing this book is facing my fear and saying to everyone this is who I am. Your opinions mean nothing to me, I love me and I realize you have ONE advantage over me. You can kiss my ass and I can't. Enjoy it.

Be careful of who you judge. You don't know the path God has chosen for them and who they will become one day. If you start to talk bad about another, before you OPEN your mouth, THINK! Would you want another to talk about YOU like that? What right do you have to say anything? What is INSIDE YOU that makes you want to take another person down by verbally ripping them apart? YOU'RE the one that is sick. Those that judge and gossip have the darkest secrets in their own closets, so if you hear another gossiping about someone, you know they are hiding something FOR SURE.

So ask them "What the hell is wrong with YOU?" People who love themselves don't talk bad about others. Relax...90% of haters are begging for love. 10% just want a little attention. The one that angers you, controls you. Don't give anyone that power, especially the one who does it intentionally. ONLY GOD CAN JUDGE ME! Don't judge me until you know me, don't underestimate me until you challenge me and don't talk about me until you've talked to me.

~Teddy

As she stood in front of her 5th grade class on the very first day of school, she told the children an untruth. Like most teachers, she looked at her students and said that she loved them all the same. However, that was impossible, because there in the front row, slumped in his seat, was a little boy named Teddy Stoddard. Mrs. Thompson had watched Teddy the year before and noticed that he did not play well with the other children, that his clothes were messy and that he constantly needed a bath. In addition, Teddy could be unpleasant. It got to the point where Mrs. Thompson would actually take delight in marking his papers with a broad red pen, making bold X's and then putting a big "F" at the top of his papers. At the school where Mrs. Thompson taught, she was required to review each child's past records and she put Teddy's off until last. However, when she reviewed his file, she was in for a surprise.

Teddy's first grade teacher wrote, "Teddy is a bright child with a ready laugh. He does his work neatly and has good manners... he is a joy to be around.." His second grade teacher wrote, "Teddy is an excellent student, well-liked by his classmates, but he is troubled because his mother has a terminal illness and life at home must be a struggle." His third grade teacher wrote, "His mother's death has been hard on him. He tries to do his best, but his father doesn't show much interest, and his home life will soon affect him if some steps aren't taken." Teddy's fourth grade teacher wrote, "Teddy is withdrawn and doesn't show much interest in school. He doesn't have many friends and he sometimes sleeps in class." By now, Mrs. Thompson realized the problem and she was ashamed of herself. She felt even worse when her students brought her Christmas presents, wrapped in beautiful ribbons and bright paper, except for Teddy's.

His present was clumsily wrapped in the heavy, brown paper that he got from a grocery bag. Mrs. Thompson took pains to open it in the middle of the other presents. Some of the children started to laugh when she found a rhinestone bracelet with some of the stones missing, and a bottle that was one-quarter full of perfume. But she stifled the children's laughter when she exclaimed how pretty the bracelet was, putting it on, and dabbing some of the perfume on her wrist. Teddy Stoddard stayed after school that day just long enough to say, "Mrs. Thompson, today you smelled just like my Mom used to."

After the children left, she cried for at least an hour. On that very day, she quit teaching reading, writing and arithmetic. Instead, she began to teach children. Mrs. Thompson paid particular attention to Teddy. As she worked with him, his mind seemed to come alive. The more she encouraged him, the faster he responded. By the end of the year, Teddy had become one of the smartest children in the class and, despite her lie that she would love all the children the same, Teddy became one of her "teacher's pets." A year later, she found a note under her door, from Teddy, telling her that she was the best teacher he ever had in his whole life.

Six years went by before she got another note from Teddy. He then wrote that he had finished high school, third in his class, and she was still the best teacher he ever had in life. Four years after that, she got another letter, saying that while things had been tough at times, he'd stayed in school, had stuck with it, and would soon graduate from college with the highest of honors. He assured Mrs. Thompson that she was still the best and favorite teacher he had ever had in his whole life. Then four more years passed and yet another letter came. This time he explained that after he got his bachelor's degree, he decided to go a little further. The letter explained that she was still the best and favorite teacher he ever had. But now his name was a little longer.... The letter was signed, Theodore F. Stoddard, MD.

The story does not end there. You see, there was yet another letter that spring. Teddy said he had met this girl and was going to be married. He explained that his father had died a couple of years ago and he was wondering if Mrs. Thompson might agree to sit at the wedding in the place that was usually reserved for the mother of the groom. Of course, Mrs. Thompson did. And guess what? She wore that bracelet, the one with several rhinestones missing. Moreover, she made sure she was wearing the perfume that Teddy remembered his mother wearing on their last Christmas together. They hugged each other, and Dr. Stoddard whispered in Mrs. Thompson's ear, "Thank you Mrs. Thompson for believing in me. Thank you so much for making me feel important and showing me that I could make a difference." Mrs. Thompson, with tears in her eyes, whispered back. She said, "Teddy, you have it all wrong. You were the one who taught me that I could make a difference. I didn't know how to teach until I met you."

If you see someone who is struggling to make friends or being bullied because he/she doesn't have many friends or because they are shy or not as pretty or not dressed in the most "in" clothes -- PLEASE step up. Say hi or at least smile at them in anyway. You never know what that person might be facing on the inside. Your kindness might just make a BIG difference in someone's life! Remember, never judge a book by its cover! You never know who that person can grow up to become. Damaged people are dangerous because they know they can survive. Albert Einstein struggled in school. Thomas Edison was kicked out of high school. Walt Disney got fired from a job because he supposedly lacked "good" ideas. Natalie Newman was labeled every bad thing you can imagine and they said I would become nothing. Understand?

Fear creates anger and rage inside us. When we can't face the fear we run from it. We become victims and abusers. You have every right to feel rage or anger. Although hanging on to it becomes a hell inside that we take out on everyone around us. Understand it is something inside you that says "HELLO YOU! PLEASE LOOK AT ME, YOU NEED HELP." Our subconscious says you need to deal with it. It surfaces because we are scared to face it. What you are spinning on is your attachments to THINGS and fear of healing it. It is so important to deal with it and stop carrying this weight on your shoulders. Everything that scares you is a chance to shed some light on who you are so you can better know yourself.

Anger and rage is a power. It is a power if we decide to use it correctly, we can see where it is coming from and how we project it. This fear you have generated into a tornado is yours and it is not correct to project it on anyone. It is clearly your fear you cannot fix. Nobody deserves to suffer because you cannot help yourself. It is what you hold inside. Everyone around you is there to support, guide and love you. We drag them through our hell and destroy them with what is inside us. People vomit their pain all over everyone else and can't even see they are mirroring themselves.

Abuse is the most common reaction we have when we are angry. We yell, give bad looks, call names, hit or hurt others just to get it out. It is your hell honey, NOT THEIRS. We find any addiction to something that makes us feel better and NOT have to look inside. As a woman with a lifetime of abuse, I tried to realize they had a hell inside that they couldn't get out, but I tried my best. You can't help everyone. What is most important is saving yourself first. Cut the cords and move on. Unless you learn to face your own shadows, you will continue to see them in others because the world outside you is only a reflection of the world inside you. Thousands of candles can be lit from a single candle and the life of the candle will not be shortened. Happiness never decreases by being shared.

~ Be careful what you water your dreams with. Water them with worry and fear and you will produce weeds that choke the life from your dream. Water them with optimism and solutions and you will cultivate success. Always be on the lookout for ways to turn a problem into an opportunity for success. Always be on the lookout for ways to nurture your dream." ~ Lao Tzu

Don't make a permanent decision for your temporary emotion. Take a time out for yourself to think when these negative emotions arise. What is really causing this? Take a moment and step out of it. Make a choice, even if you are not ready. Look at the situation if you are to continue to carry this fear or if you fix it. See how it feels when you walk away from it. Then see how it feels if you stay in it. Ask yourself if this will even matter a year from now? Don't get trapped to any attachments. Evil wants to survive and thrive inside you. You are allowing it an open door to come on in and take over. You can't "live" in that life.

What's really sad is if you don't wake up because your lower self says "NO, I AM NOT READY TO FACE MYSELF YET". Unfortunately, you still have to process that fear and look at it.

It will NEVER go away until you heal it. You can run but you can't hide from yourself. It is your decision how long you want to live in that hell you have created with fear. Remember a seed must fall to the ground, then completely destroy itself before it can spread its roots and grow into a beautiful tree. Not until we are lost do we begin to understand ourselves. SOMETIMES YOU JUST NEED TO ALLOW YOURSELF TO FALL APART IN ORDER TO BE ABLE TO PUT YOURSELF BACK TOGETHER AGAIN.

~ Anger cannot be overcome by anger. If someone is angry with you, and you show anger in return, the result is a disaster. On the other hand, if you control your anger and show its opposite – love, compassion, tolerance and patience – not only will you remain peaceful, but the other person's anger will also diminish. ~ Dahlai Lama

Even when you do something wrong, even when you fail, even when you make poor choices, you are loved. God is not a punisher. No doubt YOU will punish yourself enough for your mistakes. The question is: Will you try to do the right thing next time? Will you learn from your mistakes? Will you keep on loving and caring to the best of your ability? Be proud of the scars in your soul. They will help you and teach you. Tragedies do happen. We can discover the reason, blame others, imagine how different our lives would be had they not occurred. But none of that is important. They DID occur and so be it.

~ Energy flows where attention goes! ~ Michael Beckwith

From there onward we must put aside the fear that they awoke in us and begin to rebuild. There are those days when it's hard to put one foot in front of the other, but those are the days when champions are created. Every little part of you is magical. Yes, even the parts that hurt and even the ones that are feeling disease right now. It's alright to love what is feeling pain. More than alright, that's exactly where your love is needed the most. So why not touch that part that hurts and smile at it. Smile at yourself through it, and whisper: "I love you."

Accept your past without regret, handle your present with confidence, and face your future without fear. Your heart can break, your soul can ache, your confidence can shake, your smile can be fake, but your life is never a mistake. Before a new chapter has begun, the old one has to be finished. Tell yourself that what has passed will never come back. Remember that there was a time when you COULD live without that thing or that person. Nothing is irreplaceable; a habit is not a need. Look in the mirror and say, "I do have negative behaviors and thoughts, I am still finding my own path, and it's okay. I am going to do the best I can to be positive and rise above them."

Before you diagnose yourself with depression or low self-esteem, first make sure that you are not, in fact, just surrounded by assholes. Most people would learn from their mistakes if they weren't so busy denying them. If you're not getting paid to hate or be miserable, stop working for free. To be a star, you must shine your own light, follow your own path, and don't worry about the darkness, for that is when the stars shine the brightest. The only restriction is the limitation in your beliefs that prevents you from breaking free from self-made imprisonment. He who angers you, controls you. Your imagination is the place where your future experiences are constructed. Your energy of love is so powerful that it can heal anything, including your future. The human spirit is stronger than anything that can happen to it. Don't let a bad day make you feel like you got a bad life.

~Define success and prosperity on your own terms. Begin to build your own life based on love, compassion and respect, both for yourself and for others.

~Nurture your spiritual foundation and build a peaceful center within, a center which will withstand the setbacks and obstacles which are a natural part of life and growth, making you stronger as you meet each challenge.

~Find out what is truly important to you, what feeds your deepest core, what builds you up inside, and follow this, do

this, no matter what anyone else says, no matter what society directs.

~You are fully responsible for your life and you can make it beautiful and fulfilling, your interior world a safe harbor you turn to and your outer world a loving gift. ~Quado

~To notice the mistakes, to criticize, humiliate and talk about others is often easier to do than to acknowledge our own mistakes. ~Luke 6:42 Bible

Furthermore, I also want to address another side of fear. Your intuition that tells you something is not right. When you feel the hair stand up or your body change to fear instantly, YOU BETTER LISTEN. That is God and your inner self warning you to protect yourself now. You are given these signs as a big alarm to help yourself immediately. This type of fear is a warning. Never discredit it and let it go to your head. When you feel the feeling of fear that is enough. When you start to think about it, then you justify it. You change it and make it something else. Then walk right into hell. If your mind says take the scenic route, then do it. You could be avoiding a car accident.

Never forget you have complete control to change the outcome. You never have to be nice if you feel fear. Humans are the stupidest creatures on Earth. Animals instantly run when they sense danger. People think about it and walk straight into it.

Reclaim your life and stop being a victim. You are smarter than you ever dreamed. You have the ability to stop many bad things from happening to you before they happen. If you do not listen it is really your own fault. When in doubt, ignore your thoughts and pay attention to your body. Your body never lies. Do not let the thoughts take you one step farther. If it doesn't feel right- LISTEN.

~There are two basic motivating forces: fear and love. When we are afraid, we pull back from life. When we are in love, we open to all that life has to offer with passion, excitement, and acceptance. We need to learn to love ourselves first, in all our glory and our imperfections. If we cannot love ourselves, we cannot fully open to our ability to love others or our potential to create. Evolution and all hopes for a better world rest in the fearlessness and open-hearted vision of people who embrace life~ John Lennon

~Be consciously aware of your thoughts and emotions and how they are translated into energy. Then take your energy out of your mind and center it in your heart and your solar plexus. Find there the light that is burning, the storehouse of energy that you are generating. Then open and allow yourself to glow.

~From your center, glow with peace and a deep understanding of your personal truth. This is who you are and you can learn to project it out energetically. And from your heart, glow with love. Take your truth and move it through love, compassion and tolerance before presenting your truth to the world.

~Consciously cease reflecting energy from others and instead move to your own storehouse of self-generated energy. You will find that the supply is endless. And the more energy you project from these centers, the more powerful and energetic you will feel. The more you glow from within, the less exhausted you will be from trying to fend off other energies you do not care for. Make your glow so strong, that you are never concerned with what others project. You are glowing with self and truth, love and peace, and it is enough. ~Quad

~People tend to think that happiness is a stroke of luck, something that will descend like fine weather if you're fortunate. But happiness is the result of personal effort. You fight for it, strive for it, insist upon it, and sometimes even travel around the world looking for it. You have to participate relentlessly." ~ Elizabeth Gilbert

~ At the center of all human beings is the place of good. That includes myself. At my very core is good. I can find this place by staying free of resentments, fear, dishonesty and self-seeking motives. ~Native American elder

~ Anytime you feel negative emotion, stop and say: Something is important here, otherwise, I would not be feeling this negative emotion. What is it that I want? And then simply turn your attention to what you do want. In the moment you turn your attention to what you want, the negative attraction will stop; and in the moment the negative attraction stops, the positive attraction will begin. And—in that moment—your feeling will change from not feeling good to feeling good.

~Don't play with woulda, coulda, shoulda, cause they won't ever play fair. Don't stress the could haves, if it should have, it would have. ~ Natalie Newman

~Wisdom is nothing more than healed pain.

~When you have done something wrong, admit it and be sorry. Nobody in history has ever choked to death from swallowing his pride.

~Discomfort is the call to set yourself free. ~ Bryon Katie

Chapter 6
The Soul Never Ends

When we come into this life we have a blueprint of our path we will walk on this earth. Our spirit came to learn certain lessons and teach certain things. The day we are born and the day that we die, also has a timeline. Yet, our biggest fear is death. Death is nothing to be feared. It is a natural process of life. You were born to die. We need to stop fearing death while we are alive. First step is just accepting it. While we are alive we say goodbye to 1000's of things along the way. Letting go and death are some of our biggest, most painful problems we face in life.

Every day of your life something leaves you to make room for something new. If we focus so much on what we lost we never can receive or see the new blessing that has been put in its place. We walk around this life blinded by fear, stress, depression and worry. We look straight ahead thinking about what we lost or are afraid of losing. Open your eyes and look all the way around you. There is so much more out there. When we hold pain inside of us we don't see all the blessings God has put in our path meant for us to see. We miss it because we are blind with negativity.

Look around everywhere. Life is there for you to experience but so is death. Death should be looked at as an achievement. They came to earth to perform certain things and have accomplished their mission. Who are you to say they needed to stay longer for you? They touched lives while they were alive and even through their death they continue to teach us. Their message stays with us forever.

When we die our spirit immediately leaves our bodies.

Many have claimed they have had an out of body experience and seeing the light on the other side. Yet, nobody listens to these stories about the beautiful place they went in this transformation. They survived this to reassure us that life after death is truly heaven and nothing to be feared. We instead just hold the fear of the "unknown".

When we die our spirits travel this earth for four days and four nights. We visit everyone, say good-bye, finish what we came to do in this life and complete our spiritual mission on earth. I always tell people when a loved one dies that within four days they will come to you and say goodbye. Most of us are so caught up in our inability to let go and so filled with depression that we don't even feel them come to us. They watch you sit and cry and cry and cry and ask WHY? Seriously, you shouldn't be crying. They succeeded in their life and they are in a very beautiful place. They are the lucky ones. We on earth have to keep fighting and it is not always a picnic down here. Anyhow, during the 4 days they are still here. When you feel them, please understand you are not crazy, what you feel is real. Talk to them and say all the things you didn't get to say. Finish with saying goodbye to them. Feel the peace and closure in your heart. Let them go fly with the angels.

One of the reasons the spirit gets "trapped" here and becomes a 'ghost' is because the guilt they feel for how much they hurt their loved ones for dying. They want to stay and take care of you. Then they miss the door home when it opens. Stuck here because you couldn't let go, when you should be celebrating their life and the blessed time you got to have them with you. Your sadness and inability to let go traps them here. Let go people! Let them go HOME! Let them return and be your guide in life on earth. You can still talk to them when they are gone. Just close your eyes, breathe deeply, open your ears and mind. Shakespeare said, "Feel the pain until it hurts no more." Allow yourself to feel it but learn to let it go and release it for healing.

Other reasons we choose not to follow the path HOME is

because we have lost our faith. When we lose our faith we just ignore the light because we do not believe in it.

Addictions to alcohol, pharmaceuticals, heroin, and meth are deaths of empty souls. They do not leave either, unless they found God before they died. Usually their soul is gone to the addiction and evil taking them over. Suicidals rarely ascend because of course they totally lost faith, unless their soul came to teach people a lesson. Another reason souls stay is because they are greedy and cannot leave their possessions. This is much more common with people of wealth. As humans they worked so hard for everything and are obsessed with it. The soul wants to protect it and watch over it. Leaving them trapped here. However, after you die they sell it off or divide it up. You lose it anyway and stay for nothing. This obsession is stronger than the will to go HOME. It's so sad when materialistic things are more important than going home to be with God. Another reason also, is they want the truth of something to come out.

Unfortunately, there are all different reasons why some souls become 'ghosts'. Now you can see the main reason we don't follow the path HOME is because we can't let go. Think about that in your present life now and let go of what is no longer worth holding on to. Free yourself from hanging on to everything so tightly. At some point everything will leave us or we will leave it. It's a natural process of life. If you happen to come upon a 'trapped soul', do not be scared. But if you are in the presence of difficult ghosts, call someone who is a paranormal expert that can help you. Most of the time when you have a ghost around, you do not need to fear it. They trust in you to guide them. Ask them why they are still here. Ask them how you can help them get HOME.

When my dad died there was so much I wanted to tell him and I wished I could have spent more time with him. Time can't come back or change. I wanted to thank him for being my father and loving me. When I was at his funeral, the one thing I learned was he had NEVER told anyone I was not his child. Everyone thought I was his real daughter. It was the most loving thought I have had in my life to know his love for me. We are always so good at not appreciating people until they are dead throughout most of our lives. Say what you feel, because you never know when they are going to leave you. Live with no regrets, show your love and appreciation always.

Six months after his death I finally was able to face it again. I had such a strong desire to tell him thank you for loving me, standing beside me, and about all the beautiful things he brought to my life. So I decided to try meditation and this was something I had never done before. I did a guided meditation to meet a dead loved one. I opened my mind and just let all my thoughts go. My Dad came and sat with me on a big log at the beach of a lake I live by. I told him everything I wanted to say. He told me many things about us, then me, also my sisters and my brothers. When I told my sister what happened and the part about her, she said "You did talk to him. Only he and I know about that, no one else." It was complete confirmation of what I'd seen and heard was real.

So if you have regrets, questions, or miss them, just call upon them. But do not selfishly hang on when they die. God and that person had a contract. You may not think it is fair. But it was the choice between their soul and God. Celebrate their life! My Dad gave me the tools to survive. He taught me to always smile, love everyone, help everyone, never say a bad word about anyone, give everyone the biggest hugs, and dance with everyone you can. What beautiful gifts he gave me to survive my life.

Our lives are so much more than we can ever imagine. We are not just a person. We are a soul. We look at each person as who they are. We never stop and try to understand that they are a soul with a purpose. Stop judging others because of their behaviors and personalities. We are all here for a purpose and most of the time we don't even know it. So please do not judge another. Disconnect yourself from the personality or ego of that body and realize there is a "soul" in there with lessons for us.

Nobody's lessons are the same either. It is so much deeper than we can ever comprehend. Furthermore, it is one of the most important things we must remember when another person dies. They physically left this earth, yes. When we can't see or touch them, we believe they have left us forever. When in fact, they left teachings and messages all throughout their lives. They are a soul that can help guide you forever. A person is never truly dead until the last person on earth stops thinking about them.

~Don't grieve! Anything you lose comes round in another form. ~Rumi

The most difficult loss to get over is the death of a child. The first things that come to every mind is why?, not fair, and too young. It is the hardest grieving process when a mother and father lose their child. Everyone looks at it as a complete tragedy. It suffocates the parents' lives and it can divide them because their pain comes out on each other. Honestly, that is the only person who understands how they feel. Everyone around them suffers in this horrible pain and it destroys everything when they allow it to get out of control. You must remember it is a soul with a purpose whether their life is only for a few minutes, 18 years or 100 years old.

I am going to take this time to explain one of those stories about how a small body, but big soul, had a HUGE message. It is my dream that millions will read this and hear her story.

My 11 month old niece died because she went to the doctor for an earache. The doctor treated her with an adult dosage of medication. It killed this beautiful, loving child to go to the doctor. It was a tragedy! I witnessed the pain it brought to everyone around me. However, after the pain cleared from my heart, I could see how her short little life carried a big huge message. Maybe more than my family will ever see. Now I will share it with you because I loved her and I care about you.

Doctors are human and all humans make mistakes. By now we all know that is a part of life. Doctor error creates higher deaths than you can ever imagine. About 300,000 a year at least are killed by doctor error. We need MADD. Mothers Against Damn Doctors. Drunk driving only kills less than 5,000 a year. Now after her death I am so careful. I thoroughly check out anything that is given to my children. I look up the amount that should be taken and what is the drug. I look it up if I have not heard about it before. I took control of what the doctor puts into my child's body. We just take the doctor's word for it and take it. We never question it. People just trust their entire lives with a doctor. We never research the history of the drug, the amount that should be given or what the effect it could have on us or our beautiful children. We just give it or take it.

Please keep this in mind. You never know you could save a life and it only takes a minute to educate yourself on what is going into your child's body and yours. Another thing I always research is a natural healing first. I believe God gave us all the things we need in nature to heal ourselves and survive on this planet. Some things are too big and do need a doctor's care, but don't hesitate to look up an alternative natural way. So many healing plants are right in your grocery store and they work. Educate yourself. I will teach you this in my book "Naturally Natalie".

Now you can see her message. Her beautiful soul came to teach this lesson. That is a HUGE lesson to teach people!!! We cannot keep ourselves connected to the physical body. We need to understand it was God's wish for her to perform this teaching. When we dry the tears we can begin to see how very, very powerful their life was. It may be a tiny body or very young adult, but they have a message. Look now at how many lives she will touch with her short visit on earth. Parents who have lost a child please remember one thing for me. Those souls chose you because you were qualified. You should feel honored to have such an enormously powerful soul who choose you to be their parent. Let go and the message or messages will come of what their soul came to teach. We cannot see the blessing that soul came to give us if we cannot end our pain to receive them.

We also need to look at the pain from losing a child. What I am going to say could also be used in the death of anyone we hang on to and the effects it has on others. As for now I will be talking about losing a child. When we lose a child we inflict this pain on everyone and most of all, on our other children. Every birthday, holiday, or big event in life, we always wish they were with us. This is bringing much unneeded sadness over the entire moment. It forces the other kids to regret being the one that lived.

Especially, when a twin or a multiple dies do you see this happening the most. The living twin/multiple has to survive under the constant reminder of the one that is no longer with us. We are filled with deep, blinding pain because they were not there for the 1st day of school, birthdays, prom, graduation, marriage and having their 1st baby. We constantly surround every life event with sadness because they should be here at this moment also.

It is a horrible pain and burden we place on the other child/children. We punish them with our inability to let go and make every event a negative energy for them. The other child/children become filled with guilt and shame because these life events cause so much pain to the people they love. We punish them for being alive without being aware of it. The life that was taken from you is a soul. Be grateful for what you do have. Love it with all the love you would have given the child you lost. You know that your baby's soul is flying with the angels. Your ego told you that you'd be safer if you remembered your past pain. Yet the truth is, that any suffering held in your awareness, magnetically attracts more of the same.

When my niece died twelve years ago she also left me with another very intense lesson. Two days after her death I was laying in my bed with my 15 month old daughter. She ran out of my bedroom into the living room where all of her toys were. Suddenly, I could hear her laughing. It sounded like she was playing with someone. My daughter was giggling and talking.

However, nobody was in our house except the two of us. A very strong voice came into my head and said "It is your niece and she has come to say goodbye." So I froze! I thought maybe I had gone a little crazy. Yet, I could hear my daughter having fun and playing with her. I decided to just leave them alone and let it happen. After about 20 minutes of her soul being with us, my daughter came back to my room. She had a gigantic smile and pure happiness in her heart. She kept repeating my niece's name over and over. I knew it had really happened. Our souls do fly when we die and come back us to say goodbye. Everything about death changed inside me at that moment. Only the physical self goes.

Now when someone I love dies I do my best to remain open to them coming to me. When I feel their presence. I tell them everything I needed to. I say my goodbyes and appreciation to them. Then I tell them how to get HOME. I am going to tell you also. Please never forget this. Hopefully you can drop all your fears about dying and where you go.

After we have traveled for 4 days and nights finishing our mission on earth, a light will appear in the south. Do NOT worry! You will not miss this if you are aware. You as a soul have the freewill to follow that light that is a trap to soul recycling, follow the path HOME, stay trapped in between because of a fear of leaving or no faith. Follow that PATH and walk through the beautiful doorway HOME. Once I have said that to them, I tell them to go HOME. I tell them they will do us no good here trying to help us. We will get through it. They need to go HOME so they can be our guiding angel. Go fly with the angels beautiful soul, fly!

~Death of those we love comes to us as a tragedy. The real tragedy is what dies inside of us while we are still alive because we are blinded by pain and fear. ~ Natalie Newman

We also need to start praying the correct way for people who ARE dying. When a tragedy happens or a disease infests our loved ones, the first thing we do is ask everyone to pray for them to heal. We send this prayer out in masses. First of all, we need to remember that everyone has a time to go. We keep them on life support, drugged up or full of chemo long after it is humanly correct because we cannot let them go. Seriously, would you want to live like that? You can heal them of their cancer but they still have a date. They will get hit by a bus or something else. You cannot change the time.

We need to pray for them and their families. Ask for God to bring comfort and peace to the situation. Surround the situation with love. Then let God take control. Never pray for an outcome. You are placing expectations on the situation. You could be asking for something that is not in their Divine Plan with God. Just ask God to help them through, fill them with comfort and do what is best for their soul's path. If they are supposed to survive the tragedy they will.

I have had the angels poking me to tell you also, that it is best to pray to God and the angels. Most souls are coming to earth at this moment to be a part of this amazing time in human history and the evolution of this planet. I can tell you one thing, I have many dead souls nudging me to talk to their loved ones to change something so they can come back to earth. That is why our population is growing so fast. Everyone wants to be here now. If you ask for them, you may feel them come to you. But, I do not want to give anyone false hope that they are talking to a soul that has already come back again. So know they are not ignoring you up there, many are already back here in another body.

In October my Irish friend's soul came to me and told me he was coming back as human. He prepared me for it and told me when. I spent the day with him, he gave me many messages, and I felt him leave me for the last time. I know exactly what day and time he was born. I also know where. He told me that one day we will see each other and I will call out his name when I meet the person who is him in human form again. I will recognize his soul immediately.

Death is not the end my friend. The blessing is eternal and their message will be with you forever. So please, live while you are here, love everyone as much as you can and forgive others. Learn to let go of them with love and faith. You have no idea when loved ones will be taken from you, so enjoy your time with them. Do not fear death, embrace it as you embrace birth. It is a beautiful process of your life on Mother Earth. It by no means is the end. Just another chapter in our journey as a soul. Everyone on earth is here to do something to teach a lesson or project a message. Everyone is here to do something big, even if it is after they die we receive it.

You could be a mother, a teacher, an animal rescuer, volunteer, counselor, a friend or anything else that involves helping another or someone. It does not have to be something extremely big, but everything we do has a big meaning to it. Everyone is here to touch the lives of others in some way. Stop and ask your soul what your job is here on earth. You will hear the message. I heard my message at 15 years old that I was going to help as many people as I possibly could heal from their pain because I understood it. I lived through it. I never allow anything to get in the way of what my soul came to do. I have a job and I will succeed in accomplishing it by writing this book to help others survive. Then I will continue on with whatever steps God guides me to next.

It is all more than you can see when you look at a physical body. Find your purpose and when you do, your heart will know it. Do not regret never knowing what your soul came to do. Find your path and do it well. Be of service. Whether you make yourself available to a friend or co-worker, or you make time every month to do volunteer work, there is nothing that harvests more of a feeling of empowerment than being of service to someone in need.

~Love the people God gave you because he will need them back someday.

~ Each morning when I open my eyes I say to myself: I, not events, have the power to make me happy or unhappy today. I can choose which it shall be. Yesterday is dead, tomorrow hasn't arrived yet. I have just one day, today, and I'm going to be happy in it." ~ Julius Henry "Groucho" Marx

~Life's journey is not to arrive at the grave safely in a well preserved body. But rather to skid in sideways, totally worn out shouting, "Holy shit... What a ride."

~Honor those that have walked before you, for it is the path you will learn from.

~HEAVEN- Don't miss it for the world.

~Life always hands you a second chance. It is called tomorrow. Be grateful for it!

~ I am grateful for the nights that turned into mornings, friends that turned into family, dreams that turned into reality, likes that turned into loves, and everyone who crossed my path along the way, no matter how long they stay. ~ Natalie Newman

~Whatever life may bring you, just thank God for the opportunity to be alive. ~Natalie Newman

Chapter 7
Children: My Promise From God I Will have a Friend Forever!!!

Do I work??? Why yes, I am a Mom! That makes me an alarm clock, cook, maid, a doctor, fashion adviser, waitress, teacher, nanny, nurse, handyman, security officer, photographer, counselor, chauffeur, a lifelong student, an event planner, a personal assistant, an ATM, healer and comforter. I don't get holidays, sick pay or days off. I work through the DAY & NIGHT. I am on call every hour for the rest of my life. I'll always need my children no matter what age I am. My children have made me laugh, made me cry, stressed me out, wiped my tears, hugged me tight, seen me fall, cheered me on, kept me strong, and drove me a little CRAZY at times!

As a mother of 3 very beautiful and busy children, I have worked hard to be the opposite of my parents. When I gave birth to each one of them I made a lifetime commitment to be their mother forever. I vowed to guide them, love them, protect them and nurture their spirit. I know it is not my job as a parent to make sure they are perfect in school or great in sports. It is my job as parent to teach them how to survive when they go out on their own. We learn everything from our parents and the surroundings we grow up in.

When we come here, we choose our parents because of the lessons they will teach us. As a mother I need to show them and teach them how to be in relationships. They are a mirror to us. When their behavior is bad you really can't keep pointing the finger at your child because three are pointing back at you. Something in their path has caused this behavior and happy children do not act badly. We also don't want to face when our children are in trouble. We cover their mistakes. We enable their behavior over and over just so we don't have to admit our own failures.

~If you see someone who is struggling to make friends or being bullied because he/she doesn't have many friends or because they are shy or not as pretty or not dressed in the most "in" clothes -- PLEASE step up. Say hi or at least smile at them in the hallway. You never know what that person might be facing outside of school. Your kindness might just make a BIG difference in someone's life! PS Remember, never judge a book by its cover!

Children learn how to be in relationships based on their parent's behavior. If you have good, healthy relationships with your family, lovers, friends and yourself; it is most likely your children will also. If you have a loving and healthy sexual relationship with your partner, your child will also have the same. Take a long hard look at your child's behavior. You can only blame yourself and the environment you have created for them. They were born innocent and you cannot blame anyone but yourself for the way they behave. If you want to show them verbal abuse, mental abuse, emotional abuse, physical abuse, sexual abuse, controlling, yelling, fighting, backstabbing, gossiping, lying, and cheating that is probably what they will behave like in relationships also. They are not taught anything different. Only what YOU show them. Your children's behavior is a mirrored reflection of your parenting and how they are treated. STOP BLAMING THE CHILDREN!

We all want better lives for our children than we had ourselves. But the only way that will happen is if you make YOURSELF better. It is what you show them. You really need to pay close attention to how you act around your children with how you treat others and yourself. I think you will see you need to change some things.

After spending my entire life in abusive relationships, I chose to not expose my children to the life I had been living anymore. I promised them they would never have to live in a home of yelling and violence. They would only have a home of peace, love and happiness. I told them until there was a man that could treat me like I deserve, I would be living alone. At this time, it is going to be 6 years living alone without a man in my home. Another thing my children don't see is men in and out of my bedroom. I keep my relationships at a distance, even when they lived in the same country.

My children feel sad for me at times. They tell me I should have someone here helping me and loving me. I reassure them it is okay because we have peace. They are the most important to me. I wish them the easiest life possible. I cannot control what they are exposed to by their fathers. They chose him for lessons also. But I can show them a different way in my home. Eventually, they see through to the truth all on their own. I do not want my daughters to follow in my footsteps thinking life should be about taking abuse or my son thinking it is right to abuse others. I want my children to have healthy, loving and intimate relationships. I have to find that on my own so they will learn what a beautiful relationship is all about.

~A truly rich man is one whose children run into his arms when his hands are empty

I admit I am not the greatest parent on earth. I do not have any money. But, I have one thing that is most important to them and that is unconditional love. Honestly, children don't care about money. They just want your love. Unless, of course, you have trained them to be materialistic like you and hand them money, instead of love. They definitely weren't born that way. Love is free.

I allow my children to be themselves. I love them each individually for who they are and guide them the best I can through their challenges. I also know my children's life lessons are not the same as mine. I must do my best for them to learn sooner than later. When problems arise with my children I try my best to handle it with peace and logic. I hear all sides to the story with an open mind. I do not point fingers unless I am sure they did it. I normally walk away from the issue so I have time to calm down and think about it rationally.

Literally, I close my eyes and count to 10. If I need 10 minutes, 10 hours or a few days, I will take it for myself until I know I am ready to handle the situation with an open mind and integrity.

~ *A child can teach an adult three things: to be happy for no reason, to always be busy with something, and to know how to demand with all his might that which he desires.*

A soft answer turns away wrath. When everyone around you seems to be in bad spirits, bickering and complaining, take a step back. It's so easy to answer the same way back. Instead, feel into your heart and answer gently. Let peace radiate from you and create peace within the situation. I put myself back to my child's age and remember what I was like. I remember what I was thinking and feeling at that time. When I feel I am ready to deal with my child's mistake I question them. I say, "Why don't you respect yourself?", "How would you feel if someone did that to you?" or "Do you think what you did was right and why?" I ask them to look at how they are hurting others, hurting themselves and how they would feel if the tables were turned on them. I make them look inside at the impact of their actions. I allow them to have a voice and an explanation. To me, that is the real punishment, having to see how stupid they behaved.

They do not learn anything from "grounding" or "time out". I want them to understand and think about what they have done to themselves and others. I do not feed useless ideas, condemnation, fear, and anger into them. That is a child who is just learning and growing. Two wrongs do not make a right. What's important is showing them and allowing them to think deeply about what they have done so they hopefully do not repeat the same mistake. Being too lenient with a child may cause them more harm than good in the long run. By being firm but fair in your dealings, you will gain not only their love but their respect as well. My child trusted me as a soul to be their mother. I am so honored. But, I must never forget their soul is here to learn also. My job is to lead as example and guide them the best I can.

~*There is no trust more sacred than the one the world*

holds with children. There is no duty more important than ensuring that their rights are respected, that their welfare is protected, that their lives are free from fear and want and that they grow up in peace. ~ Kofi Annan

My children are lucky enough to have a beautiful home in the woods. I have not had television for over three years. I do not have time or patience to watch it. If you ask my children, they will tell you they don't want it. When they are in the house they are fighting, wild and negative. Then I force them out the door into nature, they laugh and love each other. I make them to go outdoors, use their imaginations and be creative. I teach them to appreciate every living thing in nature and be grateful for it.

Too many parents are using the television as a babysitter. Do not get me wrong, I will put a movie in when it is needed for myself to calm them down or when things are really busy. Our television is full of subliminal crap we stuff down our children's throats. It just repeats fear, terror, eat terrible, sue somebody and take a pill for everything. The less they see, the healthier their minds will be as they grow. Same goes with their time on the internet. Pay attention and monitor it. There is a lot of evil out there ready to corrupt them. How will you feel if you child gets hurt because you were too busy with YOUR life to pay attention to theirs?

Furthermore, I never speak badly about their fathers. No matter what bad or stupid things they have done, it is not worth filling my children's heads with more negative. Yes, their father says the most horrible things about me all of the time. Even after 5 years, terrible lies are told to my children about me. You think a person could move on after all of that time. My children see and tell me "Dad was lying about you again." What's sad is, he does not get it. His children think he is a liar. What he drags my children through because of his choices, inner issues, and behaviors are heartbreaking. Yet, I never talk bad about him to the children. I try to say positive things or explain he has a problem he needs to fix.

I also refuse to play the pissed off, revengeful parent game. I watch so many parents play a tug of war with their children. Using their children as weapons in a relationship break-up. These people should really think long and hard about why they are dragging their children through hell.

First of all, what did that child do? I grew up without my father because of my mother's choices to keep him away from me. I know how it feels. She felt it was the best choice for me. Yet, it was so damaging and painful because I thought he did not want to be a part of my life. It was a very big, empty hole of rejection left in my soul. I truly wish I could have made that decision myself instead of my mother making it for me. I will never do that to my children, ever. By separating from the other parent you already made a choice to change their world forever because you cannot make your relationship work. You tear their life in two, stripping them of their security, family and their home. Then you want to threaten the other parent with the child/children.

Many parents refuse the other parent to see their child/children. In my eyes it is just a selfish way to behave. Your revengeful game is played by using your children. It is a horrible form of abuse to that child. Are you proud? Then we question why the children are such a mess. They are learning from their parents how to behave.

Some think it is best for the child to keep them away from the other parent and to play these games because we are only thinking of ourselves. Who are you to decide? Let the child decide that. Because you hate the other, does not mean the child does. You feel pain and claim you love the child/children. Then pour out your anger and hurt onto them because of your feelings towards another.

One of the reasons children go into such deep depression and addiction during a divorce is because of how you emotionally abuse them and use them to hurt the other. Both parents have EQUAL rights and the child should have a say in his/her life. The ex and I have 50/50 custody and at first I thought it was a terrible idea. Instead, I found it creates a balance in them. They love us both. It is about what is best for them, not your ego or inability to get over it.

Respectfully so, I do know that there are some parents out there that do not deserve to see their children. I am speaking about child abusers and molesters. They SHOULD be kept from their children until they have had extensive help and prove they have changed completely.

Drug addicts and alcoholics have a deep, deep pain they are covering up. They need help to release the pain inside them and once they do this the addiction will also leave them eventually. They will not need the addiction to hide the pain anymore. Do your best to help them. You loved that person long enough to have a child with them. You choose that person to be the father/mother of your child. YOU made that choice, nobody else. Why can't you like them enough to provide a better life for your child? Only allow supervised visits if they are too bad. Remember we need people who behave badly in your life to teach you how NOT to behave.

Do not take the child away from them. That will only darken their hearts causing them to go deeper into their addiction. We all want what is best for our children. BOTH parents living healthy lives is the best thing possible for them. It is about raising the most incredible children we can. Sometimes we have to swallow our pride to do what is best for our beautiful baby. They are only with you a very short time of their life. Then they are out the door on their own and you do not get a second chance at doing it right. Remember, they learn from your behaviors. They learn how to be a parent from you. You are the most influential parenting teacher they have. What are you teaching them?

Violence Statistics with Children:

Each year 3.3 million children witness domestic violence.

Estimates show 3-5 children in every classroom have witnessed a woman being abused.

Average child witnesses 200,000 acts of violence and 16,000 murders on T.V. by age 18.

Child abuse is the leading #1 cause of death in children under

1 year old.

~"Mommy, I colored your sheets with lipstick!" In anger she started to hit her child until he was unconscious. Then, she regretted what she had done, and crying said to her child, "Please open your eyes!" But it was too late, his tiny heart had stopped beating. When she walked into her bedroom, the sheet said "I LOVE YOU MOMMY."

Play with your children. Build a fort, paint, color, climb trees, hike, swing, laugh or whatever they want to do. Not only is this a fabulous way to bond with them, but also an amazing way for you to relieve stress and heal yourself. Your inner child needs attention too. Who said you had to grow up? I climb trees and build snow forts when my children are not home. It sets me free inside. Nurture your soul and play with your children. You have fifteen minutes a day in your very busy schedule, shut the television off. Watch the amazing changes in your relationship with them and your own life. Children are the greatest excuse to keep playing. So stop being such a grown up. Who really wants to grow old anyways? Keep your spirit young and have fun.

~*It's not only children who grow. Parents do too. As much as we watch to see what our children do with their lives, they are watching us to see what we do with ours. I can't tell my children to reach for the sun. All I can do is reach for it, myself.* ~ Joyce Maynard

Our children are the future of this planet. They are the ones who will inherit our mistakes in every way. The saddest thing I see is humans not educating themselves on their children. A new world of children is being born. We are labeling them with disorders and bad behaviors. Then we drug them up, stopping their souls from doing what they came here to do. We are labeling them with issues when they are just being being children.

However, it is actually the TYPE of children that are coming to earth that makes them so powerful. They are here to perform a mission. You may want to look at your child and do some research. If you are a parent to one of these children, then they have chosen you and you are fully qualified to raise them well. Do not worry. Just try to understand them rather than label them. Start looking at your child as a beautiful child of God. Embrace and love them through their setbacks. They are a precious gift. How are you treating this gift? What did they do to deserve what we are giving them? We need to solve this on a personal and global level. It is time to make the future of our children as wonderful as possible.

~**Please protect our children. They are our beautiful blessings from God. They are precious gifts we were given when they were born. Through us they experience everything. They are innocent and always suffer the most. Never judge them, you do not know what God sent them here to do. Be very careful it could be an angel you are destroying because of your choices.**
~ **Natalie Newman**

Please educate yourself before you label and medicate your child because of their behaviors. I have been surrounded by these different types of children. I have studied them and worked with them. It is time to take a long hard look at the children of our future. They are blessings of God and should be treated like angels. We need to stop destroying what they are here to do because we cannot figure out how to control them.

This insert is taken from -namastecafe.com- but there are many more websites and books you can find on this subject. Please do not just take my word for it, do your own research.

How do you know if you, or someone you know, is an Indigo or Crystal Child or Adult?

We will describe the main features and characteristics of these people. But we want to stress that the Indigo/Crystal phenomenon is the next step in our evolution as a human species. We are all, in some way, becoming more like the Indigo and Crystal people. They are here to show us the way, and so the information can be applied more generally to all of us as we make the transition to the next stage of our growth and evolution.

The Indigo Children have been incarnating on the Earth for the last 100 years. The early Indigos were pioneers and way showers. After World War II, a significant number were born, and these are the Indigo adults of today. However, in the 1970s a major wave of Indigos was born, and so we have a whole generation of Indigos who are now in their late twenties and early thirties who are about to take their place as leaders in the world. Indigos continued to be born up to about year 2000, with increasing abilities and degrees of technological and creative sophistication.

The Crystal Children began to appear on the planet from about 2000, although some date them slightly earlier. These are extremely powerful children, whose main purpose is to take us to the next level in our evolution, and reveal to us our inner power and divinity. They function as a group consciousness rather than as individuals, and they live by the" Law of One" or Unity Consciousness. They are a powerful force for love and peace on the planet.

The Indigo and Crystal Adults are composed of two groups. Firstly, there are those who were born as Indigos and are now making the transition to Crystal. This means they undergo a spiritual and physical transformation that awakens their "Christ" or "Crystal" consciousness and links them with the Crystal children as part of the evolutionary wave of change. The second group is those who were born without these qualities, but have acquired or are in the process of acquiring them through their own hard work and the diligent following of a spiritual path. Yes, this means that all of us have the potential to be part of the emerging group of "human angels".

The following extract describes the difference between Indigo and Crystal Children. It is from Doreen Virtue's article, Indigo and Crystal Children I found during research that best describes these children.

The first thing most people notice about Crystal Children is their eyes, large, penetrating, and wise beyond their years. Their eyes lock on and hypnotize you, while you realize your soul is being laid bare for the child to see. Perhaps you've noticed this special new "breed" of children rapidly populating our planet. They are happy, delightful and forgiving. This generation of new light workers, roughly ages 0 through 7, are like no previous generation. Ideal in many ways, they are the pointers for where humanity is headed ... and it's a good direction!

The older children (approximately age 7 through 25), called "indigo Children", share some characteristics with the Crystal Children. Both generations are highly sensitive and psychic, and have important life purposes. The main difference is their temperament. Indigos have a warrior spirit, because their collective purpose is to mash down old systems that no longer serve us. They are here to quash government, educational, and legal systems that lack integrity. To accomplish this end, they need tempers and fiery determination.

Those adults who resist change and who value conformity may misunderstand the Indigos. They are often mislabeled with psychiatric diagnoses of Attention Deficit with Hyperactivity Disorder (ADHD) or Attention Deficit Disorder (ADD). Sadly, when they are medicated, the Indigos often lose their beautiful sensitivity, spiritual gifts and warrior energy..........In contrast, the Crystal Children are blissful and even-tempered. Sure, they may have tantrums occasionally, but these children are largely forgiving and easy-going. The Crystals are the generation who benefit from the Indigos trailblazing. First, the Indigo Children lead with a machete, cutting down anything that lacks integrity. Then the Crystal Children follow the cleared path, into a safer and more secure world.

The terms "Indigo" and "Crystal" were given to these two generations because they most accurately describe their aura colors and energy patterns. Indigo children have a lot of indigo blue in their auras. This is the colour of the "third eye chakra", which is the energy center inside the head located between the two eyebrows. This chakra regulates clairvoyance, or the ability to see energy, visions, and spirits. Many of the Indigo children are clairvoyant

The Crystal Children have opalescent auras, with beautiful multi-colours in pastel hues. This generation also shows a fascination for crystals and rocks......

Indigo Children can sense dishonesty, like a dog can sense fear. Indigos know when they're being lied to, patronized, or manipulated. And since their collective purpose is to usher us into a new world of integrity, the Indigos inner lie-detectors are integral. As mentioned before, this warrior spirit is threatening to some adults. And the Indigos are unable to conform to dysfunctional situations at home, work, or school. They don't have the ability to dissociate from their feelings and pretend like everything's okay ...unless they are medicated or sedated.

Crystal Children's innate spiritual gifts are also misunderstood. Specifically, their telepathic abilities which lead them to talk later in life.

In the new world which the Indigos are ushering in, we will all be much more aware of our intuitive thoughts and feelings. We won't rely so much upon the spoken or written word. Communication will be faster, more direct, and more honest, because it will be mind to mind. Already, increasing numbers of us are getting in touch with our psychic abilities. Our interest in the paranormal is at an all-time high, accompanied by books, television shows, and movies on the topic.

So, it's not surprising that the generation following the Indigos are incredibly telepathic. Many of the Crystal Children have delayed speech patterns, and it's not uncommon for them to wait until they're 3 or 4 years old to begin speaking. But parents tell me they have no trouble communicating with their silent children. Far from it! The parents engage in mind-to-mind communication with their Crystal Children. And the Crystals use a combination of telepathy, self-fashioned sign language, and sounds (including song) to get their point across.

The trouble comes about when the Crystals are judged by medical and educational personnel as having "abnormal" speaking patterns. It's no coincidence that as the number of Crystals are born, that the number of diagnoses for autism is at a record high.

It's true that the Crystal Children are different from other generations. But why do we need to pathologize these differences? If the children are successfully communicating at home and the parents aren't reporting any problems... then why try to make a problem? The diagnostic criteria for autism is quite clear. It states that the autistic person lives in his or her own world, and is disconnected from other people. The autistic person doesn't talk because of an indifference to communicating with others.

Crystal Children are quite the opposite. They are among the most connected, communicative, caring and cuddly of any generation. They are also quite philosophical and spiritually gifted. And they display an unprecedented level of kindness and sensitivity to this world. Crystal Children spontaneously hug and care for people in need. An autistic person wouldn't do that!

In my book "The Care and Feeding of Indigo Children", I wrote that ADHD should stand for Attention Dialed into a Higher Dimension. This would more accurately describe that generation. In the same vein, Crystal Children don't warrant a label of autism. They aren't autistic! They're AWE-tistic!

These children are worthy of awe, not labels of dysfunction. If anyone is dysfunctional, it's the systems that aren't accommodating the continuing evolution of the human species.

If we shame the children with labels, or medicate them into submission, we will have undermined a heaven-sent gift. We will crush a civilization before its had time to take roots. Fortunately, there are many positive solutions and alternatives. And the same heaven that sent us the Crystal Children can assist those of us who are advocates for the children.

NEW CHILD LABEL- APPRX. BIRTH DATES - APPRX.AGE

Indigo Scouts	1940's – 1960's	65 – 45 years old
Indigos (1st wave)	1970's	35 -25
(2nd wave)	1980's – late 1990's	25 - 8
Crystals Late	1990's - now	8 – 0 yrs old

~Never, never be afraid to do what's right, especially if the well-being of a person or animal is at stake. Society's punishments are small compared to the wounds we inflict on our soul when we look the other way."~ Martin Luther King Jr.

~If every 8 yr old in the world is taught meditation, we will eliminate violence in one generation.

~ The withholding of a child from a loving and fit parent is child abuse. Being ignored causes the same chemical reaction in the brain as experiencing physical injury. Make time for your children.

Chapter 8
Love Comes When We Stop Searching for It

~Sometimes people come into your life and you know right away that they were meant to be there, to serve some sort of purpose, teach you a lesson, or to help you figure out who you are or who you want to become. You never know who these people may be. Perhaps a neighbor, professor, long lost friend, lover or a complete stranger. But when you lock eyes with them, you know at that very moment they will affect your life in some profound way. Sometimes things happen to you that may seem horrible, painful and unfair at first, but on reflection, you find that without overcoming these obstacles you would never have realized your full potential, strength, willpower or heart. Everything happens for a reason. Nothing happens by chance or means of good luck. Illness, injury, love, lost memories of true greatness and sheer stupidity all occur to test the limits of your soul. Without these small tests, whatever they may be, life would be a smoothly paved, straight, flat road to nowhere. It would be safe and comfortable, but dull and utterly pointless. The people you meet who affect your life, and the success and downfalls you experience, help to create the person who you are and who you become. You can even learn from the bad experiences. In fact they are probably the most poignant and important lessons. If someone hurts you, betrays you or breaks your heart, FORGIVE THEM, for they have helped you learn about

trust and the importance of being cautious about when and to whom you open your heart. If someone loves you, love them back unconditionally, not only because they love you, but because in a way they are teaching you to love and how to open your eyes and heart to things. Make every day count. Appreciate every moment and take from those moments everything that you possibly can, for you may never be able to experience it again. Talk to people you have never talked to before and actually listen. Let yourself fall in love, break free and set your sights high. Hold your head high, because you have every right to. Tell yourself you are a great individual and believe in yourself. If you don't it will be hard for others to believe in you. You can make your life anything you wish. Create your own life and then go out and live it with absolutely no regrets. Most importantly if you love someone, tell them, for you never know what tomorrow may have in store. (I love you) And learn a lesson in every day you live. Today is the tomorrow you were worried about yesterday. Was it worth it?
~Author Unknown

I am not fucking stupid. I mean I used to. But we broke up. Be careful what you ask for. Every day I see people begging for true love. If you aren't happy being single, you won't be happy taken. Happiness comes from within, not from another. Everyone is dreaming and wishing for their 'soul mate', 'the one', or their 'twin flame'. Dreaming of the perfect love for themselves. Hate to tell you, the perfect love is within you and your relationship to God. Then you find another to share it with you. Let me tell you this, your soul mates are here to teach you a lesson, work on your fears, put a mirror up to see yourself and settle past-life issues. Roll up your sleeves and put on your boots because you are going into battle knee deep in shit. Oh yes, the beginning is a fabulous honeymoon. Beginnings are exciting and thrilling. However, when the love high has ended, we have to face ourselves with all the things we do not like because they became a mirror to us.

It is not fair to start a relationship with someone when you are all screwed up. I tell the girls I work with this, "You do not want a relationship because you are filled with bullshit, you need to heal the shit or you will end up with shit. When you are healed and love yourself, true love with find you. You want a great relationship then you have to realize you have to empty your bags before you go destroy another person's life with your baggage. It is not fair to someone else."

~You need to love yourself before you can truly love another. If you cannot love yourself and be happy ALONE, you will never be happy in a relationship. You still have to live with yourself forever. ~ Natalie Newman

Follow your heart, but take your brain with you. We have many soul mates that come at certain times to help guide us to a higher level. When that lesson is over the relationship will fall apart or quietly end. At this time, we are to learn our lesson they came to teach us and let go. Too many people cannot let go and never realize there is something else for them if they just quit crying and suffering over it. So many people sit in front of the closed door hanging on for dear life with anger, jealousy, pain and fear. When God closes one door, another door opens. But it sure can be hell in the hallway. When that door closes it is time for you to sit in that hallway and get over it. Work on yourself. Find what you want different or want to change. At that time we should be grateful for the moment with them and the lesson they gave us. Forgive them and yourself so the NEW and BETTER door can open.

How long you want to hang out in that hallway is your choice. You are only keeping yourself from a better life. I always call myself Alice in Wonderland. I see an ending and learn as fast as I can because I cannot wait to see what is behind the next door. The person who arrives into our lives are the right ones. Meaning that nobody arrives by chance in our lives, all the people which surround us, that interacts with us, are in for a reason. They are here to do something, to make us learn and to advance in each situation! Be it family, friends or people we just meet.

Soul mates are here to teach you lessons. They are going to put the mirror up to your face and make you take a long hard look at yourself. They make you aware of everything you need to change. Normally, soul mates after a time argue and fight because we do not want to face what they show us or fear it. Sadly, many people do not even understand their anger towards the lessons given. Until you learn it, it will not go away. The lesson will just keep coming up in arguments or pain. Who the hell wants that?

Remember that is what you are asking for, 'the one' to take you to the next level. Yes, the love can be very beautiful, but you do not get there for free. You have to dig deep and work hard on yourself to adjust to the situation to stay in it. You have to work hard to make the relationship strong and meaningful. Most of our soul mate relationships we secretly know in our hearts it is not exactly what we wanted. If you feel that, then your intuition and spirit is telling you what you need to hear. This person is not doing your higher self any good. If you are with 'the one' you are supposed to spend the rest of your life with, there will be no question in your heart.

Soul mates can bring out the best and worst in each other, depending on their issues, and often no matter how hard someone tries to hold on and help, the lesson is to let go. As we search for that love, we tend to think of a soul mate as 'The One' (which is actually God), to complete us and fulfill us. If you start thinking that everything in a soul mate relationship is going to be magic the minute you meet, or if you imagine everything will be perfect or have no problems, I really hope you think again. You are setting yourself up for some serious disappointment.

Another danger in believing in the concept of soul mates is taking your relationship for granted. There can be temptation to get out of an unhappy relationship if you think your partner isn't your soul mate. However, if you think that being with your soul mate will mean a life free from hard times and conflict, you are not facing reality. If you think you haven't married your soul mate, don't just walk away from the relationship for that reason alone. Learn why it is time to go and what you need. Then leave it with integrity and gratitude. Spend some time getting to know yourself a bit better first.

You can't find your perceived soul mate if you haven't found yourself first

A soul mate bears gifts in the form of life lessons. We have many soul mates, not just one, and they are each part of our soul group. ~James Van Praagh

Soul mate is sometimes used to describe a feeling we have that is a feeling of deep and natural affinity, friendship, love, intimacy, sexuality, and/or compatibility. Soul mates can have various types of relationships, which do not always include romantic love. They can be close friends, co-workers, a teacher, anyone who influences your life one way or another. They play the emotional, spiritual, physical, and mental, games of a third dimension with you. They can affect relationships in a positive or negative way depending on the emotional issues of the people concerned. Souls often come together to work out issues or play reverse roles that they are experiencing elsewhere.

Anyone who is in your biological family, or adopted family, or pseudo-family, is a soul mate to you. You feel closer to certain souls, because you have attracted them into your life. Either they are on the same frequency as you or because you want to work out issues with them. Karma refers to responsibilities shared by soul mates. Some people are just here to challenge you and force you to grow.

~Never before have relationships been as problematic and conflict-ridden as they are these days. As you may have noticed that they are not here to make you happy or complete. If you continue to seek relief in relationships, you'll just be disappointed again and again. But if you accept that the relationship primarily exists to make you aware, and not happy, you can actually find relief in the relationship and become available to the higher consciousness that would manifest itself in the world.~ Eckhart Tolle ~

We are so disconnected with our body's messages and our intuition. Sometimes in our life we will date or marry our brothers, sisters, mothers, grandparents, etc., from a past life. When we meet a soul mate the feeling goes right to our stomach. That is where your intuition hits. Our intuition tells us we know this person. Our intuition feels this person, recognizes it, and most times we feel love for them. Often called 'feeling of butterflies in your stomach', this feeling is exciting. As this feeling hits our stomach it will begin to travel in all directions throughout the body.

The first place it will hit is our genitals, seeing they are closest to the stomach. Our body feels the excitement, gets confused, and relays it as sexual. This confusion leads to 'one night stands' or short relationships. If we can get past the genital excitement it will move up into our hearts causing you to feel the familiarity and love between your spirits. Your body gets a rush from it. Heart is racing. We fall in love even if it is for a second. Humans are so desperate for love that we will attach immediately to the familiarity and BAM we are not thinking. Now you are thinking about starting a relationship with somebody you should not. We need to let it travel to our minds before we make any decisions about anything with any person. Put your feet back on the ground. Let the message get to your head about who this person is.

When I meet people I let it travel through to my head. I think about how they feel and usually within seconds, minutes or few hours of meeting them I can tell exactly what they are to me. You need to let it travel up to your third eye (located between your eyebrows) for you to "see" and then to your brain to "hear" who they are. We always hear of people who say "he's like my brother" or "we are like sisters". That is because he/she was your brother/sister in another life.

I have people all over the world that the minute they meet me call me sista or momma. I know this is family from another life. I feel love for them but it is because they were my children, friends or family in another lifetime. Allowing my mind and intuition to work like it is supposed to; I get my answer to who that person is to me. I have made enough mistakes in my life with relationships I should not have been in. I wish I would have understood this because I would have saved myself a lot of heartache. Now I think it through and listen. Your intuition will also tell you when to run when something does not feel right.

So please listen to yourself. Fate controls who walks into your life, but you decide who you let walk out, who you let stay and who you refuse to let go of. The only way to get what you want is to let go of what you don't want. It is better to have loved and lost, then live with a psycho the rest of your life. Find a heart that will love you at your worst and arms that will hold you at your weakest. That is 'the one' for you.

Twin flames are the relationship we are all looking to find. They are the most magical relationships. This is the true fairytale love story. When our spirit is born it splits into two becoming a female and a male. Their first life they spend together in pure, innocent and perfect love. After that twin flames are rarely ever together again. One usually incarnates while the other acts as their spirit guide. Normally, they guide them through every life incarnated. They will guide them and assist them on their journey through that lifetime. When they choose their last life incarnated, they will come together, heal all unresolved pain, balance all karma, then begin their work towards a higher purpose of helping humanity and the planet.

Twin flame relationships are extremely rare on this planet. According to the experts they are not millions, or thousands but only hundreds of sets of them on earth. Sadly, only one in 100 stay together. But as our souls are evolving faster, more are coming together sooner. Honestly, most people will never be ready for the intensity of this relationship. First, you must heal all your past unresolved pain and all karma from all your soul's lifetimes. It is deep digging and very painful to survive. It is enormous amounts of work at the highest level of spirituality, trust and unconditional love.

One of the main reasons that twin flame relationships will not work is the amount of emotional baggage one or both are carrying. Also, another reason is they are under a spiritual awakening, which is extremely challenging on its own. It is normally a painfully, dramatic story of strength, patience, and unconditional love with these relationships. Twin Flames have to PROVE their love and work hard for it. They are completely opposite with half of everything and exactly the same in every way with the other half of everything. Their connection is a telepathic and at a soul level of love. They 'complete' each other and only few lucky people are able to find their twin flame. Once your twin flame has been found your heart will know instantly.

~It does not matter where you are or what your lifestyle is, if one is in reclusion and one is on public display, when it is time for your Union it will happen. You do not have to go out and look for it. You do not have to wonder if every person you pass on the street is your Twin Flame. It is not in your hands to orchestrate this Union, but it lies strictly in the hands of the Divine Mind and within your Sacred Heart and your Covenant with God.~ Unknown

Relationships of all kinds are like sand held in your hand. Held loosely, with an open hand the sand remains. The minute you close your hand and squeeze tightly to hold on, the sand trickles through your fingers. You may hold onto some of it, but most will be spilled. A relationship is like that. Held loosely, with respect and freedom for the other person, it is likely to remain intact. But hold too tightly, too possessively, and the relationship slips away and is lost. Always give respect to others in your life. Do not disregard what they came to teach you because of your ego. When your reaction to them is pain or anger that is when you really need to look in the mirror at your own self. What is wrong inside of you that triggers this negative feeling? Acknowledge it and change yourself.

When you change yourself the situation will also change. Surround it with love no matter how bad it feels. Give them a chance to try to change. If they cannot do it, then end it. You deserve to have the life you dream. They may not change, but YOU will. Everything will have a positive outcome if love surrounds it. Do not lose yourself in the process of treasuring someone too much and forgetting that you are special and valuable too. Really, we won't know the right person unless we meet the wrong ones. You do not need the right one to complete you. You need to find the one that accepts you completely.

At any moment your relationship could be over. How are you going to handle it? Sometimes we see it coming, sometimes it is death, cheating or unexpectedly it ends. We need to learn to live without attachments which are connecting ourselves to outcomes we cannot control. Be grateful for what you have today. Tomorrow never comes, it will always be today. So live for everything you have at this moment because it is all you have. Be thankful for everyone around you, because they are there for YOU. You cannot say you will be in the relationship forever because only God knows that. Keep an open mind.

Remember your journey and lessons will never be the same as theirs. They have lessons in life too. Those lessons may hurt you deeply but it is theirs, not yours. Your lesson is how you react to it. Are you open and forgiving or are you filled with pain and anger? If you love someone you guide them through their lessons with a loving, forgiving, and understanding heart. Look at yourself and see what you need to learn through it. Learning helps everything to heal. Do not selfishly hang on. Why do most people continually force themselves upon another when they know it is not right or that person does not want them? When you stop chasing the wrong things, then you give the right things a chance to catch you. We can't beg someone to stay when he/she wants to leave and be with someone else. However, the end of LOVE is not the end of LIFE. It should be the beginning of understanding that LOVE LEAVES FOR A REASON BUT ALSO LEAVES WITH A LESSON.

~The moment you see how important it is to love yourself, you will stop making others suffer." ~ Siddhārtha Gautama

We do not know the rules. We struggle, we search for love and happiness. We use material things and others to find this feeling. When all we need to do is look up and say "Thank You" and love yourself. God will take care of you. You can only give away what you already have inside yourself. True giving happens when you are overflowing from the inside, and cannot help but share. When there is so much love within you that it has to flow to others or you would burst open. There is no thinking involved and no willpower in such sharing. It just flows out. If you have to force yourself to be kind, to love, to feel compassion, you've missed the first step of filling your own Self with these emotions. They might hurt you and it may end, but you still have YOURSELF.

I promise each day will grow lighter with more love and freedom in your heart. That is when beautiful things happen. Just love yourself the most. I always choose God first but I know I have to be #2. If I am not good then nothing or nobody is good around me. I have to stay strong and healthy to take care of everyone. Trust me, I know it is the hardest thing to do. But when you love and trust yourself the most, then the pain does not hurt so deep. Life changes from broken hearts that take forever to heal, to just a scratch of pain that is not so deadly and heals quickly. Protect your heart because you were only given one. Be very careful who you give it to. When you change, you will only give your heart to those who are worthy of it.

~Do not make a woman cry, because God counts her tears.

~The woman came from a man's rib, not from his feet to be walked on, not from his head to be superior, but from the side to be equal. Under the arm to be protected and next to the heart to be loved.

~ If you can't forget your 'EX' you Will Never Trust your 'next'

~ One person that wasn't supposed to ever let us down, probably will. You'll have your heart broken and you'll break others' hearts. You'll fight with your best friend or maybe even fall in love with them, and you'll cry because time is flying by. So take too many pictures, laugh too much, forgive freely, and love like you've never been hurt. Life comes with no guarantees, no time outs, no second chances. You just have to live life to the fullest, tell someone what they mean to you and tell someone off, speak out, dance in the pouring rain, hold someone's hand, comfort a friend, fall asleep watching the sun come up, stay up late, be a flirt, and smile until your

face hurts. Don't be afraid to take chances or fall in love and most of all, live in the moment because every second you spend angry or upset is a second of happiness you can never get back.

~ Each relationship between two persons is absolutely unique. That is why you cannot love two people the same. It simply is not possible. You love each person differently because of who they are and the uniqueness that they draw out of you.

~ Romance, for most people is what they do when they want something. But sacred love is a function of giving not taking. Romance is a sacred way of giving love. The conditionality of most love is that romance stops if the response we get is not what we expect. But sacred love is about giving, not giving to get, giving to love.

~Falling in love is like jumping off a bridge. Your brain tells you it is not a good idea and your heart tells you that you can fly.

~Guys: take time to love her or somebody else who has more time will come and take her off your hands.

~I see, so if I don't have sex with you I am a prude bitch, if I use the pill I am a slut, if I get pregnant I am an idiot, and if I get an abortion I am Satan. Yay!

~Somebody said to me, "You're too pretty to be single." I said, "No, I am too pretty to be lied to, cheated on and played with." ~Natalie Newman

Chapter 9

God Gives Us People to Love and Things to Use, Not Things to Love and People to Use

Why does a woman work ten years to change a man's habits and then complain that he's not the man she married? HELL NO! Neither are you. We spend so much time trying to change another to become what WE WANT. We forget to let them be themselves. Then complain because we do not like who they are years later. Just because someone doesn't love you the way you want them too, doesn't mean they don't love you with all they have. Maybe your journey together at that point should be over if you cannot look at them and say I am so proud of the person you have become. Many marriages would work if the husband and wife clearly understood they were on the same side.

You also need to be able to look at yourself and see the person YOU have become while the two of you have been together. If it is not a good feeling then maybe it is time to open your eyes a little wider to your feelings. Understand that they come and they go, you learn and you grow, and then LET IT GO. Pray for God to take it. It will either heal itself or God will assist you in ending it peacefully. The most secure way to keep love is to give it space and care to grow. If you hold it too tightly, you will lose it. Put a smile on your face. Be grateful for the adventure. They are your teacher.

Most relationships were not meant to hang on to forever. You know in your heart when it is time. You are not alone with your pain. Reach out for help. EVERYONE on this earth has had a broken heart. God doesn't give you the people you want. He gives you the people you need. To help you, to hurt you, to leave you, to love you and make you the person you were meant to be.

We take a risk when we open our hearts because the truth is, if we open our hearts, we will get hurt. You can't open your heart and not have some hurt because you're in a human experience. Even if it's the love of your life and you have many wonderful, deepening, growing, powerful years together, it's a human experience and that person will pass over. Love takes courage. Be courageous. ~Mary Manin Morrissy

Love is the opposite of ego. Ego is argumentative and aggressive upon the mind. It splits the world into right and wrong, us and them. Love is generative, compassionate, and embracing all creation. Ego pays attention to what is being said. Love pays attention to how things are said. Ego leads to debate. Love leads to communion.

My Swede and I faced many issues that were very difficult together. However, with each problem we got better, our attitudes got better, we grew spiritually, our self-esteem grew, our parenting got better, our relationships with our families got better, our gratitude for life got better, our friendships got better, and our faith in God grew with every shitty moment we faced. We stand beside each other when the other was knee deep in shit. We crawled and fought our way through it. With each moment our souls grow. I step back and realize he made a mistake. We all make mistakes, myself included. I did not try to make him suffer for something he had to learn from. I vowed to support him through every horrible and beautiful moment. I made a promise and I keep my promises.

Some moments I would rather run than face it. Each moment was a step closer to a better self and relationship. There is no force greater than unconditional love. Our love upheld the greatest enemy to it, ourselves. We kept learning and working very hard together. When God feels we are ready and strong enough, then maybe we will come together. Situations may not be pleasant at times in a relationship, but as long as you see it is moving forward, then you know it is worth fighting for.

The most important thing you can give a relationship is time and space. Accepting who they are and realizing you cannot control anyone. However, you can be lovingly honest about your feelings. Think before you speak. Realize you are not the same. Their lessons are different. Men and women DO NOT think the same at all. So take that into consideration when you do not like their actions. Let them change on their own. Tell them how you feel. Stop bitching about it continuously. They will just rebel against you. Handle the situation with integrity as you want to be treated. Then surround it with love. Give them the freedom to want to be better and that is when you get change. Encouragement and patience does pay off. When you don't yell at each other, beautiful outcomes will rise from it.

<u>Natalie's 5 Rules For Lovers</u>

1) Hug them once a day- it gives you a feeling of relief, comfort, love and security.

2) Kiss them hard once a day- keeps the erotic passion flowing, keeps the relationship alive.

3) Smile at them once a day- If it sucks for you, it also sucks for them too. You will survive it TOGETHER.

4) Tell them I LOVE YOU every day while looking into their eyes- Reminds the both of you about the commitment of your spirits together and keeps your love untouchable.

5) NEVER, NEVER go to bed angry- It is the worst feeling to in the world to both of you. Get your ego out of the way and fix it enough without arguing, so you can have a peaceful sleep.

Sometimes you have to take a step back and look at the bigger picture and the people that you're stressing over. Get rid of your toxic relationships. It's time to cancel their subscriptions to your life. The people in your life should only enhance your quality of living. When you know it is over, then it's time to pack up your lessons from your partner or friend. Cry, scream, throw things (not at others of course, but pillows work well), and do whatever you have to do to get those emotions out. FEEL IT!!! It is important to feel it and you have the right to. Do not keep it locked up inside to grow into a ticking time bomb. Don't be afraid of the shadows, because that only means there's a light nearby.

~God always has something for you, a key for every problem, a light for every shadow, a relief for every sorrow & a plan for every tomorrow. ~Unknown

Next, you have to sit and look at what lessons you needed to learn, pick up all the pieces of you scattered all over the floor and put yourself back together again. You died inside and now it is time for rebirth. You do not see the caterpillars crying because it is over and refusing to become butterflies. So why the hell do you resist change? If you do not make a transformation you cannot become something more beautiful. When you get through it all, you will be even better than you were before you met them. Let them go forward on their journey. Don't cry because it is over, smile because it happened. Forgive them so your fear can stop and you can be grateful for what they taught you. Do not shut love out of your life by saying it is impossible to find and keep. The quickest way to find love is to give love. If you want it too badly, you will not find it.

Now, get ready for the new doors of adventure to open. Heal your heart and don't drag your baggage to the next relationship. Nobody deserves that. When you open a new door, you are graduating to a higher level and it is always better for you than the last. Smile, open that door, and keep walking your path knowing you tried your best at that moment. Be grateful for the new beginnings that come your way.

~Before you diagnose yourself with depression or low self-esteem, first make sure that you are not, in fact, just surrounded by assholes. ~William Gibson

I have much sympathy for those who cannot pull themselves out of the hole. They never let go and continuously create unneeded suffering for themselves. They get comfortable in the hell and forget about what they need to make them happy. They hang on and cry over it. They post it on Facebook or constantly whine about it every day. Complaining they cannot get over that person and they cannot live without them. Why? Why? Why? Dragging every single person around them through their misery and filling others with their negativity. They are always looking for sympathy and people to feel sorry for them. When people walk away from you let them fucking go. Your destiny is never tied to people who leave you and it doesn't mean they are bad people. It just means their part in your story is over. Forget what hurt you, but never forget what it taught you.

Did you look in the mirror and ask why? Did you deserve it? Did you treat it right? Did it treat you right or deserve you? Did you just hang on because you are scared? Do you fear with 7 billion people on earth there was nothing else for you? Or is your fear of being alone? What do you need to learn and you do not even realize it? Was it healthy for you? Where do you think the relationship would be 10 years from now? Why you sit and cry over something that DOES NOT want to be a part of your life? IS THIS PERSON ENCOURAGING AND SUPPORTING THE PERSON YOU WANT TO BE? Why would you want to make someone your everything when you are only their something?

Cheating is never an accident. You don't just trip and fall into a vagina. People who are in happy relationships do not cheat. They cheat because they are missing something from their partner. They are craving attention which they are not getting from the one they love. Why do we always feel sorry for the one who got cheated on? The question is why did that person cheat? What were they lacking at home to make them go get it from somebody else? Stop pointing the finger at the cheater and point at both people. Each of them made mistakes to get that relationship to that point of cheating.

Normally, affection and sex is what they are missing at

home. That is why they go somewhere else to find it. So if you want to keep it at home, then you have to take care of it. Studies say that 68% of American women would cheat if they knew they wouldn't get caught. 8 out of 10 marriages in America one cheats. Seriously, what have we become in relationships and as a people? Why are people in relationships when they want to go find pleasure with someone else? Your partner is supposed to be YOUR BEST FRIEND who you are sharing your life with. If you wouldn't treat your best friend like that, then why are you treating the person you say you love and have a relationship with, like that? Cheating is behavior like flirting, talking dirty, kissing, or sex, that you would not want your partner to do. I never do to another without thinking to myself, "How would I feel my man to did that behind my back?" Then if you take any actions after the answer is no, then you have cheated yourself and your partner. Don't forget the karma coming back to you for your behavior also. If you have sex with a married person, be careful when you love someone enough to marry. Karma is a bitch and you need to learn a lesson about breaking another person's heart and destroying their life. Just sayin!

62% of married men in America have affairs with someone they work with. The man is not getting the attention at home from the wife, who is probably overwhelmed, bitching all the time and has withdrawn from sex. People spend most of their time at work so you create a relationship with them. Most spend more time with co-workers than their spouse. Just a little flirting and things begin to get out of hand. It feels good and they cannot get that from their spouse anymore. This goes for both women and men.

54% of Americans know someone who is cheating. I have many people from other countries ask what the hell is wrong with Americans. We look like out of control idiots. Americans have no value in a relationship or family. I watch women hop from bed to bed being afraid to be alone. I call them 'bed hoppers'. Most already have the other bed ready before they leave the one they are in. Most times they find someone within a week to replace the last one. AFRAID TO BE ALONE!

~You are going to feel alone, until you can live alone with yourself, only then can you feel complete and whole. *That is when you open yourself to another who is also comfortable with their self.*-Natalie Newman

~It is easy to take off your clothes and have sex, people do it all the time. But opening up your soul to someone, letting them into your spirit, thoughts, fears, future, hopes, and dreams............THAT IS BEING NAKED!

~ Love is like a precious plant. You can't just accept it and leave it in the cupboard or just think it's going to get on by itself. You've got to keep on watering it. You've got to really look after it and nurture it. ~John Lennon

Experience is what you get when you are looking for something else. There are 7 billion people on this earth. So you know there is someone else out there to love you. That person is NOT the last one on earth. And PLEASE, do not think that having a baby is the way to keep a relationship together. A baby will not going to save anything.

Also, seriously look at how that person treats you and others. That is how they will be towards a child. Think before you destroy an innocent life for selfish reasons. If it is meant to be, it will be. God will never leave you all alone and you will always have someone to help you through. But it is ONLY you who understands how you really feel. Others can't help you, only you can help yourself. No one can drive you crazy if you don't give them the keys. If you aren't happy being single, you won't be happy taken. Happiness comes from within, not from another.

We forget about what we need to make ourselves happy. Letting go is the most heart-wrenching experience. But hanging on is a much greater hell we create for ourselves. How long do you want to hang on and exist in the hell before you decide you need better? You do deserve better. Let go of the negative energy that nobody could love you better. We have many loves in our life and each one will be different. Still each one will be better than the last. Don't be a person that needs someone, be a person someone needs. If they miss you, they will call you. If they care, they will show it. If not, then they can't be worth your time because you are obviously not worth theirs.

If you don't treat yourself with respect other people will follow your example. Being single doesn't mean you're weak. It means you're strong enough to wait for what you deserve. The best thing you can do is be alone and have some damn patience. Wait for somebody to respect you and treat you right. Don't settle for only half of what you dream. Let go and love yourself first. Let the Laws of Attraction work for you. One day someone will walk into your life and you will see why it never worked out with anyone else.

~A true friend doesn't care when you're broke, being a bitch, what you weigh, if you don't see them for months, if your house is a mess, what you drive, about your past, or if your family is filled with crazy people. Your conversations pick up where they left off, even if they have been years apart. They love you for who you are. ~ Unknown

You will always have a group to support you on your journey. That is why people come and go. You lose common ground. You just begin to drift off to more like-minded people. Our circle of support changes as you change. They no longer serve your purpose. If you are trying to get better why would you stay at a lower level of support? You want people who think like you. As you grow and change so does the people in your life. You move off to different people of your new interests so you have someone to talk with, so you can continue to grow and better yourself. Why would you close yourself off to better relationships?

Somewhere out there could be your new best friend or a new and better lover? But until you let go, God cannot give you better than what you have. You have freewill to decide what you want. Everyone says that love hurts, but that's not true. Rejection hurts. Losing someone hurts. Envy hurts. Everyone gets these things confused with love, but in reality, love is the only thing in this world that covers up all the pain and makes someone feel wonderful again. But you need to find that love within yourself. If you can't figure out to love yourself then how the hell do you expect someone else to do it for you or know how to love you?

Everything changes, Go with the Flow. Sometimes we have to lose something precious to gain something priceless. In this new era of evolution of this planet, relationships are now forced to be truthful and honest. Always tell the truth, even if the other cannot handle it. Do not fear the consequences. You will be rewarded with freedom if you are always honest in your relationships. Never hurt the ones you love. Never!

I know when most of you read this chapter you will think of your loving relationships. Now you should also read it again thinking of your other relationships with friends, co-workers, and family. We have many kinds of relationships in our life. These words can be used with any one of them.

~There are dreamers and there are realist's in this world. You'd think the dreamers would find the dreamers and the realist's would find the realist's but, more often than not, the opposite is true. You see the dreamers need the realist's to keep them from soaring too close to the sun. And the realist's well, without the dreamers they might not ever get off the ground.

~Everything is backwards in society. Lust is mistaken for love, profits over people, greed over compassion, and happiness is measured by the "things" you accumulate. Where is the compassion, self-respect, and pride in oneself that resonates through seeing humanity as a reflection of the self? Females need to stop letting these insecure guys control their every move and take away their individuality... and then call it love. At the same time males need to de-condition themselves from these egotistical societal standards that have been perpetuated upon them. You are NOT measured by the amount of females that you have had, the type of cars you own or how many Nike's you possess. You're not a player. As a matter of fact you're playing yourself into a shallow existence that dilutes your purpose of life and what you were destined to achieve. Kill the insecurities and embrace your imperfections for our uniqueness is the bond that holds us all close together!
~Free Your Mind and Think

~If I knew it would be the last time that I'd see you fall asleep, I would tuck you in more tightly and pray the Lord your soul to keep.

If I knew it would be the last time that I'd see you walk out the door, I would give you a hug and kiss and call you back for just one more.

If I knew it would be the last time I'd hear your voice lifted up in praise, I would tape each word and action and play them back throughout my days.

If I knew it would be the last time I would spare an extra minute or two to stop and say "I love you," instead of assuming you know I do.

So just in case tomorrow never comes and today is all I get, I'd like to say how much I love you and I hope we never will forget.

Tomorrow is not promised to anyone young or old alike and today may be the last chance you get to hold your loved one tight.

So if you're waiting for tomorrow, Why not do it today? For if tomorrow never comes You'll surely regret the day that you didn't take that extra time for a smile, a hug, or a kiss and you were too busy to give yourself to someone. ~Unknown

~ The greatest degree of inner tranquility comes from the development of love and compassion. The more we care for the happiness of others, the greater is our own sense of well-being. ~Dalai Lama

~ Everyone is my teacher. Some I seek. Some I subconsciously attract. Often I learn simply by observing others. Some may be completely unaware that I'm learning from them, yet I bow deeply in gratitude. However, as soon as anyone tries to 'Impose' their beliefs on me, attempting to convince or convert me, I walk away; for this is someone who wishes to control my mind, NOT Enlighten it. Remember, Learn from Every one you meet, but let NO ONE 'Tell You' what or how to think. ~Eric Allen

~ Love comes when manipulation stops; when you think more about the other person than about his or her reactions to you. When you dare to reveal yourself fully. When you dare to be vulnerable." ~ Dr. Joyce Brothers

~ If nothing ever changed, there'd be no butterflies.

~ That family is not a name for a group of people, but the quality of relationships between them. Relationships grounded in mutual love, trust, caring and forgiveness. In all the ups and all the downs of life. Look closely, - who is really your family, and who in truth are just strangers in for the ride?

~It only take seconds to hurt someone, but sometimes it takes years to repair the damage. Cherish the ones who love you.

~True love doesn't have a happy ending. True love doesn't have an ending.

~I wonder how many couples would still be together if they traded phones for the weekend?

~ I am grateful for the nights that turned into mornings, friends that turned into family, dreams that turned into reality, likes that turned into loves, and everyone who crossed my path along the way, no matter how long they stay. ~ Natalie Newman

~ Dear Human, You got it all wrong. You didn't come here to master unconditional love. That is where you came from and where you'll return. You came here to learn personal love, universal love, messy love, sweaty love, crazy love, broken love, and whole love infused with divinity. Lived through the grace of stumbling. Demonstrated through the beauty of... making mistakes often. You didn't come here to be perfect, you already are. You came here to be a beautiful human flawed and fabulous. Here to rise again into remembering.

~Some people are just missing a screw, they are missing the whole fuckin tool box.

~ Everything that tries to kill me makes me feel alive.

Chapter 10

The World Opens to Us All

Our relationships are now started, reunited and destroyed by the internet. I remembered a decade or so ago when someone said we will look at people while we talked to them on the phone. I did not want anyone seeing me when I am on the phone. I never wanted any part of it. Now it has become a way of life. Back in 2008 my adventure with the internet began. I walked into a world I had no idea about.

As I spread across the world in the last 4 years I now have two profiles with 9000 friends just on one site. Because of having so many friends, I have been invited and joined so many social networks. I have studied the behaviors of everyone. I have watched the human race become something completely different because of social networking. I have been a part of people's heartbreaks, weddings, engagements, babies, children, backstabbing, pain, happiness, successes and losses.

The internet had become my psychological study of human beings. I may not have a damn degree in psychology, but I had the world and real people to teach me. I learned as it was happening, not in some book. I helped 1000's and 1000's of people through their pain. I have helped people with every problem you can imagine. I felt their pain for them, I prayed for them, and I tried to help them even if I did not talk to them. Almost every day I pray for every friend I have all over the world. I truly love my online friends. They have carried me through so many horrible moments. They taught me enormous amounts of information from almost every country on earth. The biggest thing I learned was we are all exactly the same. We all suffer. Nobody on earth is exempt from suffering. We are here to learn remember? Everyone is filled with some sort of hidden pain that they project on themselves or another. There are very few people on this earth who have pain free lives. They do not evolve much. Those who have pain will make changes so pain will finally stop.

3 Rules to Live By

Don't shop when you're hungry.

Don't date when you're horny

Don't update your status when you're drunk or hurt

We all want to be loved. It does not matter what damn color you are or where you're from. WE ALL WANT TO BE LOVED. Love begins as a rough stone in the ground. You have to scrub the dirt away. Then you have to carefully start chipping away at the stone. Day after day you chip at this stone. Dreaming of the beautiful results you will have when you finish. Years later you are still chipping and each day it gets smaller. As it starts to look more like a gem you start to believe in yourself. You put all your time, heart and soul into chipping this stone. Suddenly, one day you look down and see it. It has become a precious diamond.

You are the diamond. That is what you need to get love. You have to work and learn as you go. It takes time to chip away the dirt and debris from your soul. Do not stop chipping until you see that sparkling perfection made only by God with your hands. You have to love yourself first. Only then can the world love you back. So instead, we are hating because we cannot love ourselves.

~We may have different religions, different languages, different colored skin, but we all belong to one human race.
~Kofi Annan

I witness the results of not loving yourself everyday

online. The amount of negative energy on my news feed completely outweighs the positive. It is fear, stress, worry, pain, anger, jealousy, judgment and everyone pouring every moment online for the world to see. You people are not shy at all. The internet gives you a power. You are not afraid to say anything anymore. But you should really pay attention to what you say. You are shooting that energy all over the world, even if you do not have world-wide friends. The energy still goes to that website and you leave it there for everyone to absorb.

Also, it is a haven for screwing people's lives. I suffer through hell on a daily basis and NEVER do you see me say a damn word about it. I always post the lesson I have just learned or something inspirational. Your friends have to read everything that is put out there and it enters their brains when they read it. Sometimes what people put out there is not right. We suddenly have the power to hurt people in front of hundreds or thousands of their friends. We cannot tell them face to face? Or send an email at least? I hope you can find some integrity. If you do not want another to say things about you online, then do not do it to others. Think before you post or comment.

However, all you crazy and funny people keep up the good work. We need more of you out there. You people make me laugh every day. Thank you for that. I can have tears rolling down my face and someone will make me laugh with their insanity. I love it!

Be aware that every single word you write online is kept and monitored. You do not own it. Whatever you write can be used against you with things like job interviews and college acceptance. The government is monitoring everything. I learned the hard way how unprivate the social networking was. My ex decided to call social services when my house fell apart last year when the Swede was here. Social services and the sheriff had gone through all 3 of my profiles on one extremely popular social network. Just think before you post. Thank God I have chosen to only post positive things but they got into my profile for my garage with all the party pictures. It can come back at you at any time and we all know how life goes. One minute life is perfect and BAM! Protect yourself in all ways always.

Another thing that blows my mind is the relationship statuses. I thought I bounced through relationships like a soccer ball. I can see half the world is doing the same damn thing. My newsfeed is 30% relationship statuses. WOW! Facebook should have a limit on how many times you can change your relationship status. After three it should default to UNSTABLE. My Swede and I waited for six months to post we were together. Still, we felt it was too early to announce to the world we were in a relationship. The main reason we did it was because I was being so harassed by men.

People are changing relationships monthly. I see the status change and then your life change. Either you are madly in love and constantly talking about it or you are filled with heartbroken pain. Most of the pain is because nobody wants to let go. Then they sadly drag their friends though everything. Friends get to watch you fall apart and stay there. It gets exhausting as your friend to watch it. It breaks my heart because you cannot love yourself. You are allowing the whole world to be a part of something deep inside you. As friends, we are here to support each other. You know who will be there for you. Think before you send it out there please.

Welcome to Facebook- The place where relationships are perfect, liars believe their own bullshit and the world shows off they are living a great life. Where your enemies visit your profile the most, your friends and family block you and even though you write what you are thinking, there is always someone who is going to take it the wrong way. Facebook needs an "I DONT GIVE A SHIT" button. People need to become real again.

If you need support or suffered a loss your friends are there to pray for you and love you. Cheer you on and help you get through it. We are there for your endings and your beginnings. We want to be a part of every moment you have. We have become so addicted to our friends lives. In many ways it is so beautiful. I have met 10,000's of people along my path of life. I am connected to so many people again because of the internet. I may not have seen them for many years but they were always a part of my heart. They all served a part of my path to get here. Of course I never add anyone I do not like.

One day I was in the gas station and two girls were talking at the counter. The one girl said to the other that she could not believe these two girls were friends but they were not even friends on Facebook. What have we become people? A social network is defining who we really know and are. I have 1000's of friends out there not on a friend lists. But because we are not friends on a social network, we are not really friends. Social networking is not your life. It is only a place to share it. Do not define your life by it.

Furthermore, the amount of porn and people exposing themselves out there is overwhelming. I cannot believe what I see. It is everywhere you look. No matter what I do I cannot get rid of it. So I know it is also available for my children. Especially, those children with internet on their phones. They have access to whatever they want. Parents are not monitoring it. Half of these people posting and posing are under eighteen years old. Parents, would you bring your child down to the bad part of the city and leave them alone? Well you are leaving them wide open and vulnerable online if you are not watching what they're doing.

I am a naughty girl. However, I am in shock at what I have seen people do to themselves all for attention because they are filled with pain. There is no limit in this category. My first feeling is sadness. The pain is so deep they have to do this to themselves. I have been asked some of the strangest things that you know if you were face to face those people would not say that to you. I have seen more penises in the last three years online than in my entire life. They email them to me, send me videos of them, and expose themselves on webcam. All the rules and values went right out the window with webcams. The world is a pain filled, selfish, and a horny place. I just want people to take a look at what you are doing for attention to kill your pain. If you have a wonderful and loving relationship it is a different story.

People are masturbating or having sex online by the 100,000's every second. It is not just men either. Couples are getting paid to have sex on cam and women have taken control of the porn industry by doing it themselves. I will tell you this. The government is watching. Every time you click a porn site they log it along with your name. If there is a sexual assault or rape in the area, the ones who watch the porn are the first ones they will question. Nothing is private. Think about what you are doing.

I have heard so many stories from my Arabic friends about American women. Most of these young men are virgins and these women put a horrible desire inside them. Giving them a sexual hunger. They do not realize what they have done to the innocent. They cannot love themselves so they mess with another person's life instead. Our children are also exposed to these types of people. These are just the stories I hear from others. This goes for both men and women. Sex is a dirty game of projecting pain. I learned that lesson in life the hard way.

Take my advice please. Have some respect for yourself. Put your clothes on, stop giving yourself away sexually and heal yourself. It does not work. You will have to face your fears or just keep destroying yourself for the "high" and power. There are better ways to get attention. Eventually, the high ends and you've only hurt yourself a million times more than you should have. Face yourself and get that life you know you deserve.

The lies are endless when it comes to the selfish on the internet. So many foreigners want a visa or green card to USA and many will do anything to get it. This is where I learned the ugly side of the internet. Half the people online are pretending to be somebody else for love, money or a green card. There are perpetrators with every disguise imaginable. Thousands fall for it. I am a very smart woman and I fell for many scams from people trying to get whatever they want. If I can fall for it, you know it would be nothing for a child to believe it.

I had someone who made me believe his heartbreaking story that his father was dying. He needed $5000 for his surgery or he was going to die. I felt so bad but I told him if it was God's will he would get the money. I do not have a dollar but I have God and I can pray for you. He got very verbally abusive to me when he could not get what he wanted. He was lying and scamming American women for money by pulling at their hearts. If you feel in your heart something is not right, believe it. Never give money to anyone online. Pray for God to do what is best for them. That is better than money and saves your wallet also. They will go away after you have nothing to offer them. Listen to your instincts. Protect your money and your heart.

Couple years ago I knew a Middle Eastern man who married an American woman. It was internet love at its finest. It was immediate marriage and complete disaster. That woman abused that man and controlled him in every way. He was literally made her slave. It took years for him to get out of it. The only person in this country he knew was me. His friend introduced us because of his problems. Some people do not even care what they look like and think life on webcam is what life will be like together. They think they can love them no matter what.

They get themselves into some very horrible situations and then I get called to help them. I can only give advice and pray for them. They do eventually get out. It is a horrible game being played by many. I have heard every lie on earth trying to get to USA. From people creating a scam saying they needed a doctor, to the 10,000's of times I have been asked to marry them. Do not get me wrong about everybody, over half the world HATES USA. I cannot blame them either.

So ladies and gentleman watch your heart, give it time, do not be so desperate for love you will do anything. It will blow up in your face and never work if you do not face the reality of it. Travel to visit each other in person. See their life before you marry someone you really do not know. God has you right were you belong for a reason. You will come together if God feels it is right for you and when the time is right. If it is worth fighting for then it is worth keeping no matter how long it takes. Patience is the only way you can survive not being together physically.

Another side of the internet it has brought many people together forming such beautiful, strong, and loving relationships without sex. You have to be strong, trusting, patient, honest and forgiving. You have to love unconditionally. If you are not ready to be best friends first, do not have an online relationship. Chatting and emails are never the real feeling, especially when your dealing with the opposite sex. Some days one is happy and one is angry. Words always interpret differently from one to another without seeing their face. Jokes can turn into nightmares. Communication hell! I have no idea how the Swede and I survived it.

Honestly, you have to just be clear and ask if you misunderstand. Be careful and be open to the fact that everyone has a different way of expressing themselves. You must have great strength to survive it. I have spent 4 years in long distance online relationships. Most of you cannot handle real life physical relationships. You have to be a million times stronger to make a long distance one work. If you cannot love yourself you will never get a healthy relationship on the internet. Try a real boy/girlfriend first. These online relationships take time, patience and all you can do is talk. It is very difficult to live without being able to touch someone for months or even years at a time. Trust me!

Today 40% of relationships are started online. Social networks are the new dating sites. It shocks me how many people are dating because of social networking. I would have never met my Swede without one. So, know what you are getting yourself into before you begin putting yourself through more pain. Every second of the day you miss someone and you have to be more powerful than the pain. My Swede and I were grateful for the pain because we felt it for good reasons. We felt it because we loved each other and that was a blessing. Constantly, you have to remind yourself you are feeling a pain and understand where it is coming from. If you cannot, it will manifest into disaster. You have to be confident and LOVE being alone to survive a long distance online relationship.

We need to stand up for our rights with the internet. We have the right to learn and communicate with the entire world. We have the right to get to know each other. We are bringing unity to humankind. Stand up for what they are trying to control and take away. We deserve to have the right to say what we feel and communicate with who we want without someone tagging every word said.

The C.I.A, got rid of 30% of their staff because Facebook was doing all the work for them. They have 30,000 employees monitoring your every word. The government passed a law that gave the cable and internet companies the right to slow you down or shut you down if they do not like what you are doing online. Facebook is targeting people posting media that is damaging to the government. What happened to freedom of speech and press? Well, while you were numb and dumb they took those rights away from you. That is an invasion of your privacy. Privacy is something you don't have anymore. Be aware and educate yourself. We need to make this work for us, not against us. All the knowledge of the entire universe is at our fingertips. Fight for it.

I have to admit that last year I watched everyone posting negative posts on Facebook all day long. I gave up hope when I was writing this book. I cried my eyes out and told my Swede, "I don't want to do this anymore. Nobody wants to get better. They don't want help. They love their misery." I wanted to quit praying for the world and helping people. I know all I could do was pray for everyone and myself. I can say to you that over the last few months, all over the entire world, people are now posting more positive things. Little bit of whining is still happening and you can definitely pick out the ones that refuse change. But most of you are changing. It is beautiful to watch. My heart fills with hope again.

You should be proud of yourself because you went through many changes to become more positive. You did not even understand you are being changed by the energies of the Universe. People alone, by the hundreds, and by the thousands are praying and meditating for you every day to feel love and to begin to awaken. We are all getting our asses handed to us to force us to better our lives. Magic to watch it working and you are awakening. The whole Earth is feeling it! I pray for every person on this earth every day and send my love to everyone. I am so proud of you. Trust that chaos is a moment of change and you can handle it.

The world is filled with beautiful people and we all want the same thing peace, love and happiness. So why are we fighting against each other? I am so grateful for the wonderful connections I have made because of the internet. The amazing amounts of information I have learned from everyone and the blessing to connect with those I love who are so far away. The internet has connected the world to teach each other. What a wonderful gift we were given. Let us use it for a better world, not abuse it. A big huge THANK YOU to each and every one of my online friends for the great education and support you have given me. You people are family to me and YOU ROCK!!! I love you all. PEACE, LOVE, and HUGS!

~Jesus said, "Love one another without judgment"! Martin Luther King Jr. said, "Love one another"! Gandhi said "Love"! Mohammad said, "Love"! Buddha said "Love"! Krishna said, "Love"! The Great Spirit said, "Love" and even the dark religions teach you to love to hate and to love dark things. For you are also a teacher on this earth, we are all messengers from above. YOU'RE HERE TO TEACH LOVE. -Natalie Newman

Chapter 11

IMAGINE

~Imagination is more important than knowledge. Knowledge is limited. Imagination encircles the world. ~ Albert Einstein

Please read this next paragraph out loud.

Thank you Mother Earth for giving us the air we breathe, the water we drink, the food we eat, wonderful smells, beautiful things to see and providing everything we need. Without you I cannot be. ~ **Natalie Newman**

You may say I am a dreamer, but I have millions behind me on this chapter. There is a team of a million of people at this moment that have dedicated their lives to healing this planet. I have been asking Mother Earth for ways I could help her. I have dedicated my life to serving Her and Father God. I asked her to guide me. I started praying for the words to write her message. I want to teach others to return our Mother Earth to its pristine state. I want to teach others to heal themselves to lift the spirit of this planet. And to let our beautiful children do their job of creating peace on this Earth. Sadly, most people don't understand the vibrations of this Earth or the energies they are giving off themselves.

First of all she is OUR MOTHER Earth. She is also a living soul just like you or me. Except, this life she chose to be a planet and host life. She chose this experience. She is mother to every living thing on this planet. Our poor Mother Earth is surrounded by her bad children. How do you treat your own mother? With love, respect and kindness? Just like your own mother, you should treat Mother Earth the same. Without her there is NO life. We couldn't breathe without all the plants, she provides our air to breathe, the waters we drink, she provides us with natural medicines to heal ourselves and she provides all our food we eat. Exactly like your real mother would. Every day of my life I step out the door of my home, I raise my arms to the sky and I thank everything around me. EVERYTHING! I send my love and appreciation out to every living thing on this planet.

Every living thing has a spirit so never forget that. EVERY living thing! Show your Mother and her family some respect. Treat her like the Queen she is. You should be grateful to have this experience on Her beautiful planet.

We have taken our HOME, the home to every living thing, and turned it into a toxic ball of polluted hell. Garbage everywhere, plowing down forests, polluting our skies, depleting our natural resources and sending a windstorm of negative energy straight out into the entire Universe. This planet generates pollution out across space. Every planet has energy and ours is negative. Our Mother needs us. She is wounded, diseased, dirty, broken hearted and dying because of it. What are you going to do to save your Mother? We need to give her HOPE. It all begins with YOU. What you do makes a difference and you have to decide what kind of difference you want to make.

~If there is to be peace in the world, there must be peace in the nations.

~If there is to be peace in the nations, there must be peace in the cities.

~If there is to be peace in the cities, there must be peace between neighbors.

~If there is to be peace between neighbors, there must be peace in the home.

~If there must be peace in the home, there must be peace in the heart. ~Lao Tzu

It all begins within YOU. You can do the smallest things to make a difference. You could smile at someone once a day. That smile will fill someone's heart with joy. Then they will want to smile at another too or maybe twenty people. People are smiling because of one small moment that you decided to be a nice person. Those people will continue to keep smiling at other people. It will snowball out to larger numbers.

Suddenly, without you even having a clue because you are normally so filled with stress or pain, you have spread happiness around the world. Think about that for a minute. A kind gesture will only take you one second and a few muscles. It will have a butterfly effect and transform into something more beautiful than you could ever imagine.

Every time I see someone I know I give them a BIG hug. I have to hug them tight. I have no control over it, nor do I want to control it. The best gift you can give is a hug. One size fits all and nobody will care if you return it. It is so simple with such a big impact to the energy of another. It will continue to keep giving. Imagine what you can do if you just relax with life a little bit. You could create miracles if you wanted to with just one smile or hug. You have never really lived until you have done something for someone who can never repay you. IF YOU WANT TO CREATE ABUNDANCE FOR YOURSELF - CREATE IT FOR SOMEONE ELSE.

This Universe needs to be uplifted to a more positive consciousness and our egos must be cleared that we are all separate. We can choose to personally hold separation thinking that we are all different. Yes, our personalities and the way each of us lives is different. We as humans are exactly the same. The only difference is what we look like, where we live and the language we speak. We are all emotional wrecks and have emotional lessons and hell.

We all have to face death, heartbreak, losses and failures. Our issues are all the same. So why you think you are any different than anyone else on this earth? A very negative energy called 'ego' tells us we are different. We have to come together and get through this. We are ALL here at this moment for a reason. Let's make it happen! If to love each other is the job, then a happy life is the salary. Each of us is an angel with one wing and we can fly by embracing each other.

> ~Waking up this morning, I smile. Twenty-four brand new hours are before me. I vow to live fully in each moment and to look at all beings with eyes of compassion. ~Thich Nhat Hanh

I have studied our planets and their positions very intensely for 25 years. I connect myself to the moon, the sun, each planet in the solar system and the energies they put off. I studied the moon for years with myself, my Swede, my children, my friends and my online friends. All of us are either full/new mooners or we are half-mooners. Most people feel the energy on the full. We all know everyone gets crazy on the full moon. Yet, we never step back and realize we all acknowledge it has an energy.

So I can tell you what I know about the rest of the moon's cycle. First, we have three very intense Full moons a year. One is usually at the end of June or beginning of July. Two more are usually in September to November full moons. I had the party when my grandfather died on one of them. Woo Hoo crazy fun! People go wild on these moons. Be aware of their intensity. The moon can be like a damn energy drink. If you learn of your cycle with the moon, you can start to use this to your advantage. Begin to control it and use it to work for you. I learned I was a new/full mooner. I would howl at the moon and get wild. My children also have high energy on full moons. Half-moons were good energy to me. I love dancing with the moon even if it is to my own tune.

After about a year I had control of the energies the moon gave me. I learned to use it to my advantage. Full/new moons I stay calm and centered. I make myself aware of my actions and mood. I stay balanced and open. The half-moons I found were the best times of the month for me to deal with issues. It has a good, positive energy for me. I handle things with much more patience and compassion. New moons represent beginnings and Full moons represent endings. There are fabulous websites and Facebook groups out there to teach you about the planetary line ups and how their energies affect us. They are pretty accurate every time. I study it with all the people around me and they respond as the planetary energies change. The information normally isn't wrong.

When certain planets are in our sky or lined up, different things happen to the energies we receive. Certain planets create loving energies and some cause us to be scattered. Others give off an energy of laziness. While others send great physical energy. Being aware will help you understand why sometimes you feel a certain way. It is not always you, believe it or not. The entire universe is connected to you. So stop to understand this magnificent Universe around you and its energies. It does affect you every day. Just because you cannot see it, does not mean it doesn't exist. If you don't believe me, at least give it a try. It is all bigger that you can imagine. Yet, so simple that we are all part of one big thing.

~Imagine a life where you´re in the center of cosmic energies and that all of us are pieces of the most living puzzle~ Erik Grondahl

I am going to talk to you about another type of energies that are happening around us at this very moment. At the end of August 2011 the world had an etheric split. One plate lifted up and one dropped down. Breaking apart the world on an etheric body level. I spent a week trying to figure out why everyone around me, and myself included, had suddenly felt overwhelming sadness. Nobody could understand why. What was unknown to our physical self was that people were slipping off. Those who refuse to change their lives and really look at themselves, went one way. Those who are willing to accept that all of their problems are really their own, went the other way. We felt the separation of those we loved choosing to not walk with us. Understand that you create your own reality with work, relationships, home, finances, self-acceptance, parenting, and spiritually. You get what you GIVE. It's about love, it's about compassion, it's about kindness, it's about faith, it is has NOTHING to do with luck. You get what you give. So give well.

Let go of the fear based system the world is giving us. You attract your outcomes. You decide how to feel. You are free. Never forget whatever energy you put around something, is the outcome you will receive. If you think negative about something, you will get negative results. People are slipping off and refusing change. God will cleanse Mother Earth of all evil, bad and negative. Within less than twenty years this planet will be cleansed of them all. Our children are here to rise up and do their job to achieve this. Peace will come to this earth. God and love will overcome evil. But evil is going to put up one hell of a fight. Hell will come in many forms. It has to get bad before it gets better.

Chaos will happen in our future, but take a look at who is creating it. Those demons can never be silenced for good. But, they must always be answered by the quiet and steady dignity that refuses to give in. Have courage and keep going. Now you know what you can do to make a difference on Mother Earth. Start by cleaning your polluted mind and soul.

~No tree has branches so foolish as to fight amongst themselves.- Native American saying

Now I am not going to waste my time writing about humans polluting Mother Earth, we all know how horrible we have treated the earth by dumping our garbage everywhere. But, I would like to tell you that nature is my greatest healer and teacher. Every single thing on this earth that is living has a soul. Every animal, fish, tree, and including your grass is a soul which chose that experience this lifetime. They chose a different form of life than you. Your ego told you that you were better than that tree because you are human.

If you look at a tree every leaf is different. If you look at an animal closely, each one is different. Every butterfly is different, even when they all look the same. Look closer because everything is different than the other. Everything is individual just like humans. God gave everything individuality, but only humans judge each other by it. The leaves on the tree are not saying, "Hey, I am bigger than you, so I am better." But humans do!

Everyone calls me a tree hugger because I really do hug trees. When I have nobody, I have nature. When I am stressed or hurt, I go to a tree. Putting your body to the tree by either hugging or leaning with your back against it, will help you. Go to a tree, lean your back to it, then feel the energy it sends through your body. Positive! Trees do have negative energy, they do not have fear. I tell people I would rather hug a tree than most humans who are filled with negative.

Another thing I find sad is that we do not touch Earth with our feet anymore. Humans get out of the car with their shoes on, walk on the pavement to wherever they are going and walk into the building. When you walk barefoot the energies of the earth can travel through you. These energies teach, help and heal you. Humans were not born with shoes. We have lost one of our most important connections to the earth. I finally got science to back me up on this one. People thought I was crazy, but scientists have proved that the energy coming off the earth is the same energy as a hands on healer.

People do not even pay attention to nature anymore. Nature is also our messenger. Scientists have now proven that plants communicate underground with chemicals. Everything is communicating on different levels. I always talk to my nature. I pay attention to how everything works and interacts. The outdoors teaches me so much more than any human on earth. Sitting in silence and touching nature is the true connection to our higher self and God. Nature has so many beautiful things to say when you stop to listen. I would rather listen to the whispers of my surroundings outdoors, then some human talking bullshit out of their mouth.

As humans we started in nature and as we evolved we moved indoors. Once we moved indoors, we went away from nature, and humans began to destroy themselves. We were not made to spend every minute inside. Get out of your box that you spend your life in. I guarantee the more time you spend outside the better and more balanced you will feel.

I was once told that when you mow your grass, if you could hear over the lawn mower, you would hear the grass cry. At first I thought that was seriously crazy. Until, I moved back to the forest and nature again. Now I do not cut ¾ of my grass until July because I realized the 10,000 butterflies, humming birds and bees need the wildflowers for food. I want them here around me. In July I have enough flowers here to feed them. Then I let it grow up again until the weather is too cold for them, then I cut it again. People judge me. They think I am lazy and can't take care of my yard. That is not the truth, the truth is I respect everything. It is sad that we believe that even our grass is less important. I apologize to my grass before I have to cut it. It makes my home look beautiful, feeds many things, and gives me oxygen. Sounds crazy yes, but when you connect yourself to nature as intensely as I do, only then you will understand we are all in this together. Every living thing has a purpose on this earth.

In my book Naturally Natalie, I will talk about how nature healed me of many horrible illnesses. I let it guide me to what I need. My internet was shut off for two months. I turned to nature for all my answers and I let Mother Earth show me what I needed to heal myself without a Doctor. Not only was I given guidance, I healed. Nature gave me the most amazing gifts while I was struggling through the many different illnesses for over a month. When I am told by angels to write a book, I know I will get a crash course in that subject I am going to write about. If I can't live it, I have no right to teach it. Nature taught me almost the entire book and guided me to answers without the internet or other communications.

Furthermore, butterflies are like angels to me and they represent new beginnings. I have the most amazing and unexplainable relationship with them. I have butterflies that just land on me wherever I am and come to me when they are hurt or dying. They walk all over me and hang onto my shirt. I help them whatever way I can or I talk to them before they die. I pray for their transition to be comforting. I tell them not to fear and I give them messages to take HOME.

Yesterday, my son brought in a butterfly that was wet

from the rain and the cats were about to have lunch with it. I brought it in and let it have time to dry its wings and gain strength. It just sat on my bed in complete comfort. Then I set it free to let it keep being beautiful. I am always communicating and caring for them. It seems I have become a butterfly magnet. It is like they say, "Hey if you need help or if you are dying, head over to Natalie's, she will take care of you." These butterflies come when I am having a hard time, or I am making a major transition in my life. They always teach me something or have a huge message for me. God created them too.

I know nature loves me because it gives me the greatest gifts that money cannot buy. I have a bird that sings all day long. Cute lil thing but it talks non-stop. He has been coming back every year for three years that I am aware of. He makes me smile. Everyone that comes here notices his chattering and thinks it is so cute. I tell them that he never stops, but it is better than listening to most humans I know.

I have a friend that lives near me and he has learned massive amounts of knowledge from nature alone. He observes how it all interacts, communicates and behaves. He respects and allows it to tell him what to do. He has been one of the greatest teachers of nature to me. The forest gives back to him in the most amazing ways for respecting and taking care of it. One day he looked down at a rock that he had passed hour before. On that rock a squirrel had taken flower petals and placed them in a perfect circle. It was proof that nature does appreciate what you do for it and gives you gifts back.

I teach people who are trying to heal their pain to get their ass out to nature. Go to water, park or to a forest! Close your eyes and feel the good energy it gives you. It will whisper better advice than your best friend can give you. Also, keep your secrets if you need to let them out. I tell nature everything and it always answers me in ways I never imagined were possible. Nature will give you purity and peace. It is so important for our souls to connect back to where we are supposed to be. It is where you truly see the work of God.

Our Mother Earth and the Universe need your help. Clean yourself up and make a commitment to clean our Mother Earth. It all begins with you. Pray for our beautiful Mother and every living thing to heal. Healing Mother Earth begins with your heart. Do your part and it will make a world of difference. IMAGINE WHAT YOU COULD DO IF YOU COULD DO WHAT YOU IMAGINE. YOU CAN!

~Twenty years from now you will be more disappointed by the things you didn't do than the things you did do.-Mark Twain

~Break down your walls. Free your mind. The only thing God wants you to do is be YOU. You are BE-YOU-TIFUL just the way you are. Celebrate it! ~ Natalie Newman

~ Do not pay attention to the "world events", they are all orchestrated to make you pay attention to them. The struggle you should pay attention to is on a personal level.

~"Peace is not a relationship of nations. It is a condition of mind brought about by a serenity of soul. Peace is not merely the absence of war. It is also a state of mind. Lasting peace can come only to peaceful people." ~ Jawaharlal Nehru

~All that we are is the result of what we have thought. If a man speaks or acts with an evil thought, pain follows him. If a man speaks or acts with a pure thought, happiness follows him, like a shadow that never leaves him. ~Buddha

~Everyday may not be good but everyday has something good in it.

~Alone we are like one drop. United we are an entire ocean

~Grandfather, Great Spirit I give you thanks that we can sit here in this circle of Life, We send Prayers and the very best thoughts about our Grandmother Great Spirit. As we raise this sacred pipe to give thanks to you and to all of your Creation. We give thanks to the spirit helpers who came and sat among us. Grandfather, Most sacred one, these are your prayers that we send to you as we sit here together and pray.
Grandmother your children are crying. Grandfather your children are dying. The hands of greed and the hands of lust for power have been laid on them. And all around is death and desolation. The gifts you made for all your children, stolen and laid to waste in a monstrous desecration. Grandmother Great Spirit, as we sit and pray together we send you this prayer of affirmation- We your children whom you created in your likeness and image- We will reach out and we will dry our tears and heal the hurts of each other. Our sisters and brothers are hurting bad and our children, they see no future. We know Grandfather, that you gave us a sacred power, but it seems like we don't know its purpose. So now we've learned as we sat together, the name of that power is love. Invincible, irresistible, overwhelming power. This power you gave us we are going to use. We'll dry the tears of those who cry and heal the hurts of them that are hurting. Yes Grandmother, we'll give you our hands and in our hearts and minds and bodies we dedicate our lives to affirmation. We will not wait nor hesitate, as we walk on this sacred earth. We will learn together to celebrate the ways of peace and harmony and tranquility that come. And in the world around us. Thank you Grandfather for this prayer.

~ Native American prayer

Chapter 12
Connecting to the World Waiting for You

Dear Self,
Please accept yourself more,
Please love yourself,
Please make the right choices,
Please know what is good for you,
And please, please know that you are not alone.

One of the greatest fears people have is praying. We were not given a manual on how to perform this when we were born. First, praying is a choice. You have been given the freewill to ask God and the angels to work with you. Until you ask, they will just patiently wait for you to allow them to come into your life.

Second, you do not have to do anything fantastic except be yourself when you pray. God already knows who you really are. Third, never ask for an outcome. Ask for assistance or guidance. Let God control how things happen and trust it will be better than your dreams. Prayer is your connection to God and the Universe. When you pray, you open the entire Universe to come together to help you. I know we could all use as much help as possible. Fifth, have FAITH in your prayers and have faith in yourself. You will never have to face anything alone again.

I am going to give you a big, huge **WARNING: Never let others pray for you.** They do not have the same intentions as you and they will pray for outcomes. These outcomes may not be in your soul's best interest. That can be dangerous. Only let others pray for comfort and peace through the challenges. People mean well, but are actually praying for things that are NOT supposed to happen. When many people are praying for someone then everything is alerted to come help. You have opened the doors for something you can't control. Guidance, strength, comfort and peace is all anyone needs to pray for another.

Once you have prayed the angels will be around you. When you feel a shiver or coldness, or flashes of lights out of the corner of your eye, animals or items in your path or other signs, they are letting you know they are there for you. Pay attention to your dreams also. Our angels speak through our dreams and help us to understand or find answers to our questions. Keep a dream journal of whatever feeling, word or story you can remember. Your dreams will start to answer your questions. Your dreams are your conscious working things out. If you could not dream, you would literally go insane. But realize that there is almost always a hidden message in your dream.

I was taught to pray by a Native American friend. I had no idea what to say or what to ask for. I took her advice and began to I learn on my own and create my own prayers. Through my own mistakes I found out how and what to ask for. Never worry about saying the wrong thing. God already knows your intentions. However, you need to ask for help for God to intervene and work for you. If you don't ask you can't expect change.

The best place to pray is in the church of Mother Nature. I know it is difficult to get outside sometimes and our living circumstances do not always allow us to pray outdoors. Water has the amazing power to take your prayers and carry them everywhere. Praying at sunrise, or when the sun is high in the sky directly above you, and when the sun sets, are powerful times to be heard.

However, anytime is good. Always face the west. East is the past and already done. The West is the future and new beginnings. Believe me this really works. I studied it for over five years. I pray to God first, everything around me and then Mother Earth. This brings everything around you together to listen and work for you.

Next, I wrote a prayer for you to use to bring all things in to you. God, Mother Earth, along with the powers of the West, North, East and South. Also, I have added the prayers that I pray to my beautiful 10 Archangels I work with. EVERY prayer I have prayed to them has been answered. Never the way have I imagined, but they are ALWAYS answered. It is your choice which Archangels you choose. You have freewill. Really, all you have to do is read these prayers out loud and the angels will surround you immediately. Feel their presence come into your life. It is time to celebrate!!! Everyone has been patiently waiting for you to ask for their help.

Natalie's Daily Prayer to Your "God" and All

~*Face upwards, and say-* God, I pray to you first. My creator and true source of everything please pity me and hear my prayers.

~*Face the West and say-* West, I pray to you. Without your power God cannot hear me.

~*Face the North and say-* North, I pray to you. Without your power God cannot hear me.

~*Face the East and say-* East, I pray to you. Without your power God cannot hear me.

~*Face the South and say-* South, I pray to you. Without your power God cannot hear me.

~*Stop and say-* Mother Earth, I thank you for all you give me to survive every day. I pray to you. Without your power God cannot hear me.

~*Face West again and say*

Dear God,

I thank you for all of my blessings. The ones that you have given me, the ones I cannot see, the ones that hurt and the ones those are to come. I ask you to vacuum away my fear and the negative energy within me and around me. Please replace this with your Divine Light and Divine Love so I can receive full faith. Please open my eyes, ears and mind to see your messages. Please fill me with your Divine Knowledge.

I ask that you fill the hearts of every person on Earth with your Divine Light and Divine Love so they can smile through their challenges. I pray for a positive outcome in/with the situation of _____ and that all hearts and minds are healed from my mistakes. I put my trust into you to do what is best for me. I will release any fears and unforgiveness to you. I will have faith you are with me. I will take your hand and let you guide me. Please show me the way. Thank you for hearing my prayers.

~May I become at all times, both now and forever
A protector for those without protection
A guide for those who have lost their way
A ship for those with oceans to cross
A bridge for those with rivers to cross
A sanctuary for those in danger
A lamp for those without light
A place of refuge for those who lack shelter
And a servant to all in need.
~Buddhist - prayer of peace

~I pledge allegiance to the world to cherish every living thing, to care for earth and sea and air, with peace and freedom everywhere. ~ Unknown

~Oh, Great Spirit,
whose voice I hear in the winds
and whose breath gives life to all the world, hear me.
I am small and weak.
I need your strength and wisdom.

Let me walk in beauty and make my eyes
ever behold the red and purple sunset.
Make my hands respect the things you have made
and my ears sharp to hear your voice.
Make me wise so that I may understand
the things you have taught my people.
Let me learn the lessons you have hidden
in every leaf and rock.

I seek strength, not to be superior to my brother,
but to fight my greatest enemy - myself.
Make me always ready to come to you
with clean hands and straight eyes,
so when life fades, as the fading sunset,
my spirit will come to you
without shame. ~American Indian - Lakota - Chief Yellow Lark

~*Make us worthy God,*

*To serve our fellow men
throughout the world who live and die in poverty and hunger.*

*Give them through our hands this day their daily bread,
and by our understanding love, give peace and joy.*

~*Mother Teresa*

My Last Words for You

Why Butterflies and Bullshit? Because life is both beautiful and full of shit at the same time. It is all how you choose to handle it. People bullied, tortured, beat, raped, kidnapped, and molested me. I never stopped believing. God took my hand, forced me up and gave me the strength to keep fighting. People told me I am nothing. What they did not understand is who I really am.

I never forget I chose this life exactly the way it is now. It was the journey my soul came to walk. I have now come to realize life is all just a show. My movie of life! You need to look at life like a movie and you are the star of your own show. God orchestrated everything for you. You must decide if you want it to be a drama, nightmare, or comedy. I created mine to be The Natalie Newman Show- an inspirational, romantic, love-filled comedy with intense suspense.

We are all here to experience everything. It is exactly what you dream your movie to be. You keep thinking it is a bad movie and it will continue to remain that way. You really came to laugh and embrace every moment as experience. You came to enjoy each experience of your life good and bad. You came to feel it. So let is swim around your head. Say hi to it and have faith in your heart you are going to get through it. Tomorrow is another day. You just have this moment right now. So what are you thinking and doing right now?

We as humans are here to experience and feel emotions. They are very powerful. You have the right to feel all of your emotions. They are a part of your being. Don't fight them, feel them. Cry, scream and get it out of you. Without these emotions you cannot change. Stop fighting yourself. Your soul is always speaking to you. If you don't listen to the message it will become a problem. Then the problem continues to grow as you surround it with negativity. Next, you have a complete internal crisis.

You need to listen and quiet your mind to hear what you need to do. Let your emotions guide you to change. But handle it with love and allow it to heal what is inside. Be honest and don't hide your feelings. You have the right to take off the mask and be a human with emotions. By facing these experiences with gratitude, we become the strongest. Then, these problems will just go away

Let life rain on you. Some days it feels like the storm will never end. But just like nature, the skies always clear and the sun shines again. Life should never be something to fear. You have what you need to survive every moment. Every moment is building you into a better you. Dance in the rain!

Do you want to experience magic like me? Then stop holding on to bullshit forever and creating unnecessary suffering for yourself. You are not here to suffer. You have created that reality for yourself. Trust me, God gives you magic every day. You just need to open your eyes and see YOU ARE ALREADY BLESSED.

~Life gets messy! Keep calm and say FUCK IT! You don't have to continue to drag yourself through the bullshit. FLUSH THE DAMN TOILET! You're just standing around smelling it and feeling sorry for yourself. When you flush the shit that weighs you down, you heal. Let it go! That is when magic happens! ~ Natalie Newman

No matter how shitty life gets, remember, you chose to be here for this Earth changing moment on the planet. What it comes down to is this, we are all doing the best we can in each moment given to what is available to us. If we could have performed better, we would have, and it's as simple as that. We often wonder how things could have been different in hind sight, but the point is to learn from the past and adjust our direction in this moment, not to dwell with judgment. Just keep moving on. You have a job to do here. Every one of you is there to love. You are all here to help create peace on this planet and change the history of the human race. Get your shit together and do what your soul came to do.

Your love will destroy the dark, evil souls and they won't be able to do bad things anymore. Evil will be stopped in its destructive path of killing, controlling, hurting and creating fear into more people. You are responsible for this. You agreed to come onto this planet and help.

~One by one the darkness will teach the light. One by one the light will illuminate the darkness. We will all unite with love. LOVE RULES ALL!!! ~Natalie Newman

Sit in silence for 30 seconds every day and love yourself, then the love entire earth. That is all you have to do. Don't tell me you don't have 30 seconds to help save the world. YOU DO!

You have the gift of life. Surround every moment with love and faith. Watch your outcomes change to positive. Your life will open to something very beautiful. Your problems will get lighter and lighter. See each shitty moment as a moment to grow. Don't fear anything and love your enemy it helps them. The only true thing you have to fear, is yourself. If you're stressed, worried, angry, sad or scared, then you are filled with a fear you don't want to face. The only person you have to blame is yourself. It is all in your own head. God has the greatest humor if you really look at it closely. Happy people are happy because they don't have fear. They face it, laugh at it and learn from it. That is how you get happy. Just forgive yourself and start over. Just keep trying your best.

~Meaning of life- Live, Laugh and Love! Nothing but positive comes from it.

What you say every day can change a life, so be positive not negative. Would you rather help someone or fuck up their day because you can't get your life straightened out? How unfair to everyone around you? Smile, say Hi, be nice and the world will return the favor. You receive what you put out. If you have nothing, means you are giving nothing.

This last holiday season I clearly observed how this is a time of gifts, love and enchantment. A wonderful time of sharing, appreciation and relationships with others. Imagine if we could live like that every day. Imagine a world of sharing. Be willing to give as well as receive.

Remember karma in all your deeds. When you give you will receive twice in return, but in many different ways that you need. When you open your heart the world responds with gifts and appreciation. Riches do not come in the form of materialistic things, but in the form of love. Love is the greatest gift you can give anybody. Open your heart to those less fortunate. Show your appreciation to those who need you and give every day. Not just on a holiday.

Nobody is perfect and nobody deserves to be. Nobody has it easy and everybody has issues. Yet, everyone is perfectly themselves. We can only understand what we know. You never know what people are going through. People change for two reasons. Either they have learned enough and they want to. Or they have been hurt enough, they have to.

So pause before you start judging, criticizing or mocking others. Everybody is fighting through their own unique war. What makes you so much better? Help them, don't hurt. This is your awakening. It is no mistake that you were guided to read this book for a reason. Because your soul is ready to move into your higher self and begin to heal yourself. It hurts my heart to see others hurt. I gave my life to God. I gave my life to helping and healing the world. I gave up my life so you could learn these lessons. I lived this life so you could live your life easier. I never regretted it for one second and I pay a very high price too.

This book was written by me yes, but these words were taught to me by many. I was taught knowledge from some of the most wonderful, powerful people on this earth and all the unseen souls around me. I take my ideas and blessings and use them to help as many people as possible all over the world. I believe if you are blessed with extra you should take that and give to bless others. That will create more blessings to come to you.

I am just going to celebrate life dancing and laughing every day. Life is way too funny to be taken seriously. I absolutely love my life. So what if I don't have any money. Every day is worth a million to me. I work hard, play hard, fuck hard, love hard, party hard and live fast. But that is exactly the way I love it. I have had more fun than 500 people did in their lifetime combined. I may be crazy, but all the best people are. I think it is better to have people think you are crazy and be remembered, then have people think you are normal and be forgotten. Well behaved women rarely make history.

Butterflies and Bullshit is a tool to help heal your mental and emotional health. Over half of the people who I let read this book before publishing it to the public, tell me they carry it with them EVERYWHERE they go. They say it has a healing energy and when they have a question, the book opens to the answer they need. When I wrote this book I prayed every day to God, Mother Earth and the Angels for them to pass healing energy to everyone who touches my book. When that book becomes yours, it takes on your energy and your healing needs. So it is best to keep your personal copy with you. Others can purchase their own. It has been blessed through 1000's of hours of prayer for you. Keep your energy with it. Also, I do not want to sell it EBook, but sadly I have to. Plastic, electronic frequencies and metal will steal the energy from it because they are not natural products. Paper is of Mother Earth and God. Their energy grew that tree it is printed on.

I just want to say thank you for taking your time to read my story. I hope you learn something from it. I also want you to know that this is my opinion and my lessons. The quotes have been taken from everywhere.

Now, I am going to take it to a whole new level for the second half of my life. I am going to wrap myself around the world, with love and celebrate life with everyone I can. The earth is my dance floor. This moment is my party and I am going to celebrate me, right now. Celebrating life is appreciating all that you have and having faith through each moment. I know God's plans for me are bigger than my dreams.

All my life I wanted others to see me for who I really am. But in reality, I was the one who really needed to see it. I know I don't have to be perfect. Just be myself because that is what I came here to do. I am extremely intense, yet very calm. I am completely crazy and incredibly sane. I am wild out of control, but filled with peace. I am highly emotional and very in tune with every one of my emotions. I love being with people, yet would love to spend a year all by myself. I am in your face and super shy. I am amazingly powerful but yet very fragile. I am extremely complicated and very simple. I am everything.

I have been guided by many, but not solved by any. Sometimes I am good and then I'm very, very good. Sometimes I am really bad and I can be downright Naughty. But I love me for everything I am and that is freedom. Freedom is power. Power is to live a life untamed without fear of the unknown with faith. I am living the true fairytale love because the entire time, it was inside me. My love and relationship with myself is the fairytale I searched for all my life. I know I will survive anything. I love ME! I fell in love with myself. It's the best fucking relationship in my life. My journey is just getting started. The sky is the limit and I have wings. I am praying for you all. Sending you peace, love and hugs my dear friends.

~ Those who don't feel this Love pulling them like a river,
those who don't drink dawn like a cup of spring water
or take in sunset like supper,
those who don't want to change,
let them sleep. ~ Rumi

Dear Universal Creative Energy,

I thank you for giving me the strength to complete the task you have trusted in me to fulfill. Thank you for guiding me through it all, to survive the painful challenges and obstacles I have encountered throughout this path of my life.

Thank you for remaining beside me and keeping my heart filled with laughter and faith. Thank you for the signs throughout my life to uplift me and continue my battle to succeed in what my soul came to do. Thank you for your protection and for holding me close in my darkest hours.

Thank you for the friendships and love I have received along the way to entertain and lighten my painful lessons. Please forgive me for the bad choices and any wrong I have done. I also thank you for any good I have performed. I hope I make you proud.

Thank you for trusting in me to live this life and giving me the honor of working for you. I have fought the best I could. I have won and I kept my faith in you through each step I have taken. Now this part of my life's journey is over. Please help me to continue my studies and walk my path according to your plan for me.

I give you this book as a tool to help others. Through me your words have been spoken. I surrender and release the outcome of its journey to you.

Thank you for helping me to learn to love myself. Thank you for showing me to love and trust in you. My life I give to you. Please hear my prayers. Thank you!

~by Natalie Newman

NOTES

NOTES

NOTES

Made in the USA
Columbia, SC
30 September 2020